CW00501191

ACADEMIA LUNARE

Not the Fellowship.
Dragons Welcome!

Edited by
Francesca T Barbini

Academia
Lunare
LUNA PRESS
PUBLISHING

Cover Image: *Smaug's Attack on Erebor* © Jay Johnstone 2013

Text © with each individual author 2022

First published by Luna Press Publishing, Edinburgh, 2022

The right of each author to be identified as the Author of the Work has been asserted by her in accordance with the Copyright, Designs and Patents Act 1988.

Not the Fellowship. Dragons Welcome! © 2022. All rights reserved. No part of this publication may be reproduced, stored in a retrieval system, or transmitted in any form or by any means, electronic, mechanical, photocopy, recording or otherwise, without prior written permission of the publisher. Nor can it be circulated in any form of binding or cover other than that in which it is published and without similar condition including this condition being imposed on a subsequent purchaser.

www.lunapresspublishing.com

ISBN-13: 978-1-913387-98-3

In Memory of Priscilla Tolkien
(18 June 1929 - 28 February 2022)

Contents

Introduction

I am delighted to welcome you to *Not the Fellowship. Dragons Welcome!* Academia Lunare 2021 Call for Papers.

As an avid reader of J.R.R. Tolkien's *The Lord of the Rings* and the studies it has generated worldwide, I am ever more aware of the world that exists – you guessed it – beyond the fellowship of the Ring. It is important to recognise the role Jackson's trilogy played in ushering generations of people from the last 21 years to Middle-earth. For many, the movies even sparked the beginning of a career in Tolkien studies, encompassing the Professor's life work.

This call was created to foreground Middle-earth characters, across ages and races, who may not be as familiar as the fellowship.

For those of you who are new to our annual calls, we include essays from academics, independent researchers, fans and creative writers, appealing to both the casual reader and the more research-oriented one. We consider this cross-disciplinary collaboration a strength, and a beginning for many more explorations. We are incredibly proud of our journey so far.

The eleven entries in this year's Call for Papers are, therefore, varied in their outlook, as we invited authors to tackle the topic from different angles to create an array of paths for leading the reader to the focussed theme.

I felt it only fitting that Treebeard should lead the way, being the oldest of the Ents, created during the Years of the Trees. Brochu's paper examines the character's role in folklore, environmental protection and eco-critical awareness.

From here we look at the elves: Dyer's Glorfindel is presented as an intertextual link between the First and Third Ages; Walls-Thumma looks at the cartography of Nerdanel; closing this section, Nicholas explores the life, influence, and legacy of Finrod Felagund.

Representing the hobbits is Ham Gamgee, by Spadaro and Toninelli: between cabbages and potatoes, his humbleness acts as a counterbalance to the main events in The Lord of the Rings.

The penultimate section is for men. McKenna explores the dyscatastrophe of Túrin Turambar, followed by a second paper from Korpua, which is a comparative study of Tolkien's Túrin Turambar and Kalevala's Kullervo. Vink looks at Tal-Elmar and the unrepresented natives of Middle-earth, while Coundjeris brings us a reading of Éowyn as light bearer and fierce defender of home and hearth. Chaussée dedicates his paper to the last Prince of Cardolan, exploring memory and meditation in the mortuary archaeology of Middle-earth.

It is the dragon Smaug who closes off our book, in Dalton's paper – a look at the nature of these creatures, their origins in literature, and as mirrors of humanity.

I hope you enjoy the journey.
Francesca T Barbini

Steward of Trees and Forests:
Treebeard's Symbolic Role in Folklore, Environmental Protection and Eco-Critical Awareness

Amie A. Brochu

Among many of J.R.R. Tolkien's writings trees have been prominently featured, not only as naturalistic representatives of the Middle-earth landscape, but as symbols of longevity, strength and resilience shrouded in myth and shaped by history. Throughout *The Lord of the Rings*, initially released in 1954 and 1955, Tolkien makes hundreds of references to trees such as those belonging to dark forests, trees with leaves covered in dew or shrouded by mist, trees bordering towns or marking a fork in the road, trees that speak, cry in pain, whisper or provide shelter. He often provides rich physical descriptions, whereby some are tall while others are stunted; some are old whereas some are young seedlings. Tolkien's mythopoeic traditions also depicted trees as humanistic with twisted branch-like appendages and hollowed trunks covered in moss and bony growths anchored by treacherous ensnaring feet-like roots. His recounting of Middle-earth's natural geographies imaginatively transports the reader into a pseudo-mediaeval world where we can feel and smell the trees and flowers of the forests, groves and grasslands imbued with significant meaning, myth and symbolism.

Tolkien's high regard for trees can be gathered from a variety of sources besides his fictional works. For example, published photographs of the author in adulthood show him sitting or standing near some of his favourite trees (Dickerson and Evans, 2006, p. 130). In his youth, pencil sketches, pen-and-ink drawings and watercolour paintings often contained trees as their subject (Dickerson and Evans, 2006, p. 130). In a letter Tolkien once stated that, "certain things and themes move me specially. I am (obviously) much in love with plants and above all trees, and always have been" (Carpenter and Tolkien C., 1981, Letter 165, p. 233). The author's connection to and affection for trees is further evidenced by his metaphorical representation of *The Lord of the Rings* as his "own internal Tree...

growing out of hand... revealing endless new vistas (Carpenter and Tolkien C., 1981, Letter 241, p. 341).

With Tolkien's reverence for trees and forests playing such a prominent role within Middle-earth and his artistic endeavours, it is not surprising that he should dedicate a character to their representation. In Treebeard he not only gives a voice to the trees and forests, but he reflects his own values around nature and ecological preservation. Making reference to the destruction of trees Tolkien said, "I find human maltreatment of them as hard to bear as some find ill-treatment of animals" (Carpenter and Tolkien C., 1981, Letter 165, p. 233). Tolkien's feelings towards this end become personified in Treebeard as a reflection of his belief that "every tree has its enemy, few have an advocate" (Carpenter and Tolkien C., 1981, Letter 241, p. 341). In that manner Treebeard becomes one such advocate.

Within *The Lord of the Rings* we can see Tolkien taking an ecocritical approach to the creation of Middle-earth and through characters like Treebeard. For eco-critics, literature is a means to a paradigm shift, which places the non-human in a central position as part of the whole; thus replacing anthropocentric worldviews with eco-centric worldviews, where the environment is viewed with respect (Brawley, 2007). The significance of anthropomorphising trees helps to establish a stronger human and nature connection. Research has shown that when a person discerns that a non-human character is able to sense and feel, they are less reluctant to harm it (Tam, Lee and Chao, 2013). Therefore, a link between the anthropomorphism of nature can be associated with connectedness to nature, which in turn leads to conservation behaviour (Tam, Lee and Chao, 2013).

According to Larrington (2015), the rebirth of the Green Man in the 1940s and 1950s, a hybrid of man and tree and fierce defender against human trespass into the wild, struck a resonant chord in contemporary culture around the growing threats of industrialisation (p. 260). The typical Euro-western image of the Green Man is that of a foliated head, a face with vines and leaves sprouting from the mouth, eyes and nose, the hair and beard formed, as well, from leaves and twigs (Varner, 2006, p. 85). Much like the Green Man, Treebeard is personified as "a large Man-like... figure... clad in stuff like green and grey bark... [with] a face covered [by] a sweeping grey beard, bushy, almost twiggy at the roots, thin and mossy at the ends... [and] penetrating... brown [eyes] shot with a green light (Tolkien, 2011, p. 603). Therefore, Treebeard as an anthropomorphised tree humanises nature thus making environmental issues more relatable which in turn can motivate eco-conservationist consciousness. Furthermore, in Treebeard the reader can glean a sense of how ecocriticism, as literature of the environment, is a mode of aesthetic representation that pays keen attention to nature and the commodification of relations (both human and non-human), which is inextricably linked to an exploitative relationship (Nwagbara, 2012). Zhang, et al. (2017), further contend that modern literary works can contain eco-environmental information which can establish an imaginary analytical and critical space to provide new angles representing environmental issues and how writers and readers of different eras are reflecting on ecologically-related problems. Therefore, in light of the above, this paper will offer a character analysis of Treebeard by looking at tree and forest symbolism in literature and myth, gendered notions of nature and the Ents, Treebeard as eco-warrior and discussions around how he contributes to critiques of neo-colonial exploitation of resources perpetuating environmental destruction and socio-economic disadvantage.

According to Cohen (2009), the use of trees in literature fits within one of four types: 1) trees appearing as they do in the real world; (2) trees that remain rooted in the ground but are able to talk, think, and/or feel; (3) trees that remain rooted but voluntarily move their branches or trunks; and (4) trees that can uproot themselves, physically moving from one place to another (p. 91). Within Tolkien's books the use of trees satisfies all four categories, from the regal White Tree of Gondor and cantankerous Old Man Willow to the wistful and nostalgic Treebeard. Along similar lines, Porteous (2002) contends that the chivalric romance literature of the Middle Ages contain many allusions to trees and forests famous in myth and enchanted forests full of magic similar to the pseudo-mediaeval world of *The Lord of the Rings*. During this time the trees of forests and woods were cloaked in mystery, intensified by the deep and solemn shadows which lay hidden within their depths. The immutable and eternal tree is representative of wisdom, history, fertility, shelter, food and fuel symbolic of eternal life and cyclical rebirth (Garry and Birkalan, 2005; Hooke, 2010). They are symbols of immortality, stability, fertility and the heavens (Varner, 2006). Trees as life-sustaining medicinal folk practices call for treatments and rituals involving tree worship or using parts of the tree to obtain cures for disease (Varner, 2006, p. 44).

The reverence and appreciation of trees through worship, fear, silviculture and anthropomorphism has established a sense of wonder and veneration for them. Some cultures have myths involving nature spirits, gods and goddesses that inhabit a tree while other societies believe that each tree possesses a soul and an intellect of its own (Varner, 2006). Tolkien furthers this where he refers to the Ents as "either souls sent to inhabit trees, or else that slowly took the likeness of trees owing to their inborn love of trees" (Carpenter and Tolkien C., 1981, Letter 247, p. 352). In this manner Treebeard and the Ents are described by Tolkien as "composed of philology, literature and life" (Carpenter and Tolkien C., 1981, Letter 163, p. 227).

The human-tree connection continues not only in mythopoeic literature, but in numerous cultural narratives from diverse societies. Nordic peoples, ancient Greeks and Romans and First Nations depicted the connection between human existence and the life of trees while reinforcing notions that humans were created from trees (Porteous, 2002; Varner, 2006). Other cultures are known for adhering to the mythology of the Tree of Life as a link between heaven and the earth, uniting above and below (Mock, 2004). In stories and folklore around the world myths about trees have created numerous legendary creatures that are closely associated with trees and forests such as fairies, elves, dryads and trolls to name a few. Varner (2006) posits that such stories reflect an ancient animistic belief system that gives every object in nature its own spirit and power (p. 28). As such, symbolic representations for speaking trees denoting intelligence and wisdom appear in folklore around the world (Varner, 2006). For instance, cultural beliefs amongst many Indigenous Peoples premise that trees possessed souls (Varner, 2006). In many countries trees are believed to utter cries of pain, and even to bleed when they are cut down or wounded in any way such as the oak tree which is said to utter a shriek and groan that can be heard for miles (Porteous, 2002; White, 2016).

Around the world, trees in myth and folklore have a tendency to be referenced in general while others have more far-reaching and pervasive symbolism. The pervasiveness of these beliefs and myths across cultures become engrained into the social fabric of our lives and consequently our notions about nature and the natural world. Universally, nature is commonly gendered as female where feminine notions of birth and motherhood are reaffirmed in allegorical names like Mother Earth, Motherland and Mother Ganges. Neumann (2015), states that notions of sacrifice, death and rebirth are attributed to psychological transformation governed by the unconscious matriarchal consciousness whose nature and symbolism are as intimately bound up with the plant world as with the world of the feminine (p. 250). When looking at trees specifically, Neumann (2015) claims that the male relationship to nature and trees is one in which the male is contained; retaining his dependency on the feminine earth-womb symbol. In this regard within *The Lord of the Rings* Tolkien places Treebeard in an interesting position. On one hand he is a tree-like representative of an un-feminised version of nature. On the other Tolkien's gendered divisions of Treebeard's race implies a male Ent dependency on the regenerative, procreative qualities of the womb-oriented Entwives. In this way we can argue that the dependence on the masculine that defines feminine identity within nature exclusively with reference to the masculine is based on relationships with men (duPlessis, 2017).

In examining the Ents and gendered divisions in nature, Treebeard's character in reference to the masculine places him in a unique perspective that can liken him to the archetypal male characteristic of the oak tree. Since the earliest ties between humans and oaks, these trees have been associated with longevity, fertility, stability, honesty and more masculine characteristics such as strength, endurance, power and justice (Leroy, Plomion and Kremer, 2020). Oak tree symbolism among the ancient Greeks and Romans associated them with important male gods like Zeus to represent the *axis mundi* or the centre of the world (Leroy, Plomion and Kremer, 2020). In art, oak tree paintings and drawings are considered a symbol of the robustness of ideas (Leroy, Plomion and Kremer, 2020). From a patriarchal standpoint, the oak is also positioned as the King of Trees, the head, heart and habitat of an entire civilisation (Stafford, 2016). In 18th century Britain, the oak tree was "celebrated as the perfect image of the manly character, because of the obvious strength of its reassuring branches, the reliable consistency of its timber and, more figuratively, its patience and good sense" (Safford,

2016, p. 96). According to Stafford (2016), the "manly oak became something of a status symbol for owners of great estates [whereby] wealthy gentlemen were increasingly portrayed in front of their own oaks in portraits by artists such as Reynolds and Gainsborough" (pp. 96-97). In this way Varner (2006) argues that the female aspect of the tree was denigrated and maligned so that the male aspects could become dominant (p. 23).

Zhang, et al., (2017), contend that within literature most writers have the tendency to feminize the natural world, thus reiterating gendered divisions of nature within their works. In this Tolkien is no exception. He once stated that "the difference of the 'male' and 'female' attitude to wild things" (Carpenter and Tolkien C., 1981, Letter 163, p. 227) undoubtedly influenced *The Lord of the Rings* and possibly the creation of certain characters like Treebeard and his race. Taking a stance from new historicism theory, I contend that an author cannot be completely divorced from the society in which they occupy as well as the cultural values and assumptions they hold. Thus, I maintain that Tolkien's gendered views on nature were strongly influenced by his upbringing and interests while writing *The Lord of the Rings* and creating his characters.

Situationally, Tolkien began his formal book writing towards the end of interwar Britain (1918-1939), an era characterised by the roaring twenties and the despair of the Great Depression. At this time a growing movement in women's liberation and activism moved women into the work world and out of the domestic sphere. However, patriarchal attitudes about the role of women in society still played dominantly. In *The Lord of the Rings* we see these beliefs played out within a distinctive divide between the sexes of the Ents by their opposing interests and inclinations. This is demonstrated when Treebeard stated his preference for "the great trees, and the wild woods, and the slopes of the high hills," (Tolkien, 2011, p. 619) as opposed to the "lesser trees" (Tolkien, 2011, p. 619) favoured by the Entwives. Treebeard's deeper explanations specifically distinguishes Entwives from the male Ents linguistically by the fact of their being wives, whereby female Ents are even further delineated along the lines of age and gender as Entmaidens (duPlessis, 2017). Treebeard's further accounts describe how the Ents roamed the wild world while the Entwives pursued more domestic interests. Thus Tolkien further genders the Entwives and Entmaidens based on their biological and societal roles as child-bearers, homemakers and agriculturalists as well as their physical appearance (Tolkien, 2011, pp. 619-620). The Entwife's world is just as emphatically domestic perhaps even sequestered and confining. Her spring is not only contained within the fields and orchards, but it is walled up in the enclosed garden (Olsen, 2008, p. 41). In this manner, Tolkien goes beyond the mere association of the masculine with wildness and the feminine with domesticity; he also associates the female with the desire to domesticate and with the male a less intrusive appreciation of nature (Olsen, 2008, p. 42).

In addition to the gendered divisions of the Ents and Entwives we can see notions of nature going beyond delineations of social roles to biblical and biological themes. The secondary world of Middle-earth was not only influenced by the sociological era in which Tolkien was writing, but also in his religious beliefs. Tolkien considered himself a devout Catholic where themes and religious undertones influence the theocentric, God-centred world of Middle-earth (Wood, 2003). In fact, Tolkien once said that *The Lord of the Rings* is a fundamentally religious and Catholic work... [where] the religious element is absorbed into the story and the symbolism (Carpenter and Tolkien C., 1981, Letter 142, p. 191). There are parallels to the Book of Genesis, the God-like character of Ilúvatar in *The Silmarillion* (Tolkien C., 1977) and biblical reference in the Resurrection of Gandalf (Wood, 2003).

While applying Tolkien's religious undertones to the conceptions of nature, Delaney (1995) contends that the system that has been dominant in the west for millennia construes nature as created by God, whom is figured symbolically as masculine; nature that is created by God, is both inferior to and dependent upon God and is symbolically construed as female (p. 182). Conceived in this manner patriarchal and paternalistic ownership and control of nature are transformed into gendered notions along the lines of procreation and birth. Men are believed to be generative agents as providing the proverbial seeds (sowing the seeds of progress and industrialisation), whereas women as the soil become a generalised medium for growth (Delaney, 1995, p. 183). To further this belief Tolkien once stated that it is women's "gift to be receptive, stimulated, fertilised by the male" (Carpenter and Tolkien C., 1981, Letter 43, p. 60). Therefore, not only are the biological differences of the sexes reiterated through the characters like the Ents and Entwives, there are far-reaching more pervasive implications within his writing. The gendering of nature along religious and biological lines can lead to objectification and commoditisation of the female body, thus establishing a generalised medium of nurture within nature itself (Delaney, 1995).

Even though there are obvious gendered notions about nature within *The Lord of the Rings* and its characters, when it comes to nature preservation Tolkien appears to challenge these ideas. Research has shown when it comes to environmentalism and nature preservation there are gendered lines along themes of activism and ecological concern (Arnocky and Stroink, 2010; Dietz, Kalof and Stern, 2002; Kalof, Dietz and Guagano, 2002). Many nature-centric movements, like eco-feminism and climate change activism are frequently led by women. Values such as altruism, self-interest, traditionalism and openness to change are more apparent among women which appear to influence the gendered pro-environmental movement (Dietz, Kalof and Stern, 2002). What is interesting in *The Lord of the Rings* is that Tolkien attempts to challenge these conceptions to a certain extent with Treebeard's character. The imperialist agenda under the guise of Saruman's deforestation and ecological destruction that Treebeard was so adamantly against transforms him into a protector and warrior. Though there are gendered notions in the Ents going to war especially when looking at the more typical associations of the male such as aggression, strength and assault, Tolkien's use of a male tree-like character turns the feminine notions of nature as solely reproductive, acquiescent and tameable on its head. Saruman as industrialist, colonist and imperialist attempts to conquer nature, which in Treebeard's case is certainly not female, nor something to be used, controlled or dominated over.

In spite of Tolkien's obvious constructions of the Ents along gendered lines, there is no doubt that Treebeard's character is created and positioned as the embodiment of the author's values regarding nature and forest conservation. Tolkien once stated, "In all my works I take the part of trees as against all their enemies" (Carpenter and Tolkien C., 1981, Letter 339, p. 462). The author furthers his stance on environmental preservation and the encroaching industrialisation on the natural landscape when he discussed "the destruction, torture and murder of trees perpetrated by private individuals and minor official bodies... [with] the savage sound of the electric saw [that] is never silent wherever trees are still found growing" (Carpenter and Tolkien C., 1981, Letter 339, p. 462). In examining *The Lord of the Rings* we can see numerous examples of Tolkien's ecocritical and nature preservationist mind-set. For instance, Brawley (2007) argues that Saruman's quest for ultimate power equates with Tolkien's negative sentiments towards environmental destruction. In this way, Treebeard's labelling Saruman as "a black traitor" and a "tree-slayer" becomes a symbolic representation for progress and the exploitation of forests, thus voicing the impingement of modernity (Brawley, 2007). With Treebeard's personification of the author's interests and values it makes the character not only relatable, but human-like, positioning nature and all trees as something worth fighting for and preserving in the face of environmental destruction. Treebeard mirrors beliefs about the appropriation of nature, a utilitarian mind-set in which nature is viewed as property without an intrinsic value (Brawley, 2007). Subsequently furthered by Treebeard's describing Saruman as having "a mind of metal and wheels; [who] does not care for growing things, except as far as they serve him for the moment" (Tolkien, 2011, p. 616). Thus, in Treebeard we encounter an environmental perspective that is suspicious of any use of the natural landscape for destructive, selfish reasons, even when the perpetrators claim some practical justification for their purposes (Brawley, 2007).

Within *The Lord of the Rings* the Ents, as shepherds of trees, are stewards of nature, tending to their flock of forests and groves. Tolkien's historical explorations of the Ents throughout his works positions the male Ents' roles as caretakers and caregivers, which is in sharp contrast to the actual role they end up playing as defenders and warriors. Wilkinson (2007) argues that in Treebeard's case, his heroic masculinity as warrior and decision-maker places himself and the other Ents as heroes in defending their land and home, thus overshadowing the life-affirming actions of the Entwives and the importance of women's roles in society in general such as growing things and child-raising. Be that as it may, I contend that what Treebeard actually draws attention to is an uneven and exploitative power dynamic between masculinity and femininity that equally mirrors the split between humankind and nature. Environmental activist Vandana Shiva (1997), claims the rise of globalisation and industrialism has ushered in the gendered construction of nature as passive, inert and valueless, not dissimilar to the characterisation of femininity (as cited in Klemmer and McNamara, 2020). In the character of Treebeard, Tolkien turns this notion on its head and not only makes Treebeard and the Ents chivalrous protectors of nature and forests, but also challenges the gendered notions of nature as meek and docile. Additionally, there is a protectionist (albeit somewhat paternalistic) narrative within the role and history of the Ents that draws away from the feminised aspect of a gentle caretaker to one of a stalwart defender. In this manner, Tolkien further distances Treebeard from any feminine, womb-like symbolisms of nature and its preservation. Therefore, images of the Ents are further reduced from peaceful, pacifistic, wander-lusting shepherds to stone-crushing, earth-churning warrior trees. Consequently, Treebeard as embodiment of nature has taken up its fight; leaves, branches, roots and all against humanity and its destructive machines.

In Tolkien's time of writing and during the medieval period from which he models his secondary world, Treebeard and the Ents reminds us that "progress originally predicated on the felling of trees to build houses and ships, to fuel workshops and factories and to turn the wild places into tame farmland" (Larrington, 2015, p. 265). Zhang, et al. (2017) claim that environmental descriptions dominating aspects of some contemporary fiction, like *The Lord of the Rings*, establish narrative settings that bears significant thematic meaning. For example, within literature we have long been embracing and celebrating works that eulogise men's power, whereby combating and conquering the natural world is a recognisable and noticeable characteristic in works by Jack London or in books like Daniel Defoe's Robinson Crusoe (Zhang, et al., 2017). Therefore, what Treebeard represents and what Tolkien's highly descriptive world highlights is the growing exploitation of natural bounties and resources through male-dominated ecological imperialism.

According to Foster and Clark (2004), ecological imperialism presents itself in the following ways: the pillage of the resources of some countries by others and the transformation of whole ecosystems upon which states and nations depend; massive movements of population and labour that are interconnected with the extraction and transfer of resources; the exploitation of ecological vulnerabilities of societies to promote imperialist control; the dumping of ecological wastes in ways that widen the chasm between the marginalised and the power-holding privileged. As Foster and Clark (2004) continue to elucidate, large fortunes were built on colonised lands by robbing the local populations of its natural wealth and exploiting ecological resources, while also enslaving local labourers to create products that feed the voracious and growing appetite of the capitalist world economy. Consequently, many nations have been left facing an ecological rift arising from the workings of the capitalist system where the history of pillage and super-exploitation of peoples is seen as part of a larger ecological debt (Foster and Clark, 2004). This debt is exacerbated by the following factors: the extraction of natural resources; unequal terms of trade; degradation of land and soil for export crops; other unrecognised environmental damage and pollution caused by extractive and productive processes; appropriation of ancestral knowledge; loss of biodiversity; contamination of the atmosphere and oceans; the introduction of toxic chemicals and dangerous weapons; and the dumping of hazardous waste in the periphery (Foster and Clark, 2004, p. 193), which threatens to undermine all existing ecosystems and species, including our own.

As someone who resists owning a cell phone and whom writes this article on a twelve year old computer, I empathise and commiserate with Tolkien's love of the simplicity of the Shire and the untouched beauty of the Old Forest and Lothlórien. As a nature-admirer, vegetarian and social worker I am keenly aware of the impacts and legacy of industrialisation and globalisation on the world around me, those I serve as clients and the communities I live amongst. Yet, I am also profoundly cognisant of how I and many others continue to benefit from the privilege of progress. That is why I find ecological imperialism a bitter pill to swallow not only because of its role in environmental destruction, but in its exploitation of people and contribution to growing social inequity around the globe.

Power and ownership are neo-liberal undercurrents within ecological imperialism, which thus lends itself to notions about land and essentially space. The geography and landscape within Middle-earth evidenced through Tolkien's richly detailed narratives and hand-drawn maps arguably situates space as something of great import to the author. His rich descriptions of not only the bucolic Shire, but also the detailed shadowy forests of Mirkwood and Lothlórien reiterates what stirs him the most and comes nearest to his heart's satisfaction; that being space (Carpenter and Tolkien C., 1981, Letter 78, p. 102). Tolkien's reverence for nature and Treebeard's character permits the reader to realise the necessity of reconciling with and preserving the natural environment. Treebeard becomes a symbolic representation of forests, trees and the spaces they occupy.

If we look at the forests depicted in *The Lord of the Rings* and Treebeard's character representing these ideological, narrative and physical spaces, we can see nature and the environment becoming a highly contested and highly representative space. Textual representations of forests imbued with cultural value distinguished from ordinary places of human residence and use can act as a gateway into the Otherworld establishing a liminal space where the actual borders the magical, thus providing transition or refuge (Morrison and Lycett, 2014; Post, 2014). The forest realm, therefore, becomes a space of mystery and supernatural harm (Kuusela, 2020). What lies under, behind, or in the past of these forests are their long-term legacies of human action: they are artefacts of human ideas about nature, expressions of economies and places mediated by institutions and their materialized practices as much as they are habitats evolving in response to evolution and planetary processes (Hecht, Morrison and Padoch, 2014, p. 5)

From a Marxist perspective our western ideologically dominant tendency divides space into separate parts and parcels in accordance with the social division of labour (Lefebvre, 1974). Space itself, is at once a product of the capitalist mode of production and an economic-political instrument (Lefebvre, 1974). Lefebvre contended that capitalism established a trinity of land-capital-labour within an institutional space; firstly a space of sovereignty where constraints are implemented, secondly a space of fragmentation and distinct localities for modalities of control and thirdly a hierarchical space of social class and privilege (p. 282). Space conceived as a forest of trees thus becomes something physical and concrete that can be controlled, produced, named and owned. Conceived in this manner Treebeard and the Ents representing trees and forests as symbols of the sacred, symbols of ownership and identity and as an extremely valuable resource, have come to work in the new deployments of power over customary common property (Hecht, 2014), through the segmenting and carving out a niche for oneself by owning one's own piece of space. Spatiality then establishes strict boundaries and limitations, imaginary lines for those that are welcome and those that are not. Space then serves as delineation between the in-groups and out-groups. There is then a hierarchical domination of those who have space and those who do not. Therefore, those without defined spheres, like the homeless or refugees fleeing persecution, are not welcomed in sharing our representative spaces.

The geographic landscapes of *The Lord of the Rings* are thus imbued with symbolic meaning, traditional rights and powers and diverging political economies and ideologies that reflect past and emerging institutional frameworks that mediate bundles of rights and powers (Hecht, 2014). There is a reproduction of actions and behaviours associated with that terrain based on ideas, values, memories and narratives linked to place (Vaz, 2016). Therefore, the physical landscape of a forest symbolises the latent drive for social distinction and social distinction expresses itself in a differentiated scale of rights to ownership, access and use of physical landscape (Kühne, 2018, p. 166). These delineations can create locations for discrimination, stigma and unequal social hierarchies which can spill over into conceptions of a global domain exploited by dominant neo-colonialist ideologies of control and ownership.

According to Krishnan (2017), space through its control and its administration functions not as an auxiliary to colonial conquest, but as a central component enacted through such conquest (p. 629). This furthers notions that the contemporary neo-liberal era has intensified assaults on resources and perpetuated the environmental and social damage suffered by the disadvantaged in ever-developing forms of neo-colonialism (Nixon, 2011). In light of this, I would argue that Treebeard and the destruction of forests in *The Lord of the Rings* goes beyond symbolising the destructive power of western imperialism, capitalism and globalisation. As a character and emblem of critical awareness he also speaks to the colonialist legacies of the past and present. Treebeard viewed as an indigenous race to Fangorn forest, while Saruman's lust for power and the industrial dwarves are situated on the opposite side of the spectrum, represents the westernised supremacy legitimised by colonialist ideology. Bringing it closer to home in Canada, similar to many other resource-rich countries around the globe, the natural resources of the indigenous people have been stripped for centuries by colonialist states and their corporate affiliates leaving the people impoverished and plundered of their resources (Watson, 2005). Ecological imperialism through colonialist practices drastically altered First Nations communities and their relationships to the natural environment with social and economic repercussions spread throughout northern Canada (Piper and Sandlos, 2007). The westernised way of knowing and understanding country, nature and land is forged by ownership, control and possession leading to land appropriation and forced displacement of many indigenous peoples. Watson (2005) makes a vividly visceral image of colonisation akin to a process of absorption and consummation, whereby the indigenous peoples are consumed by the state and its colonialist invaders. This can be likened to how Saruman's appropriation of the land around Isengard has consumed the trees of Fangorn in the name of power and industrial progress. In many ways Treebeard as indigenous to Entwood signifies the same colonialist practices on his fellow Ents and tree-kin as Watson does of her own people and the many colonised spaces around the globe.

Conclusion

Over the ages and passing eras, our species has had a long tumultuous history with nature. Our relationship has been at times reverential through worship and veneration, mystifying through fear and wonder and oppressive through taming and control. As our species has aimed for higher heights through institutions of modernity where progress is of utmost importance the natural world has become increasingly abused through exploitation and destruction. Deforestation from the encroachment of farmland threatens the lives of millions of indigenous people and their traditions around the globe. The clear-cutting of old growth forests and their thousand-year-old inhabitants robs the world of ancient memories and myths.

Throughout this paper we saw how Treebeard raises awareness about gendered constructions around nature within *The Lord of the Rings*. The exploration of Tolkien's beliefs and Treebeard's character further evidences themes that nature needs preserving. The analysis also took us into critiques and the symbolism behind Treebeard as an eco-warrior ending with his call to action against the destruction of our natural world while countering the pernicious practices of neo-colonialism and capitalist accumulation.

Arguably the greatest contribution of Treebeard is his portrayal that nature is not passive. As a representative to trees, forests and people around the world he gives a voice to the voiceless. Treebeard shows that trees, forests and nature are not silent. The whispers of leaves, the swaying of branches and the creaking of trunks are the speeches and conversations of venerable oaks, shady elms, towering sequoias and their many kin. As a defender of trees and forests, Treebeard represents the passionate fight of a fiery maple and the resilience of a lithesome willow. His timelessness history and myth is reminiscent of the lives some of the most long-lived and enduring foliaged residents in our world. What Tolkien and Treebeard reiterate is not a necessity to return to the Shire-like world of *The Lord of the Rings*, but rather an obligation to focus on the interconnectedness of all living things; that in order for us to continue to benefit from living in this world there is a need for reciprocity like that in Middle-earth.

References

Arnocky, S. and Stroink, M., 2010. Gender differences in environmentalism: the mediating role of emotional empathy. *Current Research in Social Psychology*, 16(9), pp.1-14.

Brawley, C., 2007. The fading of the world: Tolkien's ecology and loss in *The Lord of the Rings*. *Journal of the Fantastic in the Arts*, 18(3), pp.292-307.

Carpenter, H. and Tolkien, C. eds., 1981. *The letters of J.R.R. Tolkien*. London: George Allen & Unwin.

Cohen, C.M., 2009. The unique representation of trees in *The Lord of the Rings*. *Tolkien Studies*, 6(1), pp.91-125. [online] Available at: <https://doi.org/10.1353/tks.0.0041> [Accessed 31 August 2021].

Delaney, C., 1995. Father state, motherland, and the birth of modern Turkey. In: S. Yanagisako and C. Delaney, eds. *Naturalising power: essays in feminist cultural analysis*. New York: Routledge. pp.177-200.

Dickerson, M.T. and Evans, J., 2006. *Ents, elves, and Eriador: the environmental vision of JRR Tolkien*. Lexington: University Press of Kentucky.

Dietz, T., Kalof, L. and Stern, P.C., 2002. Gender, values, and environmentalism. *Social Science Quarterly*, 83(1), pp.353-364.

DuPlessis, N., 2017. To grow together, or to grow apart: the long sorrow of the Ents and marriage in *The Lord of the Rings*. *Mythlore: A Journal of J.R.R. Tolkien, C.S. Lewis, Charles Williams, and Mythopoeic Literature*, 35(2), pp.25-44.

Foster, J.B. and Clark, B., 2004. Ecological imperialism: the curse of capitalism. *Socialist Register*, 40, pp.186-201.

Garry, J. and Birkalan, H.A., 2005. Trees, various motifs. In: J. Garry and H. El-Shamy, eds. *Archetypes and motifs in folklore and literature: a handbook*. New York: M. E. Sharpe. pp.464-471.

Hecht, S.B., Morrison, K.D., and Padoch, C., 2014. From fragmentation to forest resurgence: paradigms, representations, and practices. In: S.B. Hecht, K.D. Morrison and C. Padoch, eds. *The social lives of forests: past, present, and future of woodland*. Chicago: University of Chicago Press. pp.1-8.

Hecht, S.B., 2014. Institutions: the secret lives of forests. In: S.B. Hecht, K.D. Morrison and C. Padoch, eds. *The social lives of forests: past, present, and future of woodland*. Chicago: University of Chicago Press. pp.277-278.

Hooke, D., 2010. *Trees in Anglo-Saxon England: literature, lore landscape*. Woodbridge, UK: The Boydell Press.

Hope, C., 2017. Robin Hood oak in frackers' sights. *The Sunday Telegraph*, [online] 1 Jan. Available at: <http://ezproxy.lib.ryerson.ca/login?url=https://www.proquest.com/newspapers/robin-hood-oak-frackers-sights/docview/1854371497/se-2?accountid=13631> [Accessed 15 April 2021].

Kalof, L., Dietz, T. and Guagnano, G., 2002. Race, gender and environmentalism: the atypical values and beliefs of white men. *Race, Gender & Class*, 9(2), pp.112-126.

Klemmer, C.L. and McNamara, K.A., 2020. Deep ecology and ecofeminism: social work to address global environmental crisis. *Affilia*, 35(4), pp.503-515. 10.1177/0886109919894650.

Krishnan, M., 2017. Introduction: postcolonial spaces across forms. *Journal of Postcolonial Writing*, 53(6), pp.629-633. 10.1080/17449855.2017.1403069.

Kühne, O., 2018. *Landscape and power in geographical space as a social-aesthetic construct*. New York: Springer.

Kuusela, T., 2020. Spirited away by the female forest spirit in Swedish folk belief. *Folklore*, 131(2), pp.159-179. 10.1080/0015587X.2019.1701280.

Larrington, C., 2015. *The land of the green man: a journey through the supernatural landscapes of the British Isles*. London: I.B. Taurus & Co.

Lefebvre, H. 1974. *The production of space*. Translated by D. Nicholson-Smith., 1991. Oxford, UK: Blackwell.

Leroy, T., Plomion, C. and Kremer, A., 2020. Oak symbolism in the light of genomics. *New Phytologist*, 226(4), pp.1012-1017. 10.1111/nph.15987.

Mock, T., 2004. Tree of life: restoration of sacred mythology. *Arbor Age*, pp.26-29.

Morrison, K.D. and Lycett, M.T., 2014. Constructing nature: socio-natural histories of an Indian forest. In: S.B. Hecht, K.D. Morrison and C. Padoch, eds. *The social lives of forests: past, present, and future of woodland*. Chicago: University of Chicago Press. pp.148-160.

Neumann, E., 2015. *The great mother: an analysis of the archetype*. Translated from German by R. Manheim. Princeton: Princeton University Press.

Nixon, R., 2011. *Slow violence and the environmentalism of the poor*. Harvard: Harvard University Press.

Nwagbara, U., 2012. Earth in the balance: the commodification of the environment in the eye of the earth and delta blues & home songs. *Matatu*, 40(1), pp.61-79.

Olsen, C., 2008. The myth of the Ent and the Entwife. *Tolkien Studies*, 5(1), pp.39-53. https://doi.org/10.1353/tks.0.0013.

Piper, L. and Sandlos, J., 2007. A broken frontier: ecological imperialism in the Canadian north. *Environmental History*, 12, pp.759-795.

Porteous, A., 2002. *The forest in folklore and mythology*. Reprint of Forest Folklore, Mythology, and Romance, 1928. New York: Macmillan.

Post, M.R.S., 2014. Perilous wanderings through the enchanted forest: the influence of the fairy-tale tradition on Mirkwood in Tolkien's the Hobbit. *Mythlore: A Journal of J.R.R. Tolkien, C.S. Lewis, Charles Williams, and Mythopoeic Literature*, 33(1), pp.67-84.

Stafford, F., 2016. *The long, long life of trees*. New Haven: Yale University Press.

Tam, K., Lee, S. and Chao, M.M., 2013. Saving Mr. Nature: anthropomorphism enhances connectedness to and protectiveness toward nature. *Journal of Experimental Social Psychology*, 49(3), pp.514-521.

Tolkien, C. ed., 1977. *The Silmarillion*. London: George Allen & Unwin.

Tolkien, J.R.R., 2011. *The Two Towers*. New York: HarperCollins.

Varner, G.R., 2006. *The mythic forest, the green man, and the spirit of nature: the re-emergence of the spirit of nature from ancient times into modern society*. New York: Algora Publishing.

Vaz, E., 2016. The future of landscapes and habitats: the regional science contribution to the understanding of geographical space. *Habitat International*, 51, pp.70-78.

Watson, I., 2005. Settled and unsettled spaces: are we free to roam? *Sovereign Subjects*, 1, pp.40-52.

White, B., 2016. Under the tree, King John decided to kill 28 Welsh hostages who were mainly children. *Nottingham Evening Post*, [online] 29 Feb. Available at: <http://ezproxy.lib.ryerson.ca/login?url=https://www.proquest.com/newspapers/under-tree-king-john-decided-kill-28-welsh/docview/1768631405/se-2?accountid=13631> [Accessed 15 April 2021].

Wilkinson, L., 2007. Tolkien and the surrendering of power. In: T. Hart and I. Khovacs, eds. *Tree of tales: Tolkien, literature, and theology*. Waco: Baylor University Press. pp.71-84.

Wood, R., 2003. *The gospel according to Tolkien: visions of the kingdom in Middle-earth*. Louisville: Westminster John Knox Press.

Zhang, J., Liu, L.R., Shi, X.C., Wang, H. and Huang, G., 2017. Environmental information in modern fiction and ecocriticism. *Journal of Environmental Informatics*, 30(1), pp.41-52.

Glorfindel: Tolkien's Intertextual Link Between the First and the Third Age

Brendan Dyer

J.R.R. Tolkien's back catalogue of secondary texts on Middle-earth gives readers deep-dive explorative material that supports the character of Glorfindel and solidifies his presence in Middle-earth as read in *The Lord of the Rings* (1954-55), Tolkien's primary text. In the books that are considered secondary to *The Lord of the Rings*, Tolkien has clarified governing rules for Middle-earth that elaborate on a striking amount of verisimilitude in the functions of disembodiment and reincarnation (Tolkien C., 1996, p. 378). These devices, though glimpsed in the primary text, are incorporated and explained much more in *The Silmarillion* (Tolkien C., 1977) and supplemental essays in *The History of Middle-earth* (Tolkien C., 1996). Aware of these establishments at the time of pursuing publication, Tolkien worked diligently in communication with publishers urging them to simultaneously print what was then *The Silmarillion* with *The Lord of the Rings*. He was certain that the texts would support one another as they do today and that the former would provide supplemental information for the latter. This is made clearer when reading *The History of Middle-earth* and applying the rules encased within to a character analysis of Glorfindel.

As a result of the delayed publication for *The Silmarillion*, readers developed inquiries that Tolkien would later go on to address in his many letters, essays, and correspondences shared with fans and scholars. A practice that would have been mitigated had a fuller understanding of Middle-earth been supplied in the first place. Had Tolkien been provided the opportunity to assemble an acceptable draft of *The Silmarillion* and related tales for publication alongside the primary text, the evolution of *The Lord of the Rings* in pop culture and in adaptations would have been different than how we see it today. One notable variance would have been readers' and film makers' considerations of characters like Glorfindel, a character who fortifies Tolkien's inclinations toward parallelism, self-sacrifice, and the motifs of Elvish reincarnation following their unfortunate disembodiment.

Before the average reader placed their eyes on *The Lord of the Rings* for the first time in July of 1954, Tolkien had already written a well-established history relating to Middle-earth and the people who live in it. These mythopoeic tales were hesitantly received by fans of *The Hobbit* (Tolkien, 1995) and *The Lord of the Rings* and drew criticism in reviews as being too overwhelming for readers (Foote, 1977). This material came to be known as *The Silmarillion* but similar tales and additional information can be found in other books like the massive, twelve volume series titled *The History of Middle-earth* (Tolkien C., 1983-1996). Despite poor reception in sales when compared to the more popular works, books in this collection—known widely today as writings related to Tolkien's Legendarium—delineate prominent events that occurred in Arda throughout the many thousands of years that preceded Frodo leaving the Shire. These events include creation stories, the darkening of Valinor, the siege of cities like Gondolin, Beren and Luthien's romance, Eärendil's voyage with the Silmaril, the tragedy of Turin, and the mention of many familiar names only referenced in passing in material from the Third Age. Alongside these stories are also editorial accounts by Christopher Tolkien and his father explaining the development of drafts, variances throughout the work, and its evolution.

Among the names mentioned in the Legendarium that are not as widely recognised as Melkor's, Eärendil's, or Sauron's among many others, Glorfindel's name is a duplication that appears in *The Fellowship of the Ring* (Tolkien, 1954a) and in *The Silmarillion*. As a result, fan speculation around this character ensued following publication of *The Silmarillion*, leading Tolkien to ultimately address the issue of both Glorfindels with an argument supporting they are the same character. As such, Glorfindel today stands as a figure of Tolkien's greater intentions with his mythologic texts when it comes to offering context within his more popular novels.

According to Tolkien (Tolkien C., 1996, p. 379), Glorfindel's name first appeared in his imaginative world between 1916 and 1917 in "The Fall of Gondolin." Despite being one of the earliest characters of Middle-earth's history, Glorfindel has gone overlooked in film adaptations and has garnered the perception of being merely another elf whose history is long and assumedly no different than any other elf's. This is the result of the initial limited information given to readers at the time of publication as well as pop culture influences lacking an understanding about him and how important he is to Tolkien's worldbuilding mechanics.

There are many instances of parallelism in *The Lord of the Rings* as it stands, but Tolkien's thematic techniques in story design extend throughout *The History of Middle-earth* and supportive texts. Glorfindel is an example of one intertextual link that's part of a parallel structure extending between *The Lord of the Rings* and the complicated events leading up to it. Publishers were, understandably, hesitant to embrace the more obscure writings and overwhelming content in which Glorfindel plays a key role, but the fabricated lost history of Middle-earth is critical to Tolkien's overall design. Moreover, these myths are imperative to character analyses and contribute to a deeper understanding of characters who are within and without the fellowship.

Glorfindel would certainly receive the praise he is deserved had his earliest exploits been widely published alongside *The Lord of the Rings*. The issue in his characterisation as it relates to a massive audience, however, is that his deeds are documented in stories that were not published until well after Tolkien's passing. A simple truth is that material about Glorfindel was not and never would be as widely produced as the trilogy or *The Hobbit* because it was not encased in a dramatic, dialogue-fuelled romance. Despite this, Tolkien frequently insisted on the importance of tales that expanded on the First and Second Ages (Carpenter and Tolkien C., 2000, Letter 124, p. 136). Unfortunately, publication of those stories was unlikely due to a lack of concrete narrative structure, complicated and obscure storytelling mechanics, and publishers' unwillingness to green light high-risk printing commitments that might not have the same monetary yield as a more accessible read. As a result, Glorfindel's earliest feats in *The Silmarillion* would go unrecognised and his importance alluded to during "The Ring Goes South" in *The Fellowship of the Ring* would remain obscure (Tolkien, 1954a, p. 289).

Glorfindel appears for the first time in publication outside of *The Lord of the Rings* in *The Silmarillion*. The book was printed posthumously in 1977 after undergoing edits by Christopher Tolkien to address inconsistencies and create a general story flow that would be accessible to readers. But by then readers had already established a strong familiarity with Middle-earth as they knew it, and associations with certain characters had emerged in pop culture. This is partly attributed to Ballentine Books' official authorised mass-market paperback release of the trilogy in 1965 (Brown, 2019). The vast popularity of the story grew once it was opened to a wider audience with a more affordable and widely printed edition. As such, the history behind it would still remain unseen for another 12 years, allowing the primary text to culturally evolve beyond its preceding tales. This left *The Silmarillion* and the other secondary material at a steeper disadvantage in reader reception.

After *The Silmarillion* was printed, *The History of Middle-earth* by Tolkien and edited by his son Christopher, saw its first volume in 1983 and its last in 1996. This was a time period in which an expanded version of "The Fall of Gondolin" and essays about Glorfindel emerged. These writings drove fan speculation, and inquiries continued to develop around the duplication of the name Glorfindel, especially because Tolkien had written two essays on him within the chapter "Last Writings" in *The People of Middle-earth*, stating there is no elf of prominence who shares a name with any other elf (Tolkien C., 1996, p. 380). By the time that all of *The History of Middle-earth* volumes were published, Tolkien had somewhat answered the question of whether or not Glorfindel of Gondolin was akin to or the same as Glorfindel of Rivendell.

Rather, for those who read all of Tolkien's work, that question was answered even without the provision of the essays on Glorfindel. His arch and actions were so similar to other themes explored in *The Lord of the Rings* that an apt conclusion can be drawn: both characters are one and the same and had experienced an episode of Elvish reincarnation. Whether or not the original readers of *The Lord of the Rings* could have arrived at that conclusion by reading *The Silmarillion* beforehand, is unknown. Any familiarity with Tolkien's governing rules, however, would have justly presented an argument that it was indeed the case. If nothing else, analyses of reincarnation would have made for interesting discussions at a time when *The Lord of the Rings* was building the cultural groundwork for what would become the Fantasy genre.

Tolkien's Legendarium received a devoted readership—albeit ones much smaller than *The Lord of the Rings*—and in exploration of the texts, Tolkien's patterns were lain bare to readers; new light on his genius was revealed and readers were prompted to see Middle-earth renewed with vigour, with stories, lore, and with new information. Each of these aspects adheres to Tolkien's initial insistence to publishers, that content in what was then considered *The Silmarillion* was companion to much of the obscure references present in the texts of *The Hobbit*, but even more so *The Lord of the Rings*. He writes in a letter to Sir Stanley Unwin when referring to *The Silmarillion*:

> Its shadow was deep on the later parts of *The Hobbit*. It has captured *The Lord of the Rings*, so that that has become simply its continuation and completion, requiring *The Silmarillion* to be fully intelligible—without a lot of references and explanations that clutter it in one or two places (Carpenter and Tolkien C., 2000, Letter 124, pp. 136-137).

The lore that readers received from all of the books finally published was how the material was meant to be presented by its author. Although *The Lord of the Rings* stands alone as an encased story, *The Silmarillion* provided new layers that were not initially seen at the time first editions of the trilogy were published. While a critical analysis of *The Lord of the Rings* itself would generate compelling arguments to support Tolkien's intentions behind thematic devices utilised in the text, those arguments would be further supported by incorporating material from a thematically similar secondary source. Especially if that source is referred to by the author as having "bubbled up, infiltrated, and probably spoiled everything" he tried to write (Carpenter and Tolkien C., 2000, Letter 124, pp. 135-137).

Of the motifs consistent among all the ages of Middle-earth, parallelism is the one most interestingly utilised in Tolkien's tool box. Several parallels exist in Middle-earth that connect intertextually the themes and motifs Tolkien harps on repeatedly throughout his work. Although these themes are realised in reading *The Lord of the Rings* as it stands alone, exploration of more expansive material excites analyses and generates more compelling arguments, revealing more of Tolkien's consistency and the fullness of his world. The more apparent and widely analysed theme is parallelism surrounding self-sacrifice (Hausmann, 2015). For instance, connecting Aragorn's and Arwen's romance to Beren's and Luthien's; romances in which one lover recedes from immortal life and in self-sacrifice lives with love for just one lifetime among Men. This sort of analysis draws out a parallel structure in Tolkien's writing and highlights consistencies that embellish the Third Age with insight from material preceding it. However, if given only *The Lord of the Rings* as a source, scholars would have very little to explore and devices in the primary text would be lost in obscurity. This is one of the firmly held positions Tolkien harboured in his pursuit to publish the books together. It's no doubt he understood the significance of Middle-earth's mythic past in evoking the themes he brought to surface in *The Lord of the Rings*. Difficulty, however, lay in conveying that to a publishing company so it might chance to risk resources on the printing of a book steeped in what were then merely private references to an imaginative secondary world.

Also, immediately recognised in a reading of *The Lord of the Rings* without knowledge of events prior is the dualistic reflection and parallel structure extant between the nine Nazgûl and the nine members of *The Fellowship of the Ring* (Tolkien, 1954a, pp. 288-289). Both reflections of the other consist of representatives of varying locale and significance with both parties being at one point mingled with Glorfindel either in thought or action. However, without a reading of events preceding Frodo's inheritance of the One Ring, this topic is limited in its confinement to events of the Third Age. Further inquiry would necessitate reading material from *The Silmarillion* and appendices published with *The Return of the King* (Tolkien, 1955) to more fully understand that duality, how Glorfindel is connected, and why Gandalf comments on his significance in the chapter "Many Meetings" in *The Fellowship of the Ring* (Tolkien, 1954a, p. 235).

The origins of the Nazgûl date among the Second Age as Men— nine mortal kings believed to be of both Númenor and Middle-earth—who were corrupted by Sauron's malice and bound by the enslaving powers of the One Ring (Tolkien, C. 1977, p. 289). The shadow of Sauron polarises them from mortality and juxtaposes them not only with their previous life and the lives of those in the fellowship, but accents them as solidified definitions of despair cursed with elongated life on the habitable earth to perform Sauron's bidding. In this, Sauron brings darkness from light, a facet parallel to Melkor's actions in the First Age. The unnaturally long life of the

Nazgûl contrasts their once transient lives as kings and it defies the Gift of Ilúvatar bestowed upon Men: to live and die unbound to the circles of the world. The Nazgúl are ever at odds with the fellowship who all willingly chose their fate in support of destroying the One Ring, a choice adverse to what the Nazgûl are, as they are forced into an existence bound to preserving it.

The Nazgûl, who might otherwise be mortal and experience Man's fateful doom, distort the Gift of Ilúvatar and cry with the voice of death in mockery of that fate. They are symbolic of destruction, they harbour fear, and cast doubt upon the living who seek hope and life above all things; they are emblematic of life and death and a perversion of the immortality of the Eldar. This is a motif that harkens to Melkor's shadow cast upon the gift that Ilúvatar sought to give Men in the embracing of death as read in *The Silmarillion*:

> Death is their fate, the gift of Ilúvatar, which as Time wears even the Powers shall envy. But Melkor cast his shadow upon it, and confounded it with darkness, and brought forth evil out of good, and fear out of hope. Yet of old the Valar declared to the Elves in Valinor that Men shall join in the Second Music of the Ainur; whereas Ilúvatar has not revealed what he purposes for the Elves after the World's end, and Melkor has not discovered it (Tolkien C., 1977, p. 42).

This same distorting malice is witnessed more concretely in Melkor's possession of the Silmarils. The jewels of the Noldor burn his hands as he clutches them, blackening his flesh as he sets them in his Iron Crown. It's in wearing that Iron Crown too that the bright Silmarils, containing the light of the trees of Valinor, are corrupted in their hallowed state to burn forever upon his head (Tolkien C., 1977, p. 81). Melkor would never be free of this pain and here is represented his very malice and the distorting way that evil functions in Tolkien's work. This passive corruption develops darkness from light and dread from hope. It is the motif at play in all major, dramatic structures present in Tolkien's Legendarium and is the central piece of the ongoing conflict between light and dark; good and evil.

The distortion of life in this way is layered as well with recurrent confrontations and assimilations of the living with death in the Legendarium and mythopoeic establishments of the primary and secondary texts. Most often these moments are fluid with self-sacrifice and layered even further with a protagonist's fateful collision with an antagonistic counterpart to fight on behalf of the greater good. Heroes who act to preserve in the face of evil the pure of heart, not fearing death, would be those least influenced by Melkor's or Sauron's distorting malice, and they live freely to act as the truly righteous would, without corruption.

Although common occurrences of these moments include the acts of Elves and Maiar, Men also are capable of such feats despite inclinations to be influenced by the Dark Lord's dreadful shadow. Boromir, for example, acts with self-sacrifice and heroism when defending Merry and Pippin after the temptation of the ring failed to corrupt him. However, it's unlikely that a Man could rise to challenge a foe like the Nazgûl. In a challenge of that measure with death incarnate, Boromir, or any other Man, would have failed. For when it happened one thousand years into the Third Age that Sauron's armies, led by the Lord of the Nazgûl, besieged the ancient kingdoms of Men called Rhudaur, Cardolan, and Arthedain, it was the Elf-lord Glorfindel who rose to challenge the Witch-King and defeated him, causing him to flee (Tolkien, 1955, p. 331). Not without prophesizing that no Man would defeat the Witch-King, though. Because Men live in the midst of light and dark, the only counterpart appropriate for a foe representative of Darkness in Middle-earth is a protagonist of equal or greater stature who is representative of far more powerful forces. Forces so powerful that their very being would disrupt the secretive nature of the fellowship's journey to Mordor (Tolkien, 1954a, p. 289).

That it was an elf and not a Man who defied the Lord of the Nazgûl is nearly to be expected if it's established that Men are fated to death and the Nazgûl are that very end incarnate. This is consistent with the duality of the Nazgûl's existence when contrasted with Men and highlights Glorfindel's significance in the Legendarium as playing a key role in combatting the enemy. The Eldar are untied to the cycle of life and death as immortal beings, only they could stand in the spectrum between both ends and challenge it. Although included in the appendices, had this confrontation been provided more accessibly in the publication history of *The Lord of the Rings*, it's likely that the impact of Glorfindel in adaptations would have evolved. Cultural references to his character would certainly develop around the chapter, "Flight to the Ford" and analyses of that chapter would be more widespread to include theses that circled Glorfindel's power as it relates to the historical events he played a part in, during Sauron's earliest movements.

There is some unseen but written power flowing through Glorfindel. This is underscored by the Witch-King's flight from their confrontation. It was understood by him that Glorfindel is a force distilled with power from the earliest ages of Arda. Readers are given a small gleam of this information when in Rivendell, and reunited with Gandalf, Frodo claimed to have seen a "white figure that shone and did not grow dim like the others" (Tolkien, 1954a, p. 289). As Gandalf accounts to Frodo in that same dialogue exchange, Glorfindel is "one of the mighty of the Firstborn. He is an Elf-lord of a house of princes." Affirming moreover Glorfindel's continuity in the Legendarium and presence in the earliest days of the Eldar. Gandalf's account to Frodo is the singular account in *The Lord of the Rings* outside the appendices that places Glorfindel of Rivendell in a time and place outside of his idle dwelling in Middle-earth. While these details stand alone for readers to realise to some extent the significance of this character, Tolkien was aware that by the time Frodo reached Rivendell, he had written much more that would serve the background of his characterisation. However, even the information printed in the appendices would not be provided until the publication of *The Return of the King*, a year after the release of *The Fellowship of the Ring*.

Although Glorfindel is notable for having confronted Sauron's most devoted servants, that action is not outside the expected bravery as seen in the earliest chronology of his development as a character. "Alas! 'Tis Glorfindel and the Balrog," became a phrase among the Eldar in reference to moments where good is fighting at odds with a force of significant evil (Tolkien C., 2015, p. 194). Similar to Gandalf's self-sacrifice when he confronts Durin's Bane in the depths of Moria on the bridge of Khazad-Dûm, the phrase refers to Glorfindel's own battle with a Balrog to ensure the safe passage of his companions.

In the chapter, "The Fall of Gondolin" in *The Book of Lost Tales, Part Two* (Tolkien C., 2015) Glorfindel's bravery led to one of the most important events in the History of Middle-earth, his securing the safe passage of Eärendil. In what is one of the farthest reaches of parallelism through all the ages of Middle-earth, the Elf-lord confronts a Balrog that approached him in the Encircling Mountains beyond the besieged city of Gondolin. He was at the time escaping the city with Tuor and his son, Eärendil, as well as a host of other refuges when they were come upon by a Balrog from the ranks of Morgoth's army. Glorfindel did battle with this foe, allowing the others to escape, most notable of whom was Eärendil. Glorfindel perishes alongside his enemy upon the mountain side much like how Gandalf and Durin's Bane fall on the heights of Zirakzigil above the fallen dwarf hold of Moria. At this point Glorfindel experiences what came to be referred to by Tolkien as disembodiment and he was sent to Mandos for his spirit to be judged before being sent to the Halls of Waiting (Tolkien C., 1996, p. 378). Gandalf, in his combat with Durin's Bane, also experiences disembodiment but is confirmed in *The Two Towers* to ultimately return to Middle-earth reincarnated with greater power and of higher standing for his deeds in life (Tolkien, 1954b, p. 98). Although Gandalf's return is expanded on in *The Lord of the Rings*, reincarnation and re-embodiment are more obscure aspects of Tolkien's governing rules within Arda. However, the publication of texts companion to *The Lord of the Rings* has enabled more exploratory studies of Tolkien's rules in Middle-earth as well as the significance of events set in the Third Age.

Specific attention is paid to Glorfindel's disembodiment and return to Middle-earth in the chapter, "Last Writings," within *The Peoples of Middle-earth*. These are some of the final essays that Tolkien had written related to Middle-earth. They address the question that had coincidentally become a widely analysed scenario layered in speculation by fans with the slow, posthumous release of the secondary texts: are there two Glorfindels? While Tolkien's answer to the question is much less an answer than it is uncertain speculation itself, it promulgated discussion of Glorfindel and highlighted him as a poignant, but overlooked, character in *The Lord of the Rings* who shares an arch with Gandalf, Tolkien's most central character in his primary texts.

Elves, like Glorfindel, were intended to be immortal and the aspect of disembodiment, as Tolkien called it, was not necessarily death. Disembodiment and re-embodiment were governing rules applied to a race of people in his secondary world. With these rules, Tolkien also established that it was the duty of the Valar to restore the lives of elves should they be deemed worthy and if they desired it (Tolkien C., 1996, p. 378). In structuring his argument, Tolkien refutes discussion that both Glorfindel's are different and goes as far to support his creative choice, writing that "it may be found that acceptance of the identity of Glorfindel of old and of the Third Age will actually explain what is said of him and improve the story" (Tolkien C., 1996, p. 380).

Indeed, additional texts about Glorfindel have changed perspectives of the character from being one tossed into the plot and overlooked by cinematic adaptations. His power is no longer fogged with obscurity and wonder. He is, with the provisional information provided by Tolkien, a character who transcends his moment in the narrative to stand as an emblematic figure representative of Tolkien's overworld rules, historical establishments, and affirms governing magical elements surrounding Elvish reincarnation. Unfortunately, because publication of these stories was delayed, scholars developed the perception that Tolkien was editorialising his work outside of his original intentions (Lewis and Currie, 2005, p. 53).

Christopher Tolkien (1996) writes on page 382 in *The Peoples of Middle-earth* in editorial notes, that notes on Elvish reincarnation were scribbled on the manuscript for the essay, "Glorfindel I," suggesting that his father was either theorising or establishing some definitive rules which Glorfindel supported. In his deeds and self-sacrifice during the events of "The Fall of Gondolin," Glorfindel ensures the safe passage of Eärendil the Mariner. Tolkien writes in a letter to Milton Waldman containing a brief summation of *The Silmarillion* that Eärendil "is important as the person who brings *The Silmarillion* to its end, and as providing in his offspring the main links to and persons in the tales of the later Ages" (Carpenter and Tolkien C., 2000, Letter 130, p. 150). Though he would not need to provide a defence of Glorfindel until many years after *The Lord of the Rings* was published, Tolkien in providing this note of Eärendil was part of the way to establishing the significance of Glorfindel, a character without whom Eärendil would not have survived, and Elrond would not have been born, meaning that the Third Age as readers know it would be vastly different.

That Tolkien defended Glorfindel post-publication and explained the duplication of names well after the story was written is unsavoury to some scholars who suggest it was an error on his behalf. This sort of post-publication editorialising often times deters fans and discredit's the author's judgement and intentions. For instance,

J.K. Rowling, who returns at times to editorialise her stories with supplemental information in ways to appeal to a wider audience, has experienced backlash from fans for revealing details about characters she doesn't include in her books or film adaptations (Shamsian, 2019). However, Tolkien had no intention of garnering a larger readership, and publication of this material occurred after his death. His defence of the single Glorfindel theory was a device intended to support the pertinence of *The Silmarillion* in the first place and how it related to *The Lord of the Rings*. It only aided his argument that he had structured compelling narrative evidence in support of his theory in his books well before he needed to defend his intentions. The theme of self-sacrifice and the parallelism in *The Lord of the Rings* made his point all the more convincing as being aspects of his writing which were consistent and unchanged.

The connections established in the First Age and Second Age material were, of course, hesitantly approached by publishers because they were expansive and covered the acts of characters who readers were seldom familiar with when *The Lord of the Rings* came out. Only after two decades of it garnering a readership was the earlier material publicised because by then there was a devoted following and a fandom that publishing houses had never witnessed before in genre fiction. While Tolkien knew well the merits of Middle-earth's history when held relative to the elusive story mechanics of *The Lord of the Rings*, it was a hard sell to publishers who were understandably far less familiar with the mythos of Arda. But as Tolkien's back catalogue of writing emerged, the information that surfaced showed that an artist grappled with foundational texts to unfurl a mythic, secondary history full of elaborate themes similarly woven throughout the primary text and supported by characters, like Glorfindel, who were intellectually and imaginatively consistent.

References

Brown, A., 2019. *How The Lord of the Rings Changed Publishing Forever.* [online] Available at: <https://www.tor.com/2019/01/03/a-new-age-the-lord-of-the-rings-by-j-r-r-tolkien/> [Accessed 15 August 2021].

Carpenter, H. and Tolkien, C. eds., 2000. *The Letters of J.R.R. Tolkien.* Boston: Houghton Mifflin Harcourt.

Foote, T., 1977. Middle-earth Genesis. *Time* [online] 24 Oct. Available at: <http://content.time.com/time/subscriber/article/0,33009,915707,00.html> [Accessed 17 August 2021].

Hausmann, M., 2015. Parallel Paths and Distorting Mirrors: Strategic Duality as a Narrative Principle in Tolkien's Works. *Mallorn: The Journal of the Tolkien Society*, [e-journal] (56) pp.31-35. Available through: JSTOR <www.jstor.org/stable/48614837> [Accessed 19 August 2021].

Lewis, A. and Elizabeth, C., 2005. *The Forsaken Realm of Tolkien: Tolkien and the Medieval Tradition.* Wimbledon: Medea.

Shamsian, J., 2019. *People are mocking J.K. Rowling for saying Dumbledor had an 'incredibly intense,' sexual relationship with Grindelwald.* [online] Available at: <https://www.insider.com/jk-rowling-dumbledore-and-grindelwald-had-sexual-relationship-2019-3> [Accessed 20 August 2021].

Tolkien, C. ed., 1977. *The Silmarillion.* Boston: Houghton Mifflin Company.
—, 1996. *The Peoples of Middle-earth – The History of Middle-earth Vol. XII.* Boston: Houghton Mifflin Company.
—, ed., 2015. *The Book of Lost Tales Part II– The History of Middle-earth Vol. II.* New York: HarperCollins.

Tolkien, J.R.R., 1954a. *The Fellowship of the Ring.* London: George Allen & Unwin.
—, 1954b. *The Two Towers.* London: George Allen & Unwin.
—, 1955. *The Return of the King.* London: George Allen & Unwin.
—, 1995. *The Hobbit.* New York: HarperCollins.

Cartography of a Character:
On (Re)Writing Nerdanel

Dawn M. Walls-Thumma

In his essay "On Fairy-stories," Tolkien (1966) portrays the creative process through the metaphors of the Tree of Tales and Cauldron of Story. Although these analogies have become familiar to many Tolkien fans and are certainly evocatively illustrated, in his letters, he often described his own story-making process cartographically: as a narrative movement into unvisited territory, at which point the potential for new "unexplained" or "unattainable vistas" open and offer further enticement deeper into the realm of story.

Writing of Tolkien's interests as an academic and philologist, Tom Shippey—himself an academic and philologist who filled the same role at Leeds University as Tolkien once did—says of Tolkien's inspiration: "One sees that the thing which attracted Tolkien most was darkness: the blank spaces, much bigger than most people realise, on the literary and historical map …" (Shippey, 2003, p. 38). Tolkien himself, writing in his letters of his creative work, spoke over and over again of using "vistas" to entice readers imaginatively deeper into his Secondary World, describing "an attraction like that of viewing far off an unvisited island, or seeing the towers of a distant city gleaming in a sunlit mist" (Carpenter and Tolkien C., 1981, Letter 247, p. 333). According to Tolkien, once tempted into the far-away, readers need to discover new vistas awaiting on the next far horizon to remain engaged in the story.

The majority of Tolkien's work is now posthumously published notes and drafts, unintentionally creating that very effect that he describes to myriad readers in his correspondence. After the narrative richness of *The Lord of the Rings* (1954-55)—over one thousand pages devoted to a single year—the rest of the Legendarium appears as a break in the mist, admitting a brief glimpse of people and places before closing in again. There are 213 named characters in *The Silmarillion* (Tolkien C., 1977); of them, a quarter are named just once. One of these characters briefly glimpsed and swiftly fading is Nerdanel, the wife of Fëanor (himself the second-most-mentioned character in *The Silmarillion*). Appearing only in Tolkien's unpublished notes and drafts, Nerdanel is written with the dim, fragmentary quality that Tolkien found so enticing. Her rewriting, first by Christopher Tolkien in the making of *The Silmarillion*, then again by hundreds of fans allured in her direction, illustrates how the cartography of a narrative can close and expand upon a character, driven in part by the (re) writer's estimation of her centrality within that narrative.

The Wanderings of Nerdanel

Several *Silmarillion* characters are mentioned or alluded to in *The Lord of the Rings*. Nerdanel is not among them. Fëanor, however, debuts—along with his sons—in Tolkien's earliest known work on the Legendarium, collected as part of *The Book of Lost Tales Part I* (Tolkien C., 1983). Thus Nerdanel's existence is at least implied, almost from the outset. It was only relatively late in Tolkien's work on the *Silmarillion* materials, however, that Nerdanel received a name and identity beyond a woman-shaped space on the page: unfilled but unable to be erased.

It is in two late documents that Tolkien writes almost the entirety of Nerdanel's character. The first is a draft of the *Silmarillion*, dated approximately 1958 and from which much of the published *Silmarillion* is drawn, that Christopher Tolkien titled *The Later* Quenta Silmarillion 2 (LQ2). Here, Nerdanel emerges in sudden and often surprising detail.

Nerdanel's singularity among Tolkien's women characters begins at her introduction, where she is stated to be "not among the fairest of her people" (Tolkien C., 1993, p. 272). There are twenty-one women or female characters in *The Silmarillion* who are named five or more times. Of them, about half are described as being physically beautiful (e.g., Finduilas and Morwen) or so alluring that men are inexplicably drawn to them (e.g., Melian and Arien). None, aside from Ungoliant, are described as unattractive. Nerdanel's appearance was such that her marriage to the ravishing Fëanor caused a scandal—euphemistically phrased as "wonder"— among "many" who apparently felt he could have done better.

Perhaps by having resisted his usual mould—or rut—for writing women as distinguished primarily by their appearances, Tolkien's introduction of Nerdanel in LQ2 continues to be remarkable:

> Of Mahtan [her father] Nerdanel learned much of crafts that *women of the Noldor seldom used*: the making of things of metal and stone. She made images, some of the Valar in their forms visible, and many others of men and women of the Eldar, and these were so like that their friends, if they knew not her art, would speak to them; but many things she wrought also of her own thought in shapes strong and strange but beautiful (Tolkien C., 1993, p. 272, emphasis mine).

While Tolkien doesn't directly state why Fëanor chose Nerdanel, he certainly implies strongly that their love grew from genuine friendship and mutual respect. Nerdanel "loved to wander far from the dwellings of the Noldor, either beside the long shores of the Sea or in the hills; and thus she and Fëanor had met and were companions in many journeys" (Tolkien C., 1993 p. 272). In the second paragraph of LQ2, Tolkien contrasts them. Nerdanel is patient; she listens to and observes others around her in order to understand rather than master them. Yet lest we mistake their marriage as one of simple affection, or as primarily intellectual, Tolkien is careful to note of their seven children that none of the Eldar had so many.

What Tolkien does directly state is that Nerdanel held a special influence over Fëanor. The line in the published *Silmarillion* about how Fëanor "sought the counsel of none that dwelt in Aman, great or small, save only and for a little while of Nerdanel the wise, his wife" originated in LQ2, as does the line about how "at first she restrained Fëanor when the fire of his heart burned too hot; but his later deeds grieved her and they became estranged" (Tolkien C., 1977, pp. 66, 64). It is significant that Nerdanel went from a mere implication—a "textual ghost," to borrow the term coined by the fanfiction writer Dwimordene and popularised by the fanfiction writer Elleth (2020)—to possessing the power to sway one of the Legendarium's most ironclad wills, that of Fëanor. It certainly suggests that, even in passing, Tolkien considered that this heretofore unnamed woman deserved a larger role in her family's tale.

Nonetheless, Nerdanel would not make a significant appearance again for another decade, in the text *The Shibboleth of Fëanor* (Tolkien C., 1996), published no earlier than 1968. Here, we see Nerdanel's established wisdom emerge once more, with an important embellishment: she is credited with foresight, a talent belonging to some of the most important characters in the Legendarium, such as

Galadriel, Finrod Felagund, and Melian. In Nerdanel's case, at the naming of her youngest twin sons, she chooses the name "fated," predicting that after Fëanor's rebellion one will not set foot on Middle-earth. In this version of the story, that twin later burns during the destruction of the ships at Losgar.

In this text, we also learn more of her estrangement from Fëanor, to which Tolkien often alluded, but on which he never fully elaborated. While we know that she did not go with him into exile at Formenos, which of his actions prior to that point "grieved her" to the point of sundering? In *Shibboleth*, we learn that her kin were among the Aulendur, a contingent of Noldor with a special devotion to Aulë, and she was counselled by her father not to participate in Fëanor's rebellion. Fëanor goes so far as to accuse her—when she confronts him at the seaside asking him to leave her the "fated" twin—of being "cozened by Aulë" and, of her warning, says to her, "Take your evil omens to the Valar who will delight in them … I defy them" (Tolkien C., 1996, p. 354). With mentions of the Aulendur occurring in concomitant texts, one wonders if Tolkien was on the verge of enlarging upon the political situation in Valinor at the time of Fëanor's rebellion.

Therefore, over the course of ten years, in fits and starts, Tolkien scribes the cartography of a character. Within his characterisation of Nerdanel are many of the "unexplained vistas" that he employed to generate interest from his readers, but with the details that he gave—her singularity as a craftswoman among the Noldor, her gift of foresight that puts her in league with some of the most significant characters in the Legendarium, intimations of the broader Noldorin political situation—he creates the potential for a character at the centre of her professional, political, and familial world, all the more notable because she is a woman.

And so Nerdanel is written.

Rewriting I: "A Scale So Small"

In October 1953, Tolkien wrote despairingly to his publisher about the maps of *The Lord of the Rings*: "It is the attempt to cut them down and omitting all their colour (verbal and otherwise) to reduce them to black and white bareness, on a scale so small that hardly any names can appear, that has stumped me" (Carpenter and Tolkien C., 1981, Letter 141, p. 171).

When Tolkien "mapped" the character of Nerdanel in a pair of drafts produced over the span of a decade, he charted features that brought her contours to life: her wisdom, her insight (and foresight), her artistic prodigy, her notable influence on her husband, and her position within the broader political situation of Valinor. With that characterization, he also effaced, ever so slightly, the mists shrouding farther vistas pertaining to her character. Tolkien's late writings admit the reader into an intimate proximity with Nerdanel and her family—a marital spat, low blows and all, that centres on commanding the affection of their children—that belies the aloofness typical of the Elves elsewhere in Tolkien's writings. These glimpses of her character distil the grandeur of *The Silmarillion* down to a reminder that much of the lives of these characters concerned the small hurts and triumphs of the everyday.

Yet none of this material was published by Tolkien. Instead, it was his son Christopher who took on the prodigious task of winnowing from decades of his father's writing the details that best represented the early tales of Arda as his father probably, likely, (hopefully?) would have wanted them told. The result was the published *Silmarillion*, a coherent, consistent narrative of the early history of Arda presented with minimal commentary. Yet the coherence, consistency, and readability of the published *Silmarillion* obscures the complexity of the editorial process that produced it. Christopher himself, in the foreword to *The Book of Lost Tales 1*, lamented the "serious misapprehension" of fans who believe he wrote *The Silmarillion* himself using just his father's notes (Tolkien C., 1983, p. 7). Other fans perceived a simpler process of selecting and stitching together finished writings with little to no editorial interference. In fact, as meticulously documented by Douglas Charles Kane in *Arda Reconstructed* (2011), the process ranged between these extremes, with some sections lifted wholesale from Tolkien's drafts, others (especially those based on very old material) almost entirely rewritten by Christopher, and many others a confusing amalgam of sentences and phrases coming from a variety of drafts.

The Western narrative, confined as it mostly is to the realm of the print and digital, plants *publication* at the end of an off-ramp exiting the swirl of constant rewriting, revision, and reconsideration that is the writing process. In Tolkien's *writing* of Nerdanel, she was never permitted to achieve this finality. It is Christopher Tolkien who effected her first *re*writing with the published *Silmarillion*, thus presenting her for the first time to the wider reading public and granting her the illusion of conclusiveness. In fact, Nerdanel as written in the published *Silmarillion* reveals *Christopher*'s interpretation and subsequent selection of his father's work—a selectivity that was better informed than any other editor could have been, yes, but ultimately interpreted and selected all the same—and cannot possibly represent how Nerdanel would have manifested had she been given a chance to be *written* into finality by Tolkien.

Christopher Tolkien's rewriting of Nerdanel pares her down significantly. His father's panic over *The Lord of the Rings* maps absent "all their colour" and diminished to "bareness, on a scale so small" could just as aptly describe Nerdanel's characterisation in the published text. Most of the details that make her so distinct in Tolkien's writing of her are stripped from the published text. She is mentioned just four times in the context of her marriage and motherhood, influence over Fëanor, and estrangement from him. Gone are her wanderings, her artistic gifts—the line about her father teaching her to work metal is rewritten so that Fëanor receives the benefits of his instruction—and most of the details about her "understanding" personality. Those attributes that mark her as distinct among Tolkien's women—her lack of beauty and her foresight—are both gone from the text. Once, a Tolkien trivia night I attended asked the "hard" question, "Who was the wife of Fëanor?" And that is what she becomes, in this rewriting: a triviality, an inconsequence, a mere name on the larger story-scape devoid of details or features that make her of much interest.

Kane (2011) is critical of Christopher Tolkien's rewriting of Nerdanel, pointing out that her character is part of a pattern in his editorial choices where the roles of women are reduced. Indis is another character who appears in the same chapter as Nerdanel, who plays a role in the same political and family situations, and is likewise diminished in the published text. He notes that the edits in the chapter "Of Fëanor and the Unchaining of Melkor"—where Nerdanel and Indis featured heavily in the unpublished drafts—are some of the most extensive in the published *Silmarillion*, making it one of the shortest chapters in the book, implying that these were not painful cuts necessary to curb an overgrown chapter but that the content itself—the *characters* themselves—were ruled unimportant.

It is perhaps more productive to ask what these edits show of Christopher Tolkien's view of the crux of the story. The diminishment of Nerdanel (and Indis) direct the focus of the story outward, to Middle-earth, leaving Aman—fittingly, the only major realm for which Tolkien did not draw a map—as but a staging ground for the main action. The vistas toward which he hopes readers watch and wonder lie over the Great Sea, not within the unworldly bounds of Faerie, of Aman. Nerdanel's plain looks, her friendship-matured-to-romance with Fëanor, their bickering on the beach before he departs—it may be that these details ground too firmly in the humdrum a land where Tolkien later seeks to convince us that the streets are spoiled only by the dust of diamonds.

The effect of this editorial choice on Nerdanel, as a character, is the opposite. It renders her not inscrutable but *forgettable*. In her classic 1984 essay "The Feminine Principle in Tolkien," Melanie Rawls argues for the elevation of many of the characteristics of women in the Legendarium. Nerdanel—especially as written by Tolkien—holds many of the traits she names. Yet Rawls identifies also the feminine *failing* as impotence, offering Aredhel and Tar-Míriel as exemplars for their inability to forestall the disastrous decisions of the men in their lives. As rewritten by Christopher, Nerdanel joins their ranks: a woman whose influence over her tempestuous husband founders, leaving her in stasis while her people depart without her (seemingly without even noticing her absence), her name having been uttered just four times before she reached a coda of abrupt failure, a mere speck on the map with no vistas worth exploring.

Rewriting II: "A Sudden Sense of Endless Untold Stories"

In 1945, as Tolkien was writing *The Lord of the Rings*, Christopher wrote to his father that he found the character of Celebrimbor inexplicably moving. Tolkien expressed little surprise in his son's attraction to a seemingly throwaway detail, identifying Celebrimbor as part of what he termed "the fundamental literary dilemma":

> A story must be told or there'll be no story, yet it is the untold stories that are most moving. I think you are moved by *Celebrimbor* because it conveys a sudden sense of endless *untold* stories: mountains seen far away, never to be climbed, distant trees (like Niggle's) never to be approached ... (Carpenter and Tolkien C., 1981, Letter 96, p. 110).

In other words, even the briefest allusion to Celebrimbor's story intimates narrative movement, necessary to produce the *geographic* movement that reveals new vistas, in stark contrast to his grandmother Nerdanel's amputated characterisation.

Within six years of publishing *The Silmarillion*, Christopher Tolkien published the first of what would become the twelve-volume *The History of Middle-earth* (Tolkien C., 1983-1996) series, in which he, in essence, showed his work in putting together *The Silmarillion*. A gift to Tolkien's fans that leaves *The Silmarillion* an ellipsis rather than a full stop, *The History of Middle-earth* published most of Tolkien's writings on Nerdanel, the material that Christopher excised from the published text. With these original writings, however fragmentary and incomplete, *re*writings other than Christopher's, using Tolkien's original material, become possible.

Transformative works or fanworks are a category of creative productions based on an existing literary, media, or other text. Due to copyright considerations, fanworks are generally presented as amateur, not-for-profit endeavours that rarely receive the sanction of the rights holder. Fanworks based on the Legendarium have existed as long as the Legendarium itself has. For much of the Tolkien fandom's existence, these efforts were collected in fanzines, amateur publications often printed, collated, and mailed by hand to a small group of subscribers. In the early 2000s, the near-simultaneous rise in home Internet use and the release of Peter Jackson's *The Lord of the Rings* trilogy created an effect on the online Tolkien fandom, described by John Lennard "as throwing a tanker-load of gasoline on a camp-fire" (Tolkien and Fanfiction, 2013). Susan Booker (2004) estimated that, by 2004, nearly 10% of the fanfiction sites on the Internet were Tolkien-related. While most of these early online fanworks focused on *The Lord of the Rings*, a contingent of Tolkien fans interested in *The Silmarillion* also emerged, many of them working with *The History of Middle-earth* texts as well as the published *Silmarillion*.

Fanworks are, by their very definition, boundary-pushing. They seek, reveal, and create anew the vistas that form an integral part of Tolkien's narrative technique. Using the details given by Tolkien— the *canon*, in fanworks terms—as loci upon a narrative map, they expand without limit into new terrain. This holds true for even characters, cultures, places, and events only hinted at by Tolkien, as well as interpretations of the details he did provide. When fan studies' scholars discuss fanworks, they often do so using terms like *criticise, transgress*, and *radicalise* that imply erasure of the boundaries drawn by the original creator or rights holder. In the case of Tolkien, this work often expands the Legendarium to allow for the voices of the marginalised: characters absent, sidelined, or vilified in the original text who are permitted, in the hands of fans, to drive the story.

Consciously or not, scholars studying Tolkien-based fanworks often adopt cartographical terminology to describe the process of creating transformative works based on the Legendarium. Writing of Tolkien in the pivotal essay on race and fantasy, Deepa D (2009) wrote of "trying to find myself in the unmapped lands in the East where the Green and Blue wizards disappeared to." Una McCormack (2015) extends Deepa D's analogy of "unmapped lands" to Tolkien-based fanfiction about women, using terms like *space* and *place* and *journey* that evoke geographical revelation as part of the fanwriting process. In my own 2016 study of Tolkien-based fanfiction, I apply Tolkien's analogy of "unattainable vistas" to characterisations that felt biased to readers, enticing them to "enter that distant, glittering city but to duck down its alleyways and plumb its catacombs for the stories only hinted at in the published narrative" (Walls-Thumma, p. 41). In studying fanfiction about Lothíriel, Karen Viars and Cait Coker (2015) observe that women characters in Tolkien are "restricted to specific loci within the text .... [with] little space left over for women with their own independent agency or ability to traverse across geographic or metaphysical boundaries as the men do," identifying women's movement geographically and narratively as vistas awaiting revelation (p. 38).

The cartographical analogy is helpful in understanding why and how fans rewrite Nerdanel. Circumscribed by her much-reduced role and marooned in a land literally excised from the map, Nerdanel possesses few vistas in Christopher's rewriting. Yet it is, by and large, not Christopher's rewriting that forms the basis for fanworks about Nerdanel. Rather, it is Tolkien's original writings that entice fans to develop her character outward from these loci, uncovering new vistas and, in some cases, endowing her with the kind of agency that effaces the impotence Rawls (1984) identified as a shortcoming of women characters like Nerdanel.

In 2006, I surveyed several archives of Tolkien-based fanfiction and found Nerdanel to be one of the favoured *Silmarillion* women among fanfiction authors, even when compared to women who receive far more mentions in the text (Aredhel and Haleth), women who do not succumb to impotence (Lúthien Tinúviel), and women, like Nerdanel, barely mentioned but associated with interesting— usually male—characters (Eärwen, Míriel Serindë, and Indis). On three archives that allowed authors to tag major characters, and readers to search for stories thus tagged, there were more stories about Nerdanel than about any of the other women of *The Silmarillion*. One of those archives also allowed visitors to filter stories by time period. Twenty percent of its stories set during the Time of the Trees featured Nerdanel as a major character. Fifteen years later, Nerdanel's popularity remains. As of 25 August 2021, the art archive *DeviantArt* contains almost nine hundred works of art featuring her. On the fanfiction archive *Silmarillion Writers' Guild*, she appears in about 8% of the stories, and in about 7% of the *Silmarillion* stories on the large multifandom *Archive of Our Own*—not inconsequential for a woman mentioned just four times in a work that spans millennia of history and contains hundreds of characters. (In contrast, Lúthien Tinúviel—the most-mentioned woman in *The Silmarillion* and a key actor in one of Tolkien's most important tales—appears in just 3% of the fanworks on both the *SWG* and *AO3*.)

In these fanworks, we can see how artists and writers build upon her character, often amplifying those elements that make her most distinct among Tolkien's cast of beautiful and ethereal women. Scrolling through *DeviantArt*'s collection of fanart featuring Nerdanel, there are certainly pieces that depict her as exceedingly beautiful, begowned with flowing crimson hair, contrary to Tolkien's pointed remark on her relative unloveliness. Other pieces focus on her marriage to Fëanor or her motherhood, details foregrounded in Christopher's rewriting. However, many other artists use not just her appearance but Tolkien's emphasis on her artistic talents to depict her as anything but an unearthly princess. Where Lúthien has flower-crowned tresses, unruly curls spring from Nerdanel's head, and where Galadriel is lithe, artists give Nerdanel broad shoulders and visible muscles. Filat's 2016 painting "Nerdanel Daughter of Mahtan" is an exemplar, showing her in a workshop, hands on her hips and wearing a stern look of authority.

When Nerdanel does appear alongside Fëanor in artwork, it is sometimes as his creative equal. In EPH-SAN1634's digital piece "Nerdanel and Fëanor" (2016), each works at a project, back to back in the workshop, comprising half of the composition in an implication of equality, both engrossed in work and seemingly oblivious to each other. Buckwheat's "Nerdanel and Fëanor" (2020) likewise shows her in the workshop, propping her head upon a bust she has sculpted of Fëanor, a brazen smirk on her face. Many artists treat her motherhood likewise. In one example, Velouriah (2019) depicts Nerdanel holding a twin on one hip while the other hand clutches a chisel, her well-muscled arm slung over a partly completed statue. Her posture here is likewise assertive, that of a woman uncowed by her prestigious husband and clearly a virtuoso in her own right. These artists use Tolkien's characterization of Nerdanel as a gifted artist, centering this detail in their own depictions of her, despite Christopher (re)writing this aspect out of the published *Silmarillion*.

Fanfiction about Nerdanel often explores how these elements shape her character and relationships. Others extensively worldbuild around them. For example, numerous stories invent university and apprenticeship systems in which Nerdanel moves. Her relationship with Fëanor, the early age of their marriage, and their youthful wanderings are contextualised by other authors within the laws and mores of the Noldorin people. Still other authors situate her within a social or political milieu, speculating on how Fëanor's position within the Noldorin royal house and Nerdanel's familial allegiance to Aulë may have impacted their courtship, marriage, and estrangement. The worldbuilding here takes the lead from Tolkien's own implications: finding, seeking, and revealing vistas anew.

Other stories specifically use Nerdanel's crafts to symbolise her internal conflicts and represent her emotional state. Because Nerdanel had a diverse set of skills, the mode and materials of her crafting create a rich semiotic language for authors to tackle complex topics such as love, grief, regret, and reparation. For example, in the story "Waste Paper," Himring (2012) explores Nerdanel's complicated feelings about Fëanor's crimes, Maedhros's reembodiment, and the trauma he endured and does so through her artistic productions. In "Our Share of the Night to Bear," set in the immediate aftermath of the Noldorin departure, Elleth (2014) uses craft to signify Nerdanel's anger and grief at her husband and sons and her attempts to cope with their loss.

Fanfiction stories about Nerdanel span from the Years of the Trees to the Dagor Dagorath and occupy nearly every era in between. As one of the few *Silmarillion* characters who does not perish, Nerdanel is a potential eyewitness to historical events of literally earth-shattering proportions. Most authors, however, focus on a comparatively narrow timespan during the Years of the Trees and immediately after. The first online *Silmarillion* fanwriters, writing only a few years after *The History of Middle-earth* reached its conclusion in 1996, were the first to use the fullness of Tolkien's writing about Nerdanel rather than Christopher's rewriting. Many of the conventions established by these early authors—Nerdanel's red hair is the most obvious example, evident in both fanfiction and fanart—formed the foundation upon which later writers built, taking new vistas revealed and building outward from there. Some of their conventions, discussed below, persist even as of this writing.

Early formative stories about Nerdanel tended to occur during the Years of the Trees and focused on her relationship with Fëanor and their sons. Ivanneth's 2003 story "The Follower" introduces readers to Nerdanel via Fingon's first encounter with her sculptures as a child. Nerdanel's work dominates her life at the expense of household responsibilities; prior to this, she is merely an occasional "raw-boned and gaunt" apparition at the edges of Fingon's awareness. Finch's 2003 story "The Image" shows how Nerdanel's relative lack of beauty incited her "lonely wandering" and how Fëanor's acceptance of it led to pride in her appearance on par with that for her art. Nol's 2004 "Unwitting, Nerdanel Sells Pearls to a Prince" describes the first meeting of the couple in a short story rich with artistic imagery and symbolism.

Interest in Nerdanel's early life and family relationships would continue into the mid-2000s, building on the work of earlier authors. Lyra's "Golden Days" (2009) is one example, covering the familiar terrain of their early years while embellishing considerably in terms of worldbuilding. Lyra creates an educational system in which Nerdanel and Fëanor participate and interact; in addition, she creates a family and household for Nerdanel and formulates courtly traditions, even inventing dances. Other work about this time in Nerdanel's life focuses on her early wanderings with Fëanor, using the notion of "wandering" to infer a willingness to push boundaries of knowledge and social expectation. Independence1776's "Discord and Harmony" (2018) shows both, as Nerdanel and Fëanor seek out forbidden lore on the *Ainulindalë* while simultaneously navigating societal expectations about engagement and marriage upon a backdrop of their sexual awakening. Nerdanel's comfort with the esoteric in this piece seems to stem from Tolkien's description of her work as "strong and strange." Oshun's "Five Times Nerdanel Said 'Yes'" (2010) begins with the couple on their wanderings, considering a marriage outside the usual bounds of propriety, and digs deep into the household negotiations needed by two illustrious craftspersons who are also two prolific parents.

Oshun's story also addresses another issue that arises in fanfiction about Nerdanel's early life, one which likely feels especially relevant to many of its writers: the tension between Nerdanel's roles as a master craftsperson and the mother of seven children. Written at the same time as the movement to urge women that they could "have it all" began to sour into doubt and cynicism, many stories about Nerdanel include conflict between her familial and household duties and her desire for a fulfilling artistic career—and the sense that no matter which she chooses, she must by necessity fail the other. Ford_of_bruinen's "Borne of Him or Me" (2007) allows Nerdanel to bluntly express her frustrations with being pulled from her work to care for an infant: "I am a sculptor, not a broodmare to my husband's lusts." These stories display an important attribute of fanwriting: the centering of the fan's experiences within a text. In Nerdanel's story, fanwriters, who are mostly women, locate a potential conflict in the text that Tolkien—himself a man with a wife at home to care for his children—might have elided.

As the history of the *Silmarillion* fanfiction fandom progressed, authors increasingly began to range beyond the years detailed by Tolkien, with newer work about Nerdanel often focusing on what her life looked like after her family left. As noted above, Nerdanel tidily fits the pattern of impotence that Rawls (1984) identifies as feminine failure in Tolkien's works. Fanfiction authors could take the literal rift of Aman from Middle-earth, as Tolkien does, as reason to consider her likewise excised from the story, "deedless for ever ... dropping vain tears in the thankless sea" (in her husband's own words about the Noldor who remained behind; Tolkien C., 1977, pp. 82-82). Instead, the glimpses given of this brilliant, autonomous woman become a vista before the mist drops down, obscuring but not eliminating Nerdanel from the story. In writing this era of her life, authors reveal her character anew and spare her from a fate of impotence.

This subgenre was not absent from the early online *Silmarillion* fanfiction fandom, though it has grown increasingly common as the fandom's history has progressed. In Deborah Judge's 2005 "The House of Fëanor," Nerdanel accepts the mantle of her house, which includes casting a vote for Noldorin involvement in the War of Wrath. Ellie's "Like Roses over a Fence" (2007) begins by seeming to confirm Rawls' theory as Nerdanel, Indis, and Anairë wallow over their failures. "We *failed* them," says Indis in the story, speaking of their husbands. "*If* we had tried a little harder, a little longer. *If* we had been more forceful with them, had not become estranged from them. *If* Nerdanel, you and I had accompanied our husbands to Formenos rather than abandoning them to their own devices. *If* ..." But this outburst is followed quickly by a turning point, where the three realize their political expertise and, in Nerdanel's case, her skill with craft can be turned to the benefit of their people. These early stories establish Nerdanel's potential influence in the realms of the political and the artistic, a pattern that later authors would continue to follow.

Bunn's "Even the Very Wise" (2017), part of the *Return to Aman* series set in the Fourth Age, provides an example of political involvement. Nerdanel is foisted into political prominence by Finarfin, new in his kingship and desperate for guidance, but desists in favor of living a quieter life as a craftsperson. "He came to me asking if I would help with the administration," Nerdanel says in the story. "... Me! I told him, I'm a sculptor, not a princess. I don't have the first idea how that sort of thing works, nor do I want to." However, with Elrond's return, he begins to contemplate if the cataclysmic Oath of Fëanor could be undone. It is ultimately Nerdanel who achieves the first step by convincing Fëanor, still in the halls of Mandos, that it is not only possible but wise. Thus, her initial failure to persuade Fëanor is redressed. Artistically, Nerdanel finds her purpose in stories like "Changing Lights" by Elleth (2009) and my story "Daytracer" (2014), which attribute the construction of the Sun and Moon, at least in part, to her. In my story "Statues"

(2007), Nerdanel fills the beach at Alqualondë with her lifelike statues of the slain Teleri, as a form of reparation on behalf of the Noldor. Elleth's "Our Share of the Night to Bear" (2014) considers the myriad implications of a world left suddenly darkened and its population severely depleted. Although the story is unfinished as of this writing, when it leaves off, Nerdanel is on her way to answer a plea for aid from Indis: "should you choose to come ... we will ease the plight of our people as well as we may, lay the foundations for whatever new world awaits," a line that captures perfectly the fanwriter's impulse not to end Nerdanel's story in grief and loss but to unfold a new road—a new purpose—before her.

Conclusion: A Place to Stand

We will never know what Tolkien intended for Nerdanel, but it matters little. As someone who began as a fiction writer long before I was a scholar, to me, his two lengthy writings about her read like the heady writing that happens when a writer seizes on an idea and runs off with it. From nothing, she emerges not just remarkably fully-formed but teeming with additional stories that beg to unfold. It may be that, untrammelled by his own limitations so frequently written into his women characters, Tolkien himself experienced a taste of what hundreds of fanworks creators would later actualise.

Christopher's rewriting of Nerdanel compels the story outward to Middle-earth. It is Bilbo stepping out his front door; it is Frodo taking the Ring; it is the quest narrative and in many ways an imperative within the Legendarium. Within this narrative schema, the characters who stayed behind must be left behind. Yet, Januslike, even as he unwrites so much of Nerdanel in *The Silmarillion*, he devotes his life to making accessible a considerable breadth of his father's unpublished work. From the details of *The History of Middle-earth*, countless fanworks creators have rewritten Nerdanel, spinning their ideas from the raw materials Tolkien gave and the work of other fanworks creators to come before them, crawling outward from a nexus like so many roads upon a map.

Una McCormack (2015) observes that the fanworks creator risks "rudely finding herself reminded that she has no real place in the text and that she has been granted only temporary permission to come along on the journey" (Exceptional Women: Reconfiguring the

Text). Yet Nerdanel offers a place in the story for many of Tolkien's women readers. Far from an ethereal princess who beguiles and enchants, she is a woman of artistic talent and purpose who achieves on her own merits, ordinary where it matters not and extraordinary where it does. She is what so many of her fans hope for themselves. Her inferred conflicts are theirs as well: how to balance work and family, how to take a principled stand within a polarized society, how to ensure that one's talents are turned to endeavours of value. In catching a glimpse of her through the mist, they ventured to where she stood. They pressed a finger to the map. *Here. Here she is. Here I am.* In words and paint and poetry, they mapped the landscape around her, ever peering out from new hills, in quest of themselves.

Acknowledgments
Many thanks to Anérea Lantíria and Elizabeth King for reading a draft of this piece and providing invaluable feedback.

References

Booker, S., 2004. Tales around the Internet campfire: fan fiction in Tolkien's universe. In: Janet Brennan Croft, ed. 2004. *Tolkien on film: essays on Peter Jackson's* Lord of the Rings. Altadena: Mythopoeic Press.

Buckwheat, 2020. *Nerdanel and Fëanor.* [online] Available at: <https://toastedbuckwheat.tumblr.com/post/614604583840481280/last-day-of-the-not-a-week-at-all-feanorianweek> [Accessed 30 August 2021].

Bunn, 2017. *Even the very wise.* [online] Available at: <https://archiveofourown.org/works/11367327> [Accessed 30 August 2021].

Carpenter, H. and Tolkien, C. eds., 1981. *The Letters of J.R.R. Tolkien.* Boston: Houghton Mifflin Harcourt.

Dawn Felagund, 2007. *Statues.* [online] Available at: <https://www.silmarillionwritersguild.org/node/73/> [Accessed 30 August 2021].
—, 2014. *Daytracer.* [online] Available at: <https://www.silmarillionwritersguild.org/node/135> [Accessed 30 August 2021].

Deborah Judge, 2005. *The house of Fëanor.* [online] Available at: <https://www.silmarillionwritersguild.org/node/1099> [Accessed 30 August 2021].

Deepad, 2009. *I didn't dream of dragons.* [online] Available at: <https://web.archive.org/web/20110905222334/https://deepad.dreamwidth.org/29371.html> [Accessed 30 August 2021].

Elleth, 2009. *Changing lights.* [online] Available at: <https://www.silmarillionwritersguild.org/node/3982/> [Accessed 30 August 2021].
—, 2014. *Our share of the night to bear.* [online] Available at: <https://www.silmarillionwritersguild.org/node/765/> [Accessed 30 August 2021].
—, 2020. *The textual ghosts project.* [online] Available at: <https://www.silmarillionwritersguild.org/node/4229> [Accessed 30 August 2021].

Ellie, 2007. *Like roses over a fence.* [online] Available at: <https://www.silmarillionwritersguild.org/node/3767/> [Accessed 30 August 2021].

EPH-SAN1634, 2016. *Nerdanel and Fëanor.* [online] Available at: <https://www.deviantart.com/eph-san1634/art/Nerdanel-and-Feanor-greek-mythology-style-641181829> [Accessed 30 August 2021].

Filat, 2016. *Nerdanel daughter of Mahtan.* [online] Available at: https://www.deviantart.com/filat/art/Nerdanel-Mahtan-s-daughter-600742182 [Accessed 30 August 2021].

Finch, 2003. *The image.* [online] Available at: <https://www.fanfiction.net/s/1231370/1/The-Image> [Accessed 30 August 2021].

Ford_of_bruinen, 2007. *Borne of him or me.* [online] Available at: <https://www.silmarillionwritersguild.org/node/3759/> [Accessed 30 August 2021].

Himring, 2012. *Waste paper.* [online] Available at: <https://www.silmarillionwritersguild.org/node/1385/> [Accessed 30 August 2021].

Independence1776, 2018. *Discord and harmony.* [online] Available at: <https://archiveofourown.org/works/15825039> [Accessed 30 August 2021].

Ivanneth, 2003. *The follower.* [online] Available at: <https://www.fanfiction.net/s/1645746/1/The-Follower> [Accessed 30 August 2021].

Kane, D.C., 2011. *Arda reconstructed: the creation of the published Silmarillion.* Bethlehem: Lehigh University Press.

Lennard, J., 2013. *Tolkien's triumph: the strange history of* The Lord of the Rings. [Kindle version] Skoobebooks. Available at: Amazon.com <http://www.amazon.com> [Accessed 30 August 2021].

Lyra, 2009. *Golden days.* [online] Available at: <https://www.silmarillionwritersguild.org/node/473> [Accessed 30 August 2021].

McCormack, U., 2015. Finding ourselves in the (un)mapped lands: women's reparative readings of *The Lord of the Rings.* In: J. Brennan Croft and L.A. Donovan, eds. 2015. *Perilous and fair: women in the works and life of J.R.R. Tolkien.* Altadena: Mythopoeic Press.

Nol, 2004. *Unwitting, Nerdanel sells pearls to a prince.* [online] Available at: <https://www.fanfiction.net/s/2041423/1/Unknowing-Nerdanel-Sells-Pearls-To-A-Prince> [Accessed 30 August 2021].

Oshun, 2010. *Five times Nerdanel said 'yes'.* [online] Available at: <https://www.silmarillionwritersguild.org/node/545> [Accessed 30 August 2021].

Rawls, M., 1984. The feminine principle in Tolkien. *Mythlore,* 10(3), pp.5-13.

Shippey, T., 2003. *The road to Middle-earth: how J.R.R. Tolkien created a new mythology.* Boston: Houghton Mifflin.

Tolkien, C., ed., 1977. *The Silmarillion.* Edited by Christopher Tolkien. London: Book Club Associates.
—, 1983. *The Book of Lost Tales, Part 1 – The History of Middle-earth Vol. I.* New York: HarperCollins.
—, 1993. *Morgoth's Ring – The History of Middle-earth Vol. X.* New York: HarperCollins.
—, 1996. *The Peoples of Middle-earth – The History of Middle-earth Vol. XII.* Boston: Houghton Mifflin Company.

Tolkien, J.R.R., 1954-55. *The Lord of the Rings.* London: Allen & Unwin.
—, 1966. *The Tolkien reader.* Reprint 1986. New York: Del Rey.

Velouriah, 2019. *Nerdanel and her sons.* [online] Available at: <https://www. deviantart.com/velouriah/art/Nerdanel-and-her-Sons-809656450> [Accessed 30 August 2021].

Viars, K. and Coker, C., 2015. Constructing Lothiriel: rewriting and rescuing the women of Middle-earth from the margins. *Mythlore*, 33(2), pp. 35-48.

Walls-Thumma, D.M., 2006. *A woman in few words: the character of Nerdanel and her treatment in canon and fandom.* [online] Available at: <https://www. silmarillionwritersguild.org/node/4225> [Accessed 30 August 2021].

Walls-Thumma, D.M., 2016. Attainable vistas: historical bias in Tolkien's Legendarium as a motive for transformative fanworks. *Journal of Tolkien Research*, 3(3).

Finrod Felagund: His Life, Influence and Legacy

Angela P. Nicholas

A few years ago, while researching the ancestry of Aragorn[1], I explored Tolkien's *The Silmarillion* at length (Tolkien C., 2013). I was led inevitably to Elf/Mortal marriages, along with the significant role played by the Elf Finrod Felagund, eldest son of Finarfin, in shaping the history of Men. Referred to as "perhaps the most appealing character in *The Silmarillion*" (Rateliff, 2008, p. 410) Finrod certainly stands out, with his deep regard for the race of Men and his courageous and self-sacrificing involvement in Beren's quest to cut a Silmaril from the crown of Morgoth, thereby fulfilling King Thingol's condition for marrying his daughter Lúthien. This article looks at Finrod in more detail studying his friendship with Men and his views on Elf/Mortal relationships, marital and otherwise. It also examines his influence (positive and negative) on the behaviour and well-being of fellow members of the House of Finarfin, other Elf Houses, and Mortals through to the Third and Fourth Ages.

In the genealogical table overleaf:

- Olwë and Thingol were brothers
- Thingol was King of Doriath. His wife, Melian, was a Maia
- Fëanor made the Silmarils which were stolen by Morgoth
- Finrod (and subsequently Orodreth) was King of Nargothrond
- Finrod acquired his epithet *Felagund* ("Hewer of Caves") after the delving of his Kingdom
- Turgon was King of Gondolin
- Eärendil married Elwing

The close relationship between Finrod and Men began with a chance encounter with Bëor and his companions, the first Men to make their way over the Blue Mountains into Beleriand (Tolkien C., 2013, pp. 162-165). Finrod watched them, unseen, while they sang to the accompaniment of Bëor's rudimentary harp before falling asleep

1. This was for my 2017 work, *Aragorn. J.R.R. Tolkien's Undervalued Hero.*

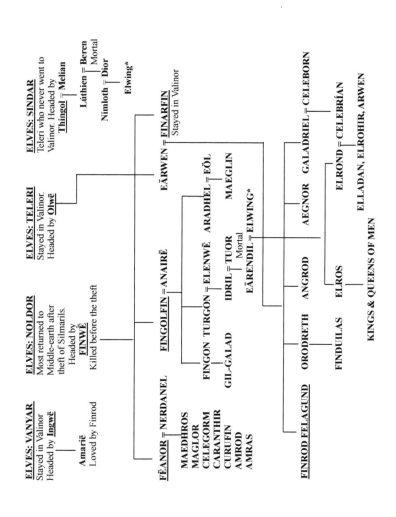

around their camp fire. He immediately felt a great love for these people and began to play his own music on the harp until they awoke. His feelings were reciprocated and one of the first things he did was to advise the Men on the best place to set up their new homes without coming into conflict with the hostile Green-elves in Ossiriand. Finrod had befriended these Elves (Tolkien C., 2013, p. 143) and knew that they were upset by the newcomers hunting and cutting down trees. A lasting alliance was formed between Finrod and Bëor's people as they supported each other in the war against Morgoth. A sobering side-effect of this new relationship was that the Elves now encountered Mortal death, described poignantly thus:

> "Bëor the Old died when he had lived three and ninety years ... And when he lay dead, of no wound or grief, but stricken by age, the Eldar saw for the first time the swift waning of the life of Men, and the death of weariness which they knew not in themselves; and they grieved greatly for the loss of their friends." (Tolkien C., 2013, p. 173).

Although the deepest level of Elf/Mortal friendship was between the Houses of Finarfin and Bëor, Finrod's influence and rapport with Men, also "rubbed off" on members of the other Elf and Man Houses. His attitude encouraged Fingolfin also to welcome and befriend Men. (Tolkien C., 2013, pp. 166, 172). In addition Finrod was a close friend of Turgon, one of Fingolfin's sons. They both had dream visitations from Ulmo (the Vala of the Seas) urging them to set up hidden cities as a retreat in the event of Morgoth breaking the Siege of Angband. (Tolkien C., 2013, pp. 129-130). Turgon subsequently created Gondolin (in the middle of a valley encircled by mountains) while Finrod delved the underground fortress of Nargothrond (in a gorge in the River Narog). Christopher Tolkien (2013, p. 185), refers to the deep affection felt by Turgon for Húrin and Huor, young Men from the House of Hador, whom he took under his protection following the Dagor Bragollach (Battle of Sudden Flame). Particularly notable was his faith in Huor's prediction of the birth of Eärendil: "This I say to you, lord, with the eyes of death: ... from you and from me a new star shall arise." (Tolkien C., 2013, p. 230). Subsequently Turgon would welcome Huor's son Tuor into Gondolin and even let him marry his daughter Idril. Although Ulmo, who had taken Tuor as his special messenger, undoubtedly played an important role in securing Turgon's acceptance of these Men, the influence of his friend Finrod can surely not be discounted.

Another significant friendship and alliance Finrod made was with the Sindarin Elf Círdan the Shipbuilder whose land bordered Nargothrond. Finrod and his people assisted with re-building the mariners' havens of Brithombar and Eglarest. (Tolkien C., 2013, p. 138). In later Ages Círdan too would prove to be of great support to Men.

Regarding Thingol, Finrod had more of a challenge as the King of Doriath was ill-disposed towards Men, and also hostile to the returning Noldor, banning the people of Fëanor and Fingolfin from his kingdom. His Maian wife Melian had woven an invisible girdle around Doriath which prevented unauthorised entry. The only reason Finrod's family were allowed in was because their mother, Eärwen, was Thingol's niece. (Tolkien C, 2013, p. 126). Nevertheless when the people of the Mortal House of Haladin were rendered homeless after an Orc raid, Finrod did manage to persuade a reluctant Thingol to allow the survivors, led by Lady Haleth, to live in the Forest of Brethil which bordered Doriath and was regarded by Thingol as his. (Tolkien C., 2013, p. 171).[2] Finrod was clearly committed to encouraging non-House of Finarfin folk to co-operate in these liaisons between Elves and Men.

An important and interesting one-to-one relationship between Finrod and a Mortal was that with the wise woman Andreth described in *Athrabeth Finrod ah Andreth* (Tolkien C., 2015, pp. 301-366), a work in which J.R.R.Tolkien uses a conversation between the pair to explore the issues of death, immortality, pity and hope. Andreth was from the House of Bëor, and it is clear that she and Finrod knew each other well and had a relationship based on intellectual compatibility and affection. Finrod is described as being the wisest of the exiled Noldor, anxious to discover all that he could concerning the history of Men. Andreth was very knowledgeable in that area and Finrod "loved [her] in great friendship". (Tolkien C., 2015, p. 305). The feeling seems to have been mutual as Andreth generally shared her knowledge, was not afraid to argue with him and was prepared to weep in his presence. The fact that this particular conversation was triggered by Finrod's grief following the recent death of the current head of the House of Bëor implies that he had turned to Andreth for support, thus further emphasising the closeness between them.

---

2. In later years Thingol did come to appreciate the courage and loyalty of Men, as shown by his fostering of the young Túrin after the boy's father was captured by Morgoth.

Unsurprisingly their conversation dwelt on the difference in lifespans between Elves and Men, comparing the short life of the latter, (after which they left the World), with the seemingly endless one of the former who, even after being "killed" in battle, would continue to exist in the Undying Lands while the World lasted. Eventually Andreth revealed that she was in love with Aegnor, one of Finrod's younger brothers, but believed that he had rejected her. Finrod said that he was well aware of this situation and knew that Aegnor returned her love, his apparent rejection being due to an unwillingness to marry during a time of war – a war in which he foresaw his own imminent death. (He and Angrod would die in the Dagor Bragollach.) This was no comfort to Andreth who "would have given all" for one day as his wife. (Tolkien C., 2015, p. 324). Finrod told her that Aegnor would never love anyone else or take an Elven bride when he went to the Undying Lands, but would keep the image of the young Andreth forever in his memory. He explained that the Elves "would rather have a memory that is fair but unfinished than one that goes on to a grievous end". (Tolkien C., 2015, p. 325). He supported his brother's attitude as he believed that Elf/Mortal unions would only occur in exceptional circumstances, telling Andreth: "if any marriage can be between our kindred and thine, then it shall be for *some high purpose of Doom*". (Tolkien C., 2015, p. 324).[My emphasis]. Otherwise he regarded such relationships as something to be avoided or cut short – rather ironic given that his desire for closeness between Elves and Men actually encouraged them.

*

The full, and tragic, significance of the mutual loyalty between Finrod and the House of Bëor was realised when Barahir, a descendant of Bëor, saved Finrod's life during the Dagor Bragollach. Aegnor and Angrod had already been killed in the battle and Finrod showed his gratitude for his own survival by giving Barahir his ring, swearing an oath of friendship and aid to him, and his kin, on production of this ring. Subsequently Barahir's son Beren requested Finrod's help as he prepared to set out on his mission to remove a Silmaril from the crown of Morgoth. Finrod realised that he was being drawn into the curse of the Silmarils instigated by Fëanor's oath of hatred against anyone who should interfere with these jewels. Nevertheless he kept his own oath and went with Beren, sacrificing not only the Kingship of Nargothrond, but also his own life in order to save Beren's, thereby enabling Beren and Lúthien between them to fulfil Thingol's condition for their marriage. By his selfless actions Finrod indirectly brought about the first of the exceptional Elf/Mortal unions[3] for "some high purpose of Doom" (Tolkien C., 2015, p. 324), as well as indirectly enabling the one between Aragorn and Arwen two Ages later[4].

Finrod's ring, known thenceforth as the Ring of Barahir, passed down Beren's line: via the Númenórean royal house, the Kings of Arnor and finally the Chieftains of the Dúnedain. It resided temporarily with the Lossoth (Snow Men) mid-way through the Third Age, being given to them by Arvedui the last King of Arnor, in recognition of their help following his defeat in battle with the Witch-king of Angmar. As agreed the Dúnedain later ransomed the ring and the last we hear of it is that Aragorn gave it to Arwen on their betrothal in Third Age 2980. (Tolkien C., 2005, pp. 1042, 1090).

*

Following the demise of Finrod in Sauron's dungeons, his legacy and influence lived on in the House of Finarfin, starting with events in the hidden city of Nargothrond where Orodreth, Finrod's only remaining brother, now ruled. (Tolkien C., 2013, pp. 250-256). It was during his kingship that another curse raised its head with the arrival of the traumatised Elf, Gwindor of the House of Finarfin, who had managed to escape from imprisonment in Morgoth's mines. He was accompanied by the Man Túrin son of Húrin whom he had encountered on his journey home. Túrin had suffered his own traumas, due to the curse of Morgoth on the House of Húrin.

Orodreth, following in his dead brother's footsteps, welcomed the Man and treated him with honour. He was greatly impressed by him (as were most of his subjects) due to his Elven appearance and noble bearing and speech (a result of his upbringing in Doriath), as well as his exceptional prowess in battle. However as time went by, Túrin started to wield more influence and become the dominant partner in the relationship. He disliked the secretive warfare methods used, based on stealth and ambush, and persuaded

3. Lúthien was actually half-Maia from her mother Melian.
4. Both were descended from Lúthien and Beren.

Orodreth to build a bridge from the doors of Nargothrond across the River Narog, thereby enabling the passage of whole armies, and of course rendering the entrance visible. Thus Morgoth now knew the whereabouts of Finrod's people.

In addition, Orodreth's daughter Finduilas, who had shared a mutual love with Gwindor prior to his captivity, now fell in love (unrequitedly) with Túrin, causing distress to all three of them. This was a rather different Elf/Mortal scenario from the Andreth/Aegnor one, influenced as it was by Morgoth's curse, such that everything Túrin did inevitably caused grief to himself and those around him. Gwindor now lectured Finduilas regarding Elf/Mortal unions in a speech which echoed, and enlarged on, the warnings given by Finrod to Andreth:

> "It is not fitting that the Elder Children of Ilúvatar should wed with the Younger; nor is it wise, for they are brief, and soon pass, to leave us in widowhood while the world lasts. Neither will fate suffer it, unless it be once or twice only, for some high cause of doom that we do not perceive." (Tolkien C., 2013, p. 251).

Two of Angrod's folk – Arminas and Gwindor's brother Gelmir – were also caught up in events, arriving in Nargothrond with reports from Ulmo and Círdan of an approaching army sent by Morgoth accompanied by the Dragon Glaurung, and begging Orodreth and his people to break down the bridge as a matter of urgency and shut themselves up in the fortress. Such was Túrin's sway over Orodreth that this advice was ignored. Thus Nargothrond was destroyed and taken over by Glaurung. A dying Gwindor, amazingly still professing affection for Túrin, begged him to save Finduilas, but when Túrin reached the remains of Nargothrond the Dragon's gaze sent him into a trance, only releasing him from it after Finduilas had been seized by Orcs and dragged off to face a gruesome death. Orodreth himself had been killed in the forefront of the battle.

The impression from these events, namely the death of Finrod and the subsequent destruction of Nargothrond, is that Finrod's generous intentions (encouragement of Elf/Mortal fidelity, friendship and respect) were poisoned by the curse of Fëanor regarding the Silmarils, and that of Morgoth on the House of Húrin. Two further victims of the latter were Elves of Doriath: the elf-maiden Nellas, and Beleg, the great archer who was a devoted and faithful friend

to Túrin. Nellas had watched over Túrin during his childhood in
Doriath, but as he grew older her feelings took on a romantic turn.
Túrin was completely oblivious to this, prompting Beleg to exclaim
in exasperation: "Indeed, I begin to think that Elves and Men should
not meet or meddle". (Tolkien C., 2010, p. 124). He had good
reason to say this as he would die at the hands of Túrin due to a
tragic "accident" which was clearly attributable to Morgoth's curse.
(Tolkien C., 2013, pp. 247-249).

*

One of Finarfin's children still lived, namely Galadriel, and it was
through her that Finrod's legacy would be passed on to future Ages
of Middle-earth.

Backtracking now to the arrival of the Noldor in Beleriand:
Thingol [as mentioned earlier] banned Fëanor's and Fingolfin's
people from Doriath, but admitted Finrod and his siblings because
their mother was his niece.

On one occasion when Finrod and Galadriel were Thingol's guests
(Tolkien C., 2013, pp. 129-130) Finrod spoke of his dreams of building
a hidden retreat beneath the hills and Thingol told him about the gorge
and caves of the River Narog. Thus Nargothrond was built, with
most of Finrod's people moving there. However Galadriel remained
in Doriath – where she had met and fallen in love with Celeborn –
living there as a pupil of Melian from whom she learnt "great lore and
wisdom concerning Middle-earth". (Tolkien C., 2013, p. 130).

Melian believed that there was something sinister behind the
return of the Noldor from Valinor to Middle-earth and plied her
pupil with questions. (Tolkien C., 2013, pp. 146-149). Galadriel
spoke of the Silmarils and the murder of Finwë by Morgoth but
kept quiet about the Oath sworn by Fëanor, and the atrocities he
had perpetrated: namely the Kinslaying (the murder of many Telerin
Elves by Fëanor's, and some of Fingolfin's, folk) and the burning
of the Telerin ships, forcing Fingolfin's and Finrod's people to
cross to Middle-earth via the Grinding Ice – with many lives being
lost. However Morgoth was now causing rumours of these events
to be spread around and Círdan informed Thingol and Melian of
their content. This happened to coincide with a visit from all four of
Galadriel's brothers, and since the rumours implicated *all* the Noldor

in the atrocities, a furious Thingol rounded on Finrod and accused him of slaying his mother's kin. Like his sister, Finrod kept quiet, being unable to defend himself without implicating Fëanor's and Fingolfin's people. Fortunately Angrod, the most hot-headed of the brothers, in a savage outburst informed Thingol of the true situation, thus repairing the relationship between Doriath and Finarfin's family.

On another occasion Galadriel travelled to Nargothrond to spend time with her brothers. During her visit she happened to ask Finrod why he had no wife, perhaps thinking that having created this impressive hidden palace he would want to marry and have a son to inherit it. Finrod replied: "An oath I too shall swear, and must be free to fulfil it, and go into darkness. Nor shall anything of my realm endure that a son should inherit" (Tolkien C., 2013, p. 150). It is then stated that "not until that hour had such cold thoughts ruled him; for indeed she whom he had loved was Amarië of the Vanyar, and she went not with him into exile". (Tolkien C., 2013, p. 150). [This was no doubt the original reason for him not marrying]. By these sudden premonitions he had anticipated his own death and the destruction of Nargothrond.

Galadriel carried on living in Doriath, where Melian continued to tutor her, and also to confide in her. For example, Thingol began to be plagued by dreams about Men, highly distressing for him given that he was determined that no Man would enter Doriath during his kingship. However Melian told Galadriel: "one of Men, even of Bëor's house, shall indeed come, and the Girdle of Melian shall not restrain him, for doom greater than my power shall send him". (Tolkien C., 2013, p. 167). Thus the coming of Beren to Doriath, and his subsequent marriage to Lúthien was anticipated by Melian and, through her, also by Galadriel.

The influence of her brother Finrod, "of all her kin the nearest to her heart" (Tolkien C., 2010, p. 297), and her friend/tutor Melian, together with the knowledge and experience she acquired from them, would equip Galadriel for her role in the marriage of Arwen and Aragorn two Ages later.

*

Galadriel's situation towards the end of the Third Age[5] was that she was the most powerful Elf in Middle-earth. Along with Celeborn

5. "Third Age" abbreviated to "TA" when citing dates. See Tolkien, J.R.R., 2005, pp.1084-1098 for Third Age dates.

she ruled the land of Lothlórien with its population of Silvan Elves. She was the keeper of Nenya, one of the Three Elven Rings made by Celebrimbor (son of Fëanor's son Curufin), and by wielding this she preserved the beauty of Lothlórien and *controlled entry to it*. There was a close understanding between her and the holders of the other two Rings, namely her son-in-law Elrond, keeper of Vilya, and Gandalf who wielded Narya (though this was not generally known).

She had also come into possession of the Elessar, a green stone with healing properties, on the understanding that she was guarding it until its rightful owner should come and claim it and take its name as his own.[6] In addition she would have been aware that Elrond had foreseen the birth of an Heir of Isildur "to whom a great part was appointed in the last deeds of that Age". (Tolkien C., 2013, p. 357). In TA 2929 the Dúnadan woman Ivorwen prophesied that "hope" might be born for the Dúnedain if her daughter, Gilraen, married Arathorn, the son of their current Chieftain. (Tolkien, 2005, p. 1057). Aragorn (the "hope") was born in TA 2931 and Ivorwen, at his naming ceremony, declared: "I see on his breast a green stone, and from that his true name shall come" (Tolkien C., 2002c, p. xii). Reared in Rivendell Aragorn, at the age of twenty, met and fell in love with Elrond's daughter Arwen just at the point when he was due to leave his childhood home to take up his role as Chieftain of the Dúnedain. Arwen, being Galadriel's granddaughter, often made lengthy visits to Lothlórien. Her mother Celebrían had sailed to the Undying Lands in TA 2510, traumatised by a vicious Orc attack from which she never fully recovered, so Galadriel no doubt also carried out a motherly role.

In TA 2980, during one of Arwen's visits, an exhausted Aragorn was returning from a perilous journey on the confines of Mordor, and heading for Rivendell to recuperate. (Tolkien, 2005, pp. 1060-1061). His route would pass near to the borders of Lothlórien. At this point Galadriel must have been recalling the words of Melian quoted earlier: "one of Men, even of Bëor's house, shall indeed come, and the Girdle of Melian shall not restrain him, for doom greater than my power shall send him". (Tolkien C., 2013, p. 167). In addition there were the words of her brother Finrod to Andreth: "if any marriage can be between our kindred and thine, then it shall be for some high purpose of Doom". (Tolkien C., 2015, p. 324).

6. There are two versions of how she obtained it (Tolkien, C., 2010, pp.321-326).

She now drew Aragorn into Lothlórien where she clothed him in silver and white, bound a gem on his brow and arranged for him to meet Arwen. Their betrothal soon followed. During the visit of the Fellowship in TA 3019, Galadriel gave the green gem to Aragorn addressing him as "Elessar" as she did so. (Tolkien, 2005, p. 375).

The purpose behind Beren's entry into Doriath is summed up in *Athrabeth Finrod ah Andreth* as follows: "Thus from the union of Lúthien and Beren ... the *infusion* of a 'divine' and an Elvish strain into Mankind was to be brought about, providing a link between Mankind and the Elder World, after the establishment of the Dominion of Men". (Tolkien C., 2015, p. 340). [My emphasis]. In TA 3019 Galadriel, using the influence and knowledge of Finrod and Melian, in addition to her own experience, observation and foresight, perceived the need to reinforce this "infusion" by bringing her granddaughter and the Mortal Heir of Isildur together again.

*

A look at Galadriel's descendants shows that mixed marriages with their resulting hybrid offspring were very much in evidence. Her daughter Celebrían had married Elrond Half-elven who wasn't a pure Elf.[7] Her three grandchildren were therefore also a mixture of Mortal and Elf and, like Elrond and his brother Elros before them, would eventually have to choose between accepting the fate of Elves or that of Men. All were well-disposed towards Men. Arwen of course married one, thus by default becoming Mortal herself. The eventual choice of her brothers Elladan and Elrohir is not recorded, but both were extremely close to the Dúnedain of the North and their Chieftains, as well as being a great support to their foster-brother Aragorn.

There were also those *not* of the House of Finarfin, who nevertheless were supportive of Mortals, possibly resulting from the influence of Finrod. For example, Elrond and Elros were of the House of Fingolfin (via Turgon of Gondolin). Elros actually chose the fate of Men and became the first King of the Island of Númenor at the beginning of the Second Age, while Elrond chose that of Elves but supported all Mortals who opposed Sauron, as well as allowing

---

7. His father was Eärendil, offspring of the Elf/Mortal union of Turgon's daughter Idril and the Man Tuor. His mother, Elwing, was the granddaughter of Beren and Lúthien.

his daughter to marry one. As discussed earlier, Turgon and Finrod had been close friends during the First Age, so this could be a further example of Finrod's pro-Mortal influence continuing down the Ages. Another Elf of Gondolin was Glorfindel, killed by a Balrog in the First Age but allowed to return to Middle-earth during the Second Age. (Tolkien C., 2002c, pp. 377-382). He was extremely supportive of the Dúnedain of Arnor in their war against the Witch-king of Angmar midway through the Third Age, (Tolkien, 2005, p. 1051), as well as helping Aragorn and the Hobbits in TA 3018. (Tolkien, 2005, pp. 209-213).

In a similar context, consider the role and friendships of Gil-galad who, as the son of Fingon, was also of Fingolfin's House. Finrod's influence could have been a factor here too, as when Men first appeared in Beleriand Fingolfin had readily followed his example of befriending the new people. During the Second Age Gil-galad was established as the leader of the Elves of Lindon, the western-most part of Middle-earth following the breakup of Beleriand at the end of the First Age. Along with Círdan, he had a close alliance with the sea-going Kings of Númenor, in particular the sixth King, Tar-Aldarion (Tolkien C., 2010, pp. 225-226). However the most significant example of his support for Men was the great friendship between him and Elendil early in the Third Age following the drowning of Númenor, after which a great storm cast up Elendil's ships on the shores of Lindon. Gil-galad befriended him and raised the three Towers of Emyn Beraid for him, the tallest containing one of the Palantíri (Seeing Stones)[8], thus enabling Elendil to look to the West "when the yearning of exile was upon him" (Tolkien C., 2013, p. 350). This was a particularly thoughtful action as Elendil's father Amandil had sailed west shortly before Númenor was destroyed hoping to plead for mercy for those Númenóreans who had remained faithful to the Valar. He had never been seen again and Elendil perhaps hoped to learn something of his fate via the Palantír. Gil-galad and Elendil founded the Last Alliance of Elves and Men and at the end of the Second Age they were killed together bringing down Sauron. (Tolkien C., 2013, pp. 352-353). There is evidence that Tolkien was considering making Gil-galad a descendant of the House of Finarfin rather than that of Fingolfin. (Tolkien C., 2002a, pp. 33-34; 2002b, pp. 242-243; 2002c, pp. 173-174, 349-351). This does fit with the depth of his friendship with Elendil.

8. Brought from Númenor by Elendil.

Círdan, who had been a close friend and ally of Finrod was supportive and friendly to all races and individuals: Thingol and Melian, Finrod and his people, Orodreth, Eärendil, the Kings of Númenor, and Gil-galad. In addition, he helped the Dúnedain during the last stage of the war which brought the North Kingdom to its end in TA 1960. This included harbouring the sons of King Arvedui and sacrificing ships and mariners in a desperate and unsuccessful mission to rescue Arvedui himself from the frozen land of Forochel. (Tolkien, 2005, pp. 1040-1042, 1051).

A specific type of mixed marriage arose through the descendants of Elrond's brother Elros. These people had considerably increased lifespans compared with other Mortals, which could be a problem if the two intermarried. For example the marriage of Aldarion, 6th King of Númenor, and Erendis, who had a normal Mortal lifespan, ended in bitterness and separation due to Aldarion's continual delay to their nuptials. (Tolkien C., 2010, pp. 223-280). During the Third Age the marriage of Valacar, 20th King of Gondor, to a woman of the shorter-lived Northmen triggered the civil war known as the Kin-strife. (Tolkien, 2005, pp. 1045-1048).

*

There follow three possible links to Finrod's influence and beliefs from Tolkien's *The Lord of the Rings* (Tolkien, 2005).

When Frodo, Pippin and Sam met Gildor Inglorion, the Elf introduced himself as being "of the House of Finrod." (Tolkien, 2005, p.80).[9] He and his companions protected the Hobbits from the Nazgûl who had been pursuing them, and later it became clear that they were in communication with Aragorn and his Rangers. Thus the support for Mortals was clearly present.

Legolas provides an interesting example of an Elf/Man relationship. Much attention is understandably given to his friendship with Gimli, but that with Aragorn is also noteworthy. After the victory at the Pelennor Fields one of Legolas's reasons for wanting to be involved in the next battle was "for the love of the Lord of the White Tree". (Tolkien, 2005, p. 878). It was around this time that his longing to go over Sea developed but he didn't actually sail until Aragorn died, well over 100 years later: "But when King

9. Hammond and Scull (2005, pp.103-104) suggest that "Finrod" should probably have been changed to "Finarfin" in keeping with similar corrections.

Elessar gave up his life Legolas followed *at last* the desire of his heart and sailed over Sea". (Tolkien, 2005, p. 1080). [My emphasis]. Although Legolas himself would not have been directly influenced by Finrod, his father Thranduil who lived in Doriath during the First Age may well have remembered him and his opinions. (Tolkien C., 2010, p. 336).

The third example is Legolas's first meeting with Imrahil, 22nd Prince of Dol Amroth. He realised, from the Prince's appearance, that "here indeed was one who had elven-blood in his veins", (Tolkien, 2005, p. 872), linking this to descent from a companion of the Silvan Elf Nimrodel.

Nimrodel and her people had fled south from Lothlórien in TA 1981, following the awakening of the Balrog in Moria the previous year, intending to make their way to the coast and take ship to the Undying Lands. (Tolkien, 2005, pp. 339-341, 1087). Further information in Tolkien, C. (2002c, pp. 220-223, and 2010, pp. 321, 409) refers to an Elf/Mortal marriage around TA 1981-2, between the Númenórean Man Imrazôr from Belfalas, and the Elf Mithrellas, one of Nimrodel's companions. When these Elves had fled some of them went astray, including Mithrellas, and when Imrazôr came upon her wandering and lost, he gave her shelter and "took her to wife". (Tolkien C., 2010, p. 321). However after giving birth to a son and a daughter she left him. Her son became the first Prince of Dol Amroth.

This marriage was clearly different from the other three Elf/Mortal unions. With Lúthien and Beren, Idril and Tuor, and Arwen and Aragorn [the last obviously still in the future at this point] the marriages were clearly based on a deep and lasting love. Although Tuor was able to marry Idril freely, both Beren and Aragorn had to achieve certain goals (the Silmaril and the Kingship respectively) before being allowed to wed. In addition their Elven brides had to become Mortal, leading to distressing, and permanent, family separations. Nevertheless it would have been unthinkable for any of them to consider deserting their spouse. The Mithrellas/Imrazôr union was less clear. Mithrellas may not have married willingly, given that she had been making her way to the Sea when Imrazôr found her. Did she fall in love with him, but dreaded what Gwindor had described as being left "in widowhood while the world lasts" (Tolkien C., 2013, p. 251), and so decided to try and find the way to the Sea again? Terror of the Balrog could also have played a part in her wish to escape. Why is there no reference to her having to become Mortal? What were Imrazôr's motives? Did he just fancy the idea of introducing some Elf blood into his line? Or did he actually believe that their union was brought about for what Finrod had called "some high purpose of Doom"? (Tolkien C., 2015, p. 324). There does seem to be a good case for this last suggestion, as the marriage took place approximately seventy years prior to the loss of Eärnur the childless last King of Gondor in TA 2050 (Tolkien, 2005, p. 1087), resulting in rule by the Stewards from then on. The House of Dol Amroth was now established, and their leaders would become "virtually independent princes, ruling over Belfalas, *but they were at all times loyal to the Steward as representing the ancient crown*". (Tolkien C., 2002c, p. 222). [My emphasis]. Thus the Ruling Stewards were backed by a line of staunch, capable and long-lived supporters. This is illustrated in *The Lord of the Rings* (Tolkien, 2005, pp. 858-893), with Prince Imrahil taking charge in Minas Tirith when Denethor and Faramir were incapacitated, and also offering support to Aragorn, the returning King.

This Silvan Elf blood of Dol Amroth, clearly still very much in evidence, spread further in the late Third and early Fourth Ages:

- Denethor married Imrahil's sister Finduilas thereby passing Elf blood to Boromir and Faramir. (Tolkien, 2005, p. 1090).
- Théoden's father Thengel married Morwen of Lossarnach who was descended from an earlier Prince of Dol Amroth. (Tolkien C., 2010, p. 371). Thus Elf blood would have passed to Théoden and his sister Théodwyn – and subsequently to their children, Théodred, Éomer and Éowyn.
- Éomer married Imrahil's daughter Lothíriel (Tolkien, 2005, p. 1070), so their children would have had Elf blood from both parents.
- The same would have applied to Faramir's and Éowyn's children.

Thus it wasn't just the Aragorn/Arwen marriage which brought Elvish blood to the rulers of the Fourth Age.

*

This final section returns to Finrod, the Elf who first befriended and loved Mortal Men, showing them compassion, respect and fidelity, and encouraging others to do likewise. By sacrificing his own life to save Beren's he fulfilled his role in what Tolkien described (in a draft letter to Peter Hastings) as "a Divine Plan for the ennoblement of the Human Race, from the beginning destined to replace the Elves" (Carpenter and Tolkien C., 1995, Letter 153, p. 194).

Regarding his life in the Undying Lands, it is stated that "Finrod walks with Finarfin his father beneath the trees in Eldamar". (Tolkien C., 2013, p. 206). He is also said to be living in Valinor with Amarië. (Tolkien C., 2002b, pp. 62, 67, 130, 243). In addition there would have been reunions with his mother Eärwen, his brothers, and later on with Galadriel when she sailed at the end of the Third Age.

But what of Men? His last words to Beren had been: "*it may be that we shall not meet a second time* in death or life, for the fates of our kindreds are apart. Farewell!". (Tolkien C., 2013, p. 204). [My emphasis]. This does not categorically rule out the possibility of Men and Elves meeting again as further indicated by the following:

- "the Valar have not seen ... the Later Ages or the ending of the World". (Tolkien C., 2013, p. 9).
- "the Valar declared to the Elves in Valinor that Men shall join in the Second Music of the Ainur; whereas Ilúvatar has not revealed what he purposes for the Elves after the World's end". (Tolkien C., 2013, p. 36).
- "The fate of Men after death, maybe, is not in the hands of the Valar, nor was all foretold in the Music of the Ainur". (Tolkien C., 2013, p. 117).

In addition Finrod himself, in his conversation with the wise-woman Andreth, refers to his own vision of a new world, "Arda Remade" (Tolkien C., 2015, pp. 318-319), where Elves and Men might indeed meet a second time. His final words to Andreth before he left to go to war were: "Whither you go may you find light. Await us there, my brother – and me". (Tolkien C., 2015, p. 326). Did he believe this? Or was it wishful thinking? A yearning to be reunited with all those Mortal men and women he'd lost and mourned?

References

Carpenter, H. and Tolkien, C. eds., 1995. *The Letters of J.R.R. Tolkien*. London: HarperCollins Publishers.

Hammond, W.G. and Scull, C., 2005. *The Lord of the Rings: A Reader's Companion*. London: HarperCollinsPublishers.

Nicholas, A. P., 2017. *Aragorn. J.R.R. Tolkien's Undervalued Hero*. Edinburgh: Luna Press Publishing.

Rateliff, J. D., 2008. *The History of the Hobbit. Part One: Mr. Baggins*. London: HarperCollinsPublishers.

Tolkien, C. ed., 2002a. *The Lost Road and Other Writings – The History of Middle-earth Vol. V*. London: HarperCollins Publishers.
—, 2002b. *The War of the Jewels – The History of Middle-earth Vol. XI*. London: HarperCollins Publishers.
—, 2002c. *The Peoples of Middle-earth – The History of Middle-earth Vol. XII*. London: HarperCollins Publishers.
—, 2010. *Unfinished Tales of Númenor and Middle-earth*. London: HarperCollinsPublishers.
—, 2013. *The Silmarillion*. London: HarperCollinsPublishers.
—, 2015. *Morgoth's Ring – The History of Middle earth Vol. X*. London: HarperCollins Publishers.

Tolkien, J.R.R., 2005. *The Lord of the Rings*. 2nd ed. London: HarperCollinsPublishers.

The Gaffer: Between Cabbages and Potatoes

Enrico Spadaro and Mauro Toninelli

Introduction – Between cabbages and potatoes.

A discussion concerning cabbages and potatoes may appear as a matter for gardeners, country people or vegetable lovers. However, the reality is that cabbages and potatoes, if placed in relation to Elves and Dragons, might provide a hermeneutic indication for reading and interpreting Tolkien's *The Lord of the Rings*, published in 1954-55. Without necessarily looking at everyone's vegetable garden, the starting point is right in the opening pages of Tolkien's masterpiece when the Gaffer, Sam Gamgee's father, at the hobbit inn *The Ivy Bush*, quotes the words he often addresses to his son:

> *Elves and Dragons*! I says to him. *Cabbages and potatoes are better for me and you. Don't go getting mixed up in the business of your betters, or you'll land in trouble too big for you*, I says to him. And I might say it to others. (Tolkien, 2007, p. 31, italics in the text).

It appears to be a very wise warning from a father to his son on how to behave in order to avoid trouble and to live a peaceful life.

When the reader begins to delve into the events of Middle-earth and its characters, he or she will discover that Sam, despite his father's recommendations, is inevitably going to have to deal with Elves, Dragons and much more, until the pages of the last chapter of the novel are reached. Once the protagonists are back at number 2 of Bagshot Row after the struggle against Saruman to save the Shire, the Gaffer cannot but repeat, as he usually does to whoever he talks to, "And All's Well as ends Better!" (Tolkien, 2007, p. 1337).

Ham Gamgee, known as the Gaffer, is a hobbit that is decidedly unfair to be called a minor character in Tolkien's Middle-earth. He enters the story on tiptoe, he remains in a corner, but he wins the affection of every reader for his bond with Sam, one of his sons.[1] In the following pages, the hidden centrality of the Gaffer,

---

1. Appendix C *Family Trees* contains a number of Hobbit families, including Sam's ancestors and descendants. (Tolkien, 2007, pp. 1444-1450).

his role as Sam's mentor and the message borne out by his few but remarkable words are going to be analysed and explained. He is decidedly a simple and humble character but such humbleness acts as a counterbalance to the main events in Tolkien's novel: a quality that is shared, though sometimes with different nuances, by other characters depicted within Tolkien's works.

In first pages of *The Lord of the Rings*,[2] according to the neighbourhood and to himself, the Gaffer is the greatest expert on roots and, in particular, on potatoes, as well as being among the most informed and listened to about the events linked to Bilbo and Frodo. At least at the beginning of the story: he had been the gardener of Bag End, Bilbo's and Frodo's hobbit hole, for forty years and, when he retired, he was succeeded by his son Sam. The Gaffer is also the first to converse with one of the Black Knights, who is looking for Frodo in Hobbiton and, from what may be inferred from Tolkien's pages, he is perfectly able to withstand the dialogue with the Nazgûl, annoyed but not afraid of the haunting presence of Sauron's servant (Tolkien, 2007, p. 91).

Ham Gamgee, though he never moves from his homeplace nor leaves the Shire (at least as far as we know), spiritually accompanies the entire journey of *The Lord of the Rings*, especially his son Sam's journey, who always mentions and remembers his father during his adventure throughout Middle-earth. Sam constantly refers to his beloved father for two reasons: to remember his land, his origins, his roots, and for the wisdom that the old man's words preserve. This is a kind of wisdom concerning country life and, at the same time, ordinary life.[3] And so it is that little by little old Ham Gamgee will carve out that little corner of sympathy and affection within the reader's heart as mentioned above. The Gaffer embodies the voice of concreteness, which has its roots in the deep connection with the land. He is a down-to-earth character whose mentality stems from such folk wisdom that can often become a guide and a key to understanding reality and most of the situations that Sam

---

2. Cf. the first chapter "A long-expected party" (Tolkien, 2007, pp. 27-54).

3. Cf. "Live and learn! as my gaffer used to say. Though he was thinking of gardening, not of roosting like a bird, nor of trying to walk like a spider. Not even my uncle Andy ever did a trick like that!" (Tolkien, 2007, p. 451). And "*It's the job that's never started as takes longest to finish*, as my old gaffer used to say. And I don't reckon that these folks can do much more to help us, magic or no. It's when we leave this land that we shall miss Gandalf worse, I'm thinking." (Tolkien, 2007, p. 470).

has to experience while helping Frodo. And the reader experiences the same moments and feel the same attachment to the Gaffer. The word "Gaffer" appears more than fifty time while reading *The Lord of the Rings*. He is not a simple hobbit as it may initially seems and he finally turns out to be an ever-felt comforting presence.

Tolkien's hobbit-centredness

"This book is largely concerned with Hobbits" (Tolkien, 2007, p. 1) – so starts the "Prologue" to *The Lord of the Rings* that Tolkien wrote at the beginning of his novel. Hobbits are the main focus of this work and the role they play within the development of the story is essential to the destruction of the One Ring and the salvation of Middle-earth. Although Tolkien's original intent, when he started composing his *Lost Tales* in the aftermath of the First World War, was to write a mythology for his own country, England, his two achieved and most successful novels deal essentially with Hobbits. Hobbits are humble and simple people, presented as a variety of humanity, known as *halflings*, almost forgotten from the rest of Middle-earth. Tolkien devised three different types of Hobbits and set their origins on the banks of the river Anduin, but his stories focus on the Hobbits living in the Shire, in the north of Middle-earth. The Shire has commonly been identified with the English countryside Tolkien lived in during his childhood, after moving there in 1895 from South Africa. "The Shire is a reflection of Sarehole" (Garth, 2020, p. 12). Tolkien loved dwelling in the rural outskirts of Birmingham as he recalled in many of his letters, and the watermill he and his brother Hilary used to play around was probably that which inspired the Mill our author described and then depicted in one of the illustrations of *The Hobbit* (Hammond and Scull, 1995, p. 106). It is not the purpose of these pages to investigate the geography of Tolkien's invented Shire, which has been efficaciously compared to British places in the latest publication by John Garth, *The Worlds of J.R.R. Tolkien*. The Shire and its lands give a sense of welcoming home, both to Tolkien and to the Hobbits leaving it for their adventures: this is what Bilbo constantly thinks of during his quest in *The Hobbit*. Moreover, the supporting and sustaining thought to Merry, Pippin, Frodo and Sam, is their roots in the Shire, a home that must be protected, saved and finally regained. If Tolkien's first novel starts with Bilbo's departure from the Shire, *The Lord of the Rings* ends with Sam's words: "I'm back" (Tolkien, 2007, p. 1349).

If the Shire represents a bucolic countryside – and there are people all over the world trying to build Shire-like areas and living like Hobbits[4] – hobbit lifestyle is a synonym for simplicity, enjoyable and peaceful life. Hobbits, who are usually unfond of adventures, are probably the most gourmet characters in literature and they live in a sort of "Epicureanism" (Smith, 2021, p. 13). They deem that prosperity does not lie in gold or money, but in good health, good company, good food and nice stories to be told around the fire. This is what Tolkien himself enjoyed as well, especially when he used to meet with his friends and colleagues at *The Eagle and the Child* (often called *The Bird and the Baby*) in Oxford, drinking beer and reading their stories to each other.[5] This passage exemplifies Tolkien's feelings about "being a Hobbit":

> I am in fact a Hobbit (in all but size). I like gardens, trees and unmechanized farmlands; I smoke a pipe, and like good plain food (unrefrigerated) […] I am fond of mushrooms (out of a field); have a very simple sense of humour (which even my appreciative critics find tiresome); I go to bed late and get up late (when possible). I do not travel much. (Carpenter and Tolkien C., 2012, Letter 213, p. 807).

In this quotation, Tolkien states he likes gardens, since the halflings are deeply concerned with horticulture: a gardener is one of the most respected jobs in the Shire. This is why the Gaffer, who is Baggins family's gardener, may be considered as the quintessential kind of a hobbit. In all likelihood, his role finds its origins in what estate gardeners used to do in the Victorian Age: they had prestigious and estimated tasks as they were in charge of the whole management of country estates. The Gaffer is assigned the title of "Master", as he is a very expert on the matter of garden and vegetable growing: Bilbo and Frodo get most of their food from the ground the Gaffer, and then his

---

4. Besides Hobbiton movie set in New Zealand, there are a few cases of people who intend to restore Shire-like villages: it could be argued whether these are speculative initiatives or merely leisure fan activities. See the case in Italy: <https://www.wired.it/lol/2021/05/08/contea-hobbit-abruzzo-intervista/>, accessed on 17th June 2021.
5. In his youth, Tolkien had already experienced such meetings with his friends of the King Edward's School in Birmingham and they had founded the T.C.B.S. (Tea Club and Barrovian Society), talking about literature and their projects to save the world. Unfortunately, only Tolkien and Christopher Wiseman survived the war, and that would always mark Tolkien's life (Tolkien, 2007, p. XXVI).

son Sam, work on. Bilbo's hole may be defined as a typical cottage garden, a furnished country house surrounded by a small garden with a seemingly casual mixture of flowers, herbs, and vegetables.

The Gaffer is a distinctive hobbit, who spends all his day working on his land and then enjoying a beer at the inn, as Tolkien used to do in the period when he composed *The Lord of the Rings*, that is the Second World War. British people that were unable to fight were encouraged to cultivate their little gardens for their own sustenance, due to rationed food in times of war. Tolkien spent a lot of time in his garden in the early 1940s and those years maybe contributed to the increasing hobbit-centredness in his life as well as in his works.

Cabbages and potatoes: the Gaffer's message

The Gaffer's words may stimulate an interesting reflection, without falling into the simple allegory that Tolkien so much wanted to avoid in his approach to *The Lord of the Rings*.

Cabbages and potatoes indicate the everyday condition in which first the Gaffer and then Sam, live. Sam's work as a gardener in the Baggins' house engages and occupies him in these chores. Cabbages and the potatoes symbolise the ordinariness of life, its routine, its habits, its merits, all its limitations, its joys and sorrows, its successes and failures. They also add a humble, earth-bound conception of the vision of life "*for me and you*" (Tolkien, 2007, p. 31).

Elves and Dragons, on the other hand, in the representation of old Gamgee's world, are everything that is out of the ordinary, out of the ordinary of Hobbit life, out of the cultivated field and the land. In other words, it is the extraordinary, that which seems unattainable "*for me and you*".

It is the beginning and the end of the novel.

The Gaffer opens the story: "*Elves and Dragons*! I says to him. *Cabbages and potatoes are better for me and you*" (Tolkien, 2007, p. 31). And the Gaffer, with his wisdom repeatedly recalled by Sam throughout his journey, closes the story by offering a reading of History[6]: "And All's Well as ends Better!" (Tolkien, 2007, p. 1337).

Everything that lies in between is a journey, a story that involves

6. Cf. *On Fairy-stories* "this element does not rise or fall, but is there, in the Cauldron of Story, waiting for the great figures of Myth and History, and for the yet nameless He or She, waiting for the moment when they are cast into the simmering stew, one by one or all together, without consideration of rank or precedence." (Tolkien C., 2008, p. 167).

everyone's cabbages and potatoes, everyday life, the ordinariness of an existence. It is from the final result, "the Better", that we understand that the story is linked to the Good. It is from the fruit, to use an image close to the Gaffer, that we understand the tree. And the tree is made up of different aspects. The roughness of difficult moments; the knots that mark fractures, deviations, the vivacity of the sap that runs through the whole of reality, the beauty and fragrance of pleasant situations, the openness to the sun, the rain, the moon, the cold and the heat.

Everything that occurs in the pages of *The Lord of the Rings* is framed by the wisdom of the Gaffer in these two sentences; what has happened to each of the characters, even the most complicated things that the Gaffer does not even imagine but which have affected everyone in a different way, as well as what has happened even to him when he is uprooted from his home (think of the difficulty of having an old man move house, especially if he is tied to the land like the Gaffer; it means destroying the certainties earned as the fruit of a life), is illuminated by the final "Better" of his statement. This is the intrinsic meaning behind the Gaffer's message, an apparently down-to-earth message unveiling unexpected wisdom. And Tolkien loves hiding precious meanings or suggestions within unsuspected people.

Not only the Gaffer, down-to-earthness in Tolkien

The Gaffer is not the only down-to-earth character in Tolkien's literary production. Almost all the hobbits are generally modest and unadventurous characters – the exceptions are the protagonists of Tolkien's two novels – however, other similar figures may be found in Tolkien's tales other than the Legendarium. Their roles might be counterbalancing the rather active protagonists of such tales, yet with different nuances. In particular two of them may deserve a mention, that is Parish from *Leaf, by Niggle* and Nokes from *Smith of Wootton Major.*

The first is the co-protagonist of the short story Tolkien wrote in 1938-39, which is often considered as the practical side of his most famous essay *On Fairy-stories*, since they were firstly published together in the collection *Tree and Leaf* in 1964 (by Allen and Unwin). The tale is usually deemed as an autobiographical representation of Tolkien's career as an artist and a writer, focusing on theme of creation and sub-creation. Although he had always denied any personal references in his works, and in letter no. 153 he stated: "I tried to show allegorically how [sub-creation] might come to be taken up into Creation in some plane in my 'purgatorial' story Leaf by Niggle" (Carpenter and Tolkien C., 2012, Letter 153, p. 713), it is doubtful whether an author displays autobiographical elements within his literary production or not. The latest studies on the relationship between Tolkien's life and work shed new lights on this approach, as it may be seen in Garth's *The Worlds of J.R.R. Tolkien* (2020) or the miscellaneous work *Something has gone crack* (2019), edited by Janet Brennan Croft and Annika Röttinger.

If Niggle is a fictional counterpart of Tolkien is not the point of interest of our text: what matters is the figure of Parish, his neighbour, who, coincidentally, owns a garden and has a particular aptitude for gardening, just like the Gaffer in the Shire. Niggle may stand for Everyman, an ordinary man who wants to achieve something extraordinary with his art and has to take a journey, which is finally summoned upon. On the other hand, Parish is bent on ordinary things, he is more worried about his wife's health and his gardens than about Niggle's paintings. The two characters form an equally balanced pair, who will end up by supporting each other: Parish is the neighbour that must be loved, according to Christian principles, and Niggle's care for him, which then appears to be intertwined with creative art, will be finally rewarded in the fictional land called "Niggle's Parish" (Tolkien C., 2008, p. 311). The tree Niggle struggles to paint cannot be achieved without this contrast between art and life that is embedded in the two characters. On the one hand, Niggle needs wood and canvas to paint; on the other hand, Parish, since his house is badly damaged, asks his neighbour wood and canvas to repair it. Parish is the practical man and Niggle is the artist, just as the Gaffer represents the humble ordinary hobbit that sets the initial frame of the story in the Shire. Samwise Gamgee will be showing his father's factual qualities all over his journey with Frodo to Mordor and will prove his presence to be indispensable for the achievement of the hobbits' quest.

Tolkien was "a man of antitheses" (Flieger, 2002, pos. 299), and pairs, both linguistically and narratively, are conspicuously found within his works. Pairings may lead to different forms of creations:

sometimes two concepts, or two characters complement each other, as it is the case with Niggle and Parish. However, it may happen that co-existence is not so peaceful: this is what is shown in Tolkien's last written story, *Smith of Wootton Major*, firstly released in 1967.

The tale sprang out of Tolkien's mind in the attempt to explain the true meaning of Faëria and the texture of fairy-tales in the preface to George MacDonald's *The Golden Key* (1867). As it had often occurred in Tolkien's creative career, the story grew in the telling and the Smith's adventures to the fairy realm, thanks to the finding of a little star in the Great Cake, turn out to be Tolkien's final testament and his fictitious farewell to Faëria. The setting is a typical English countryside village, Wootton Major, which is very close to the forest, one of the potential accesses to the fairy realm, as Tolkien explains in the long apparatus of notes and in an essay, finally published in the 2005 expanded edition, edited by Verlyn Flieger. Few are the characters depicted in the story, but among them one stands as the opposing figure to the wandering protagonist Smith: this is Nokes, who, at the beginning of the tale becomes the Master Cook of Wootton Major. According to the village tradition, the cook in charge is supposed to choose an apprentice who will then take over his position: however, the initial Master Cook in charge, Rider, takes the sudden decision to leave and Nokes is chosen by the villagers since the current apprentice, Alf, is deemed to be too young to become the Master Cook.

Although Nokes is able to cook, Alf's precious work as an apprentice proves to be essential in the upcoming preparation of the Great Cake for the Feast of Good Children. The cake is finally decorated with trinkets and coins and with a special silver star, which Smith finds and will let him travel to Faëria. Nokes is the typical factual man who does not believe in the powerful qualities of the star and denies the existence of the elves and their kingdom. He is sceptical and incredulous and finds no explanation as to why the star has disappeared after the Feast, but believes that Alf has concealed it. He embodies the figure of the down-to-earth man who does not accept what he cannot see nor touch; he is described as coarse and vulgar, insensitive and arrogant.

Only at the end of the tale, when he is old and retired, and Alf has replaced him as Master Cook, the former apprentice reveals the truth about Smith's finding of the star which granted his access to the faery realm. Despite Alf's accusations and warnings, Nokes does not want to accept the existence of fairy beings and defies Alf, who actually reveals to be the King of Faëria. Frightened, the old Nokes begged Alf not to harm him and falls into sleep. After his awakening, he still won't admit to what he has experienced and thinks he has had an awful nightmare, a repetition of which can only be avoided by fasting. This is why he begins to lose weight: from then on children will call him old Rag-and-Bones.

Nokes is the counterpart of Alf, the fairy King, and of Smith, a simple man who can enjoy the beauties of Faëria. He is the contrasting side of the pair, the dark that lets light live: his name, which etymologically indicates someone "living near the oak" (Tolkien, 2007, p. 154), is the typical characterisation of a simple-minded man, almost ignorant, who cannot accept what stands beyond mere reality and is bound only to his personal account. He may remind readers of Dickens's Mr GradGrind, the school board Superintendent in *Hard Times* (1854), whose name generally refers to someone concerned by facts, numbers and profits.

Moreover, Nokes immediately evokes those hobbits who are profoundly bound to their land and to mere facts: if the Gaffer relies only on his "cabbages and potatoes", the old Noakes of Bywater clearly represents the hobbit equivalent for many reasons. First of all, their names are almost identical – "Noakes" in *The Lord of the Rings* and "Nokes" in *Smith of Wootton Major* – and then their personal beliefs and attitudes show great similarities. During the discussions at *The Ivy Bush* that open *The Fellowship of the Ring* (Tolkien, 2007, p. 28), Noakes wonders about Frodo's parents' death and Bilbo's family and fortune. He embodies the typical suspicious ordinary man, who lacks fantasy and that Secondary Belief that is necessary in order to access the faery realm Tolkien creates. Biases, stubbornness and ignorance distinguish such characters who cannot but live imprisoned within the reality, if we want to paraphrase Tolkien's words in *On Fairy-stories*.[7] The accessibility to the fantastic

---

7. " [...] It is part of the essential malady of such days— producing the desire to escape, not indeed from life, but from our present time and self-made misery— that we are acutely conscious both of the ugliness of our works, and of their evil. So that to us evil and ugliness seem indissolubly allied. We find it difficult to conceive of evil and beauty together. The fear of the beautiful fay that ran through the elder ages almost eludes our grasp. Even more alarming: goodness is itself bereft of its proper beauty. In Faerie one can indeed conceive of an ogre who possesses a castle hideous as a nightmare (for the evil of the ogre wills it so), but one cannot conceive

world is not something simply psychological, as Todorov stated in his *Introduction à la littérature fantastique* (1970), but it implies the acceptance of a different world that exists next to the Primary one and that only a few selected people may enter. However, this world may come into being only as a sub-creation based on the real world: as a matter of fact, a realistic attachment is then compulsory, which the fantastic realm may stem from. If "cabbage and potatoes" are one of such realistic elements necessary for the existence of the Secondary World, so are the village of Wootton Major close to the Forest, as well as the fact-concerning nature of Nokes/Noakes.

Conclusion: Spiritual message inherent in the figure of the Gaffer

Doing what belongs to everyday life, coming to terms with one's own reality, one's own situation, is sometimes complicated. It is difficult to see in it that Good which will unravel the story, of which everyone is a part, to the Better. Everyone's cabbages and potatoes make sense because they can and do live in the light of something greater, Elves and Dragons.

It almost seems as if a spiritual path of meaning is here proposed, as much for Sam and the Hobbits as for those who find themselves challenged by *The Lord of the Rings*. To confirm this idea, it is necessary to refer to other texts in which Tolkien himself expressed certain principles and reflected on his work. Among these are certainly the letters, where Tolkien appears to become himself an interpreter of his novel.

Tolkien's letters 180 and 181 may be taken into consideration. Both are dated 1956, probably early in the year.

> The hobbits had been welcomed. I loved them myself, since I love the vulgar and simple as dearly as the noble, and nothing moves my heart (beyond all the passions and heartbreaks of the world) so much as "ennoblement" (from the Ugly Duckling to Frodo). I would build on the hobbits. And I saw that I was meant to do it (as Gandalf would say), since without thought, in a "blurb" I wrote for The Hobbit, I spoke of the time between the Elder Days and the Dominion of Men (Carpenter and Tolkien C., 2012, Letter 180, p. 651).

of a house built with a good purpose—an inn, a hostel for travellers, the hall of a virtuous and noble king—that is yet sickeningly ugly. At the present day it would be rash to hope to see one that was not—unless it was built before our time (Tolkien, 2008, pp. 221-222)

In this passage, Tolkien expresses his considerations about Hobbits, underlining their ordinariness, humility and nobility. If one is not surprised by the first two characteristics, one is perhaps a little more surprised by the term noble associated with the people of the Shire. Then, Tolkien adds a note about Frodo, about the sustained enterprise that led to his ennoblement, where the term is placed in inverted commas. The graphic sign says that with that term Tolkien wants to indicate something particular, something that semantically is not immediately perceptible within the term but that may be understood.

In order to understand what he means we have to rely on the following letter, when he comments on Frodo and Sam's arrival at the chasm of Mount Doom.

> The Quest was bound to fail as a piece of world-plan, and also was bound to end in disaster as the story of humble Frodo's development to the "noble", his sanctification (Carpenter and Tolkien C., 2012, Letter 181, p. 656).

Here it seems that noble means holy. An assumption that is confirmed by another occurrence in the same letter.

> I regard the tale of Arwen and Aragorn as the most important of the Appendices; it is pan of the essential story, and is only placed so, because it could not be worked into the main narrative without destroying its structure: which is planned to be "hobbito-centric", that is, primarily a study of the ennoblement (or sanctification) of the humble (Carpenter and Tolkien C., 2012, Letter 181, p. 666).

Three occurrences where Tolkien clearly says that there is for some characters a spiritual path and he defines this path as sanctification.

From these specific statements concerning the Hobbits and Frodo, Tolkien clearly affirms the possibility that history progresses towards the Better, that the ordinariness of cabbages and potatoes can only be in close relation to and within something greater, something that allows it to exist and that achieves, at the same time, History.

In the ordinariness of everyone's life, something greater is at work. What everyone is, with all his or her strengths, limitations, successes and failures, allows the extraordinary to happen and be finally achieved. Even in the darkest and most complicated moments. Cabbages, potatoes are to be thought in the light of Elves and Dragons, "And this may be an encouraging thought" (Tolkien, 2007, p. 73).

References

AA. VV., 2003. *Dizionario dell'universo di J.R.R. Tolkien*. Milano: Bompiani.

Arduini, R. et al., eds., 2015. *Tolkien e i classici*. Roma: Effatà Editrice.

Carpenter, H., 1977. *J.R.R. Tolkien: A Biography*. London: George Allen and Unwin.

Carpenter, H. and Tolkien, C. eds., 2012. *The Letters of J.R.R. Tolkien*. [iTunes version] London: HarperCollins Publishers. Available at: Apple.com <https://www.apple.com/uk/apple-books/> [Accessed 31 August 2021]

Curry, P., 2004. *Defending Middle-earth. Tolkien: Myth and Modernity*. New York: Houghton Mifflin.

Drabble M. ed., 1985. *The Oxford Companion to English Literature*. Oxford: Oxford University Press.

Drout, M.D.C., 2007. *J.R.R. Tolkien Encyclopedia. Scholarship and critical assessment*. New York: Taylor & Francis.

Fimi D., 2009. *Tolkien, Race and Cultural History*. New York: Palgrave.

Flieger, V., 2001. *A Question of Time. J.R.R. Tolkien's Road to Faërie*. Kent State Univ Press.
—, 2002. *Splintered Light: Tolkien's World, Revised Edition: Logos and Language in Tolkien's World*. [Kindle version] Kent State Univ Press. Available at: Amazon.co.uk <https://www.amazon.co.uk> [Accessed 31 August 2021].
—, 2015. *The Story of Kullervo*. London: Harper Collins.

Garth, J., 2003. *Tolkien and the Great War: The Threshold of Middle-earth*. London: Harper Collins.
—, 2020. *The Worlds of J.R.R. Tolkien*. Princeton: Princeton University Press.

Gulisano, P., 2001. *Tolkien. Il mito e la Grazia*. Milano: Ancora.

Giuliano, S., 2013. *J.R.R. Tolkien. Tradizione e modernità nel Signore degli Anelli*. Milano: Bietti.

Hammond, W.G., 1993. *J.R.R. Tolkien: A Descriptive Bibliography*. Winchester: Oak Knoll Books.

Spadaro, E., 2021. *La Littérature-monde de J.R.R. Tolkien*. Paris: L'Harmattan.

The Tolkien Society. [online] Available at: <https://www.tolkiensociety.org> [Accessed 31 August 2021].

Todorov, T., 2015. *Introduction à la littérature fantastique*. Paris: Points essais.

Tolkien, C. ed., 1977. *The Silmarillion*. London: Allen and Unwin.
—, 1980. *Unfinished Tales*. London: Allen and Unwin.
—, 1983. *The Monster and the Critics and Other Essays*. London: Allen and Unwin.
—, 1988. *The Return of the Shadow – History of Middle-earth Vol. VI*. London: Harper Collins.
—, 2008. *Il Medioevo e il fantastico*. Milano: Bompiani.
—, 2018. *The Fall of Gondolin*. Boston-New York: Houghton Mifflin Harcourt.

Tolkien Gateway. [online] Available at: <https://www.tolkiengateway.net> [Accessed 31 August 2021].

Tolkien, J.R.R.,—, 2007. *The Lord of the Rings*. London: Harper Collins.
—, 2015. *The Hobbit*. London: Harper Collins.

Tolkien Italia. [online] Available at: <https://tolkienitalia.net> [Accessed 31 August 2021].

Toninelli, M., 2019. *Colui che raccontò la Grazia*. Assisi: Cittadella editrice.

The Dyscatastrophe of Túrin Turambar

Elise Caemasache McKenna

Christopher Tolkien, in the Introduction to *The Children of Húrin*, opened with "the character of Túrin was of deep significance to my father" (Tolkien C., 2007, p. 13). Dr. Dimitra Fimi (2010, p. 53). noted that, "the tale of Túrin Turambar [remains] one of the pivotal legends of the First Age." The significance of this tale to Tolkien and to the entire Legendarium requires an investigation. As one of three longer narratives[1] from the First Age, the story concerns the life of Túrin Turambar[2], the only son of Húrin and Morwen of the race of Men. The tale *Narn î hin Húrin* or *The Children of Húrin* brings together some of the longer parts of the *Narn* from the scattered versions into one chronological cohesive narrative, telling the longer story of that family and their woes. In an important essay for the Andrew Lang Lecture in 1939, Tolkien presented his theory on the origins of fairy-stories (Tolkien, 1966, p. 33). Expounded in his "On Fairy-stories," he labelled four key elements of the literary construct of fairy-story as Fantasy, Recovery, Escape, and Consolation. Tolkien then split the final element, Consolation, into eucatastrophe and dyscatastrophe. I propose an in depth look at J. R. R. Tolkien's character Túrin throughout the story to illustrate how the author exemplified his theory of the four key elements of a successfully crafted fairy-story.

Túrin's tale takes the reader down a spiralling path of chanced encounters, missed opportunities, bittersweet loves, and a final Consolation that is anything but consoling. 'Of Túrin Turambar' embodies the dyscatastrophe of a would-be hero, where one would usually expect a eucatastrophe. Túrin attempts to do the right thing, but on many occasions he makes decisions and acts for the wrong reasons or because he is misguided. That final outcome, or

---

1. These are 'Of Beren and Lúthien' 'Of Túrin Turambar,' and 'Of the Ruin of Beleriand and the Fall of Fingolfin.'
2. (Both *The Silmarillion* (Tolkien C., 1977) and *The Children of Húrin* (Tolkien C. 2007) will be used throughout this essay since they are most similar in detail with one being told in brief and the other more fully.)

Consolation, is foreshadowed through the actions of the hero while he experiences events that reveal the first three functions of a fairy-story: Fantasy, Recovery, and Escape. Using Tolkien's essay, this article will attempt to identify, qualify, and substantiate the tale of Túrin in terms of those elements of fairy-story to arrive at an answer to the question: Is the tale of Túrin a fairy-story?

Fantasy

Tolkien's definition of the Fantasy element in "On Fairy-stories" is multi-faceted. He clarifies what is and is not Fantasy and why it has negative connotations. Its association with Imagination is the chief reason he proposes for the lack of literary status fairy-stories have in literary circles. However, "fantasy does not blur the sharp outlines of the real world; for it depends on them" (Tolkien, 1966, p. 97). Once Tolkien divests Fantasy from "the mental power of image-making" (Tolkien, 1966, p. 68), he develops what Fantasy is by stating that the element is "not to be found in our primary world, [must have] an arresting strangeness" (Tolkien, 1966, p. 69), and must be part of the sub-creation not "merely for decoration" (Tolkien, 1966, p. 70). However, he also states that to successfully create it, "will probably require labour and thought, and will certainly demand a special skill, a kind of *elvish craft* [my emphasis]" (Tolkien, 1966, p. 70).

The potential difficulty in finding the fantasy element in the story harkens back to what Tolkien explained in "Tree and Leaf," when speaking about the witches in *Macbeth*. If the witches are a natural part of Macbeth's world, then they cease to be fantasy (Tolkien, 1966). How can fantasy be found then in the story where talking dragons can hypnotize and demigods talk to elves and men? Dragons are all too commonly known as part and parcel of fantasy stories from Ann McCaffrey's *Dragonriders of Pern* to George R. R. Martin's *Game of Thrones*. So, when modern readers read Tolkien's *The Hobbit* and *The Silmarillion*, they would recognize those as fantasy elements. However, they would be incorrect. Dragons and gods or demi-gods are the norm for the diegesis.

Further analysis can also cast aside Melian, the Maia who marries the elf, Thingol. Although she has powers of perception beyond elves and men, and she cast the Girdle of Melian, keeping

Thingol's dominion safe from evil, she is like Macbeth's witches. Túrin's mother Morwen is feared by the Easterlings as being "perilous and a witch skilled in magic and in league with the elves" (Tolkien C., 1977, p. 234). Yet again, she is part of the normal world of Arda. When Húrin, Turin's father is constrained on a high throne by Morgoth and made to see through the Vala's eyes all his family come to ruin, it is an unusual event. For that family, it is the turning event that leads to utter tragedy. Still, it is not Fantasy because the Vala who does this has the power by his nature and is part of the diegesis. Although Túrin is plagued with ill luck and 'crazy random happenstances'[3] that prove ill or keep him alive until further ill can be put on him, that is not Fantasy either. The Fantasy element must be concrete. This excerpt from *Interrupted Music: The Making of Tolkien's Mythology* verifies Tolkien's diegesis as containing:

> many things besides elves and fays, and besides dwarfs, witches, trolls, giants, or dragons: it holds the seas, the sun, the moon, the sky; and the earth, and all things that are in it: tree and bird, water and stone, wine and bread, and ourselves, mortal men, when we are enchanted (*EPCW*, 1947, p.42 cited in Flieger, 2005, p.122).

Flieger (2005, p.122) asserts that Tolkien's description of Faërie above is "about as good a description of Tolkien's Middle-earth as can be found" and she is right on the mark, since it is the author's own words. Therefore, as Tolkien says, "that argument concedes the point" (Tolkien, 1966, p. 71). Where then does one find the Fantasy element?

When looking at all seemingly fantastic things in the story "Of Túrin Turambar", the one item that fits the Fantasy element is the sword that Beleg chooses. When Túrin goes missing after an altercation that resulted in the death of an elf named Saeros, Beleg is sent by Thingol to find Túrin and bring him back to the safety of the halls of Menegroth. Beleg does but cannot convince Túrin to return. Beleg then asks to return to Túrin to guard and guide him. He requests "a sword of worth" (Tolkien C., 1977, p. 239; Tolkien C., 2007, p.96). This sword is not "merely for decoration" (Tolkien, 1966, p. 70). So, from the start, it is revealed that this is no ordinary sword. In fact, "it was made of iron that fell from heaven as a blazing star; it would cleave all earth-delved [earth-dolven] iron" (Tolkien

3. Words borrowed from Joss Whedon's *Dr. Horrible's Sing-Along Blog*, 2008.

C., 1977, p. 239; Tolkien C., 2007, p.96). This item is not a part of this world, and it can damage things of this world, being other in origin. In fact, it was created by elvish craft, being forged by Eol, the dark elf. When the sword called Anglachel is looked upon by Melian, she reveals something disquieting about it. "There is malice" and "it will [not] abide with you long" (Tolkien C., 1977, p. 240). One of the reasons people dismiss fantasy, according to Tolkien is because it is arresting (Tolkien, 1966, p. 69). Finding out the sword's origins, that it has malice, and will not be with Beleg for very long are all disquieting. It does not seem like a safe choice of weapon. As the story progresses, its malice is turned against Beleg when Túrin, wrongly thinking Beleg a foe, wrestles Anglachel away and kills Beleg on a dark stormy night after being captured and tortured by Orcs. Thus Melian's two predictions come to fruition. However, the final bit of evidence comes at the end of the story. Túrin turns the sword on himself, and in doing so, he spoke to the sword…and it spoke back in a cold voice saying, "I will slay thee swiftly" (Tolkien C., 1977, p. 270). This is not something common to the world. The talking sword is in the Kalevala, and Túrin's sword is modelled after it, but it is an anomaly in this story and in the Legendarium and consequently the Fantasy element in Tolkien's sub-creation.

Recovery

The next element Tolkien felt was required is Recovery. According to Tolkien, "Recovery (which includes return and renewal of health) is a re-gaining—regaining of a clear view…seeing things are we are (or were) meant to see them […] as things apart from ourselves" (Tolkien, 1966, p. 77). This is the part in a story where the protagonist gets to rest and recuperate. It also allows the reader to rest and take stock of what has happened. It is now commonly known as an element in the 17 stages of the hero's journey, as written by the late Joseph Campbell in *The Hero with a Thousand Faces* (1949). However, that was well after Tolkien was writing this story, which is dated as early as 1918. It is in Recovery where we start to perceive a pattern of behaviour exhibited by Túrin—a pattern that will lead to the ultimate tragic ending.

Thrice Túrin is afforded an opportunity to re-gain. The first is early on when his mother Morwen sends him to Doriath to seek entrance to Thingol's halls. Sending him away was her chance to give him a safe new life, away from the enslavement and further tragedy that the Easterlings brought to Dor-lómin, after Túrin's father Húrin and the men of Hithlim did not return from the Nirnaeth Arnoediad. Certainly being fostered by Thingol allowed Túrin a renewal of health in both body and mind, and "he grew fair and strong" (Tolkien C., 1977, p. 236). However, Túrin longed for his family, especially his mother and baby sister. This clouded his vision to the point that he only wanted to go and bring them to safety. When old enough, he stayed out in the wilds and borderlands killing orcs and enemies. This single-minded focus on his family, while seeming for the right reasons prevented Túrin from what might have been more fruitful endeavours in Doriath. During his fostering, all the wisdom and crafts of the elves was at his fingertips, and he did not stay in the halls, but wandered instead in the forests with the company of Nellas.

As he grows older and fights evil in the lands surrounding Doriath, his appearance changes and he becomes "uncouth of raiment and wild of locks" (Tolkien C., 1984, p. 76). He returns to Menegroth, again for a renewal of health and gear, but so tired is he that he makes a social faux pas, angering one of the high council members named Saeros, who never liked Túrin. When an evening of sarcastic tone and scathing words are hurtled at Túrin, he seemingly lets it slide, until the insult is aimed at the women of his clan, with Saeros calling them ugly and unkempt (Tolkien C., 1984, p. 76) or "running naked in the forest clad only in their hair" (Tolkien C., 1977, p. 237; Tolkien C., 2007, p.87). This strikes too close to home and Túrin lashes out, throwing a tankard at Saeros and harming the elf. Túrin's pride and focus on family, overshadowed his better judgment. Thus he finds no renewal or clearer vision of how thing are. Instead of seeing the fallout of the event, the accidental death of Saeros, as something apart from himself as Recovery meant, Túrin lays it on himself with a change of name and laments how wronged he is by it. In truth, Túrin would be pardoned, as it was not his fault, and the altercation was created by Saeros alone. However, Turin could not see that and thus the much-needed clarity is subverted.

The second opportunity is after Saeros is killed accidentally, and Beleg Strongbow searches for and finds Túrin's band of outlaws while Túrin was away. When Túrin sees Beleg tied to a tree and

nearly killed by the outlaws that were Túrin's companions, "he was
stricken as with a shaft, and as if at the sudden melting of a frost
tears long unshed filled his eyes [and] he was angry and grieved"
(Tolkien C., 2007, p. 113) at recalling all his lawless and cruel or
evil deeds against other men and elves. This shows a change in
Túrin, a re-gaining of a clear view. Yet once again, it does not last.
Beleg assures Túrin that he is pardoned and could return in "honour
and to the service of the King" (Tolkien C., 2007, p. 114). Túrin,
however, is not joyful at the news Beleg brings, and again in pride
of his kin, turns down Beleg to stay with the outlaws, rather than
"bear looks of pity and pardon, as for a wayward boy amended"
(Tolkien C., 2007, p. 115). The opportunity to recover and possibly
avert further heartache is not taken. Túrin does accept the dragon
helm and begrudgingly the lembas of Melian, but neither change his
intent. Beleg does meet up with him again, and Túrin welcomes the
company, but he is no longer interested in renewal. He continues to
fight evil in the wilds with Beleg, until Beleg leaves for Doriath once
more, begging Túrin to come with him.

Through chance Túrin is taken to a hidden cave by Mîm, a petty
dwarf, whose son Khîm was killed by the outlaws. There he is given
succour in the wild and shows pity for Mîm's loss, thus gaining
the dwarf's admiration. After orcs come to waylay the group and
capture Túrin, Beleg attempts to rescue him. This is ill-fated and
even the atmosphere is set to thwart Túrin's ability to see things as
they were meant to be seen. Túrin struggles with and slays Beleg
with Anglachel, "thinking him a foe" (Tolkien C., 1977, p. 247;
Tolkien C., 2007, p.154). Only in a flash of lightning does he get a
brief glimpse of what he has done. It is the second death of an elf by
Túrin, and it was his best friend. This act was enough to put Túrin in
shock. Luckily, he was led by Gwindor of Nargothrond to Orodreth's
kingdom. He takes Túrin to Beautiful Mere and Eithel Ivrin springs,
where he tells Túrin there is "endless laughter" (Tolkien C., 2007,
p. 157). This harkens back to the fields and stream of Nen Lalaith
and his long dead first sister Lalaith and drinking from its healing
waters cures his madness and grief as only laughter can. This brief
respite gives hope of Recovery, as Gwindor continues to guide Túrin
to Nargothrond.

The third opportunity for Túrin to recover appears while he is in
Nargothrond. He changes his name fittingly, but he does not change

his view. He has Anglachel reforged as Gurthang, thus going from Iron of the Flaming Star to Iron of Death. What was potentially a gift from outside the walls of the world is now remade into the worst nightmare possible: Death. The significance of this change foreshadows the rest of the tale. When elves come bearing prophetic words of warning from the Vala Ulmo, Túrin counsels the King to ignore it. Pride in his constructed bridge caused Túrin to give that advice. Thus, doom is brought to Nargothrond, since the enemy now has clear access, and the Kingdom is destroyed. One final shot is given at redemption for Túrin, in the words of Gwindor, "save Finduilas […] she alone stands between you and your doom. If you fail her, it shall not fail to find you" (Tolkien C., 1977, p. 254; Tolkien C., 2007, p.177). Túrin is given the final chance at Recovery. Sadly, Túrin is beguiled by the dragon Glaurung on that very bridge, and instead of saving Finduilas, who looked like the people of Hador with golden hair and for whom Túrin felt a familial love, he rushes off to Dor-lómin for his mother and sister, not knowing they already were gone. The last chance afforded Túrin is squandered, until it is too late to save Finduilas.

This pattern of pride and internalising things, which should be seen as apart from himself, prevents Túrin from being able to accept the positive opportunities afforded to him by the Recovery stage. In each of these opportunities he could have turned his life around, seen things with a clearer vision, and strived for the greater good, but Túrin continued to look only inward at his own sorrows and losses. He goes so far as to change his name each time as well to pull the focus back onto his own suffering of injustice. He never truly regains that vision, so although Recovery is evident, the opportunities it affords him are not as successfully used by the character for all too human reasons—familial love and hubris. Verlyn Flieger (2012, p.122) verifies the effect of the story aptly in *Green Suns and Faerie: Essays on J. R. R. Tolkien*:

> What gives Túrin a special poignance […] is that his tragedy need not have happened. What he becomes makes us constantly aware of how different he might have been. Tolkien has made Túrin a paradigm of modern alienation, a self-exiled outsider driven by emotions he does not understand, wilful and conflicted, coming to painful awareness only at the end of his life.

The longer Túrin continues his path, the more internalised he

becomes. Where Recovery is meant to clarify and renew, Túrin
becomes more insular and galvanised in his beliefs and actions.

Escape

The third element Tolkien felt was evident in a faery-story is
Escape. This element is discussed at length in "On Fairy-stories"
and contains many levels. The simple desire to Escape ranges from
"noise, stench, ruthlessness" to a more "grim and terrible" desire to
Escape "hunger, thirst, poverty, pain, sorrow, injustice and death"
(Tolkien, 1966, p. 83). As Tolkien concludes this section, he states
"the oldest and deepest desire [is] the Great Escape: the Escape from
Death" (Tolkien, 1966, p. 85). Tolkien offers fugitive spirit in lieu
of escapist as an example or mode of Escape (Tolkien, 1966). In the
several iterations of Túrin's story, one thing is consistent; Túrin can
be seen as a fugitive throughout the *Narn* as he constantly evades
Death and (unsuccessfully) his Doom.

Evidence of being a fugitive can be found early on after Túrin's
father fails to return from war. His flight to seek asylum in Doriath
is instigated by his mother. This is Túrin's first instance of fleeing
potential thraldom as he escapes the servitude and potential torture
of the Easterlings. It also sets up Túrin's dislike of being held
captive, whether or not by a beneficent King. While in Dor-lómin,
Túrin spends much of his time with Sador outside in nature. While in
Doriath, he continues the same activity with Nellas learning "much
concerning the ways and the wild things" (Tolkien C., 2007, p. 80),
and again Beleg would come to bring him "far afield" (Tolkien C.,
2007, p. 81) to teach him. In this way, Túrin escaped from the Halls
of Menegroth, which were built by the dwarves in memory of the
woods. The Halls are a safe alternative to the wilds, but they are the
captured images "the beeches of Oromé, stock, bough, and leaf"
(Tolkien C., 1977, p. 101) not the real thing. This in effect is like
escaping confinement for wide open spaces and freedom.

Túrin tells Thingol, "Beyond the marches of Doriath my heart
urges me" (Tolkien C., 2007, p. 84). He is not given aid, but neither
is he a fugitive because Thingol allows him freedom. It is the point
after Saeros is accidentally killed that Túrin becomes a self-made
fugitive, fleeing into the wilds "lest he be held captive" (Tolkien
C., 2007, p. 91). Túrin joins an outlaw band after killing one of

them and engages in a lawless existence, a fugitive from justice and civilised society. He exhibits the fugitive spirit, ever on the run from his Doom. Yet he cannot escape it. Thus, Túrin's tale shows a failure to Escape. Tolkien does say, "our stories cannot be expected always to rise above our common level" (Tolkien, 1966, p. 85), meaning there is not always going to be a happy outcome which is explored further in the next section.

It is said that Túrin "received many wounds by spear or arrow or the crooked blades of the Orcs" (Tolkien C., 2007, p. 85) while fighting. However, "his doom delivered him from death" (Tolkien C., 2007, p. 85). While the Escape is from Death in battle, it is not through a wish to escape Death specifically or a desire to live particularly. His Doom is not to die—his Doom is to suffer. All that Túrin wishes to escape is his Doom. This is one of the more poignant things from which to escape. It is revealed that, "Saeros ...would have slain him" (Tolkien C., 2007, p. 90), but Túrin's bests him, thus avoiding death yet again. Once Túrin takes up the Dragon-helm of Dor-lómin, he is almost legendary. This status is afforded to him and with it a kind of immortality, which falsely mimics the Great Escape. Túrin is fierce in battle and "Elves said he could not be slain, save by mischance, or an evil arrow from afar" (Tolkien C., 2007, p. 164). Near the end of the *Narn*, Túrin stabs Glaurung and the worm's venom lands on his hand, while Glaurug's eyes "focused such malice that it seemed to [Túrin] that he was smitten by an arrow [...] and lay as one dead" (Tolkien C., 2007, p. 239). We know that indeed his is not dead because he has yet to suffer the worse of his Doom. It is prophetic that the arrow imagery comes into it.

Just when Túrin seeks for his dead sister/wife, Mablung appears and states, "though you have escaped many perils, I feared for you at the last" (Tolkien C., 2007, pp. 253-4). Túrin has indeed escaped many dire situations and for a time Death and Doom, but now is the time of reckoning. Túrin claims, "my heart also is slain" (Tolkien C., 2007, p. 254) since learning of Niniel's alleged death and lineage. When the truth is confirmed by the elves, Túrin falls on his sword. Symbolically, this type of death is meant to show how deeply held are your beliefs, as a soldier would be willing to fall on his sword for a noble cause; however, for Túrin it is death as a surrender of defeat. He has lost everything—family, friend, wife, and honour.

Túrin is of the race of Men and therefore mortal, so there should not be an expectation of the Great Escape. In fact, Túrin only tries to escape "pain, sorrow, [and] injustice" (Tolkien, 1966, p. 83) throughout the *Narn*, and therein lies not only the tragedy of it, for the struggle is futile, but the common level Tolkien states. Tragically, Túrin is unable to escape any of these since they were his Doom.

Consolation

The final element of the four is Consolation. In "Tree and Leaf," Tolkien describes in detail the consolation of the happy ending, "or more correctly [...] the good catastrophe, the sudden joyous 'turn'" (Tolkien, 1966, p. 86). By extension, there must be a bad catastrophe or sudden tragic turn. Indeed, the term catastrophe is commonly used to describe a tragic event of monumental proportions like many of the natural disasters or when loss of human life or property is high. It is destruction on a grand scale. However, Tolkien was using the Greek definition of an overturning. For the purposes of this paper, and in keeping with Tolkien, the Consolation is the ending or denouement of a story. While Tolkien recognised that fairy-stories have happy ones, he noted too that tragic ones tend to appear in Dramas, as found in Greek tragedies, Shakespeare, and other writers of Dramas.

In Letter 89, Tolkien is clearest in his idea of joy and sorrow and how they come from the same source. He states that he 'coined the word 'eucatastrophe': the sudden happy turn in a story which pierces you with a joy that brings tears" (Carpenter and Tolkien C., 1981, p. 100). Since catastrophe in the Greek definition is "an overturning; a sudden end" (Harper, 2021), it fits within the idea of an ending. This is a cataclysmic event that happens at the end, and by adding the prefixes *eu* and *dys* to the word catastrophe, Tolkien delineates the good and bad event under the umbrella term, Consolation.

Dyscatastrophe then "of sorrow and failure" (Tolkien, 1966, p. 86) with its tears is not so different from eucatastrophe, as Tolkien describes it as an experience of Joy as "poignant as grief" and indeed this sheds more light on *The Lord of The Rings*, as Gandalf says, "not all tears are an evil" (Tolkien, 1977, p. 310). They originate from the same place, but they turn towards different paths. Eucastatrophe is the best that could ever be expected or hoped for. This is the way 'Of Beren and Lúthien' ends. Shippey (2000, p. 254) indicates in

Author of the Century that, "the tale of Beren and Lúthien [is] the philosophical antithesis of Túrin." Tolkien seems to shy away from philosophical debates in the Recovery section of "Tree and Leaf" (Tolkien, 1966).

If Eucastatrophe is the best that could ever be expected or hoped for, then Dyscatastrophe is the utter worst that could happen or be experienced. Flieger (2003, p.12) in *Splintered Light* expounds on Tolkien's phrase about joy being, "'poignant as grief'" by adding "(thus light and dark) as the two halves of the same circle, reversals of one another." There is merit in this view. Light and dark are a binary, and it is the absence of one that defines the other. Tolkien explained that there are places where "joy and sorrow are at one, reconciled" (Carpenter & Tolkien C., 1981, p. 100). This seems to describe them as two parts of a whole.

While Flieger is taking a view of "On Fairy-stories" through a particular lens to find Tolkien's aesthetic of light and dark used in his mythology, Tolkien introduces the term catastrophe in the sense of a turning, and indeed uses that very word in his explanation. This does not clearly equate to a circle or being two halves of a whole. Catastrophe is separated into eucatastrophe and dyscatastrophe. They seem more like two divergent paths originating from a common place, as Tolkien also states. The Consolation or ending, which can be seen as light and dark, joy and grief, eucatastrophe and dyscatastrophe is still a catastrophic or turning event. Although turning does not itself indicate a linear movement, the term catastrophe itself also has the definition of down + turn (Harper, 2021). This comes from the Greek 'kata' and 'strophe.' The downward turn of dyscatastrophe might mirror an alluded to upward turn of eucatastrophe, but with this diagram, it can be looked at as splitting off from the main term underneath the umbrella of Consolation.

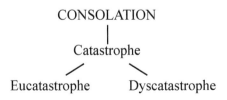

Or even more simply as:

CONSOLATION

Eucatastrophe   Dyscatastrophe

Clearly the ending in "Of Túrin Turambar" is a dyscatastrophe. He
and his sister die in the end and by their own hand, which for Tolkien
as a devout Catholic, is a mortal sin—a death beyond redemption.
This can only be the worst possible outcome, a dyscatastrophe. This
story was based on the Finnish story of Kullervo the hapless and
was important to Tolkien as noted by Fimi, Shippey, and Flieger.
The ending is of little comfort, except as a cautionary tale of failure
and sorrow brought on by a curse of hubris that began with Túrin's
father Húrin when he faced Morgoth and defied him. But it is a little
more than this. Húrin defies Morgoth's command to spy and reveal
the elvish kingdoms. This was noble and thus he was called Húrin
the Steadfast. However, it was the manner in which he refused the
servitude that earned him and his family the curse. It was because he
was haughty. Túrin's mother also shows that she was proud in much
the same way as Túrin was, when he refused to return with Beleg.
She did not leave Dor-lómin for Doriath because, as Shippey notes,
"she would not yet humble her pride to be an alms-guest, not even of
a great King" (Shippey, 2003, p. 264; Tolkien C., 2007, p.70). Túrin
is definitely his parents' son, Shippey points out, and is described
as being like in mood to his mother (Tolkien C., 2007, p. 39), while
his defiant actions with Glaurung are reminiscent of Húrin's with
Morgoth.

Where then does the turn happen in the tale? The trajectory
seems to go from bad to worse incrementally. However, there are
a few brief respites for Túrin, where like Beren, he could turn from
his path and thus potentially avoid his Doom, but neither hero
does so—to the joyous eucatastrophe of Beren's tale and the utter
dyscatastrophe of Túrin's. However, if the turn can be found, it
ought to be near the end of the story and it should be sudden. The
best scene that demonstrates the turn is when Mablung appears with
a band of elves and hails Túrin gladly. Túrin says, "Say on! And be

swift […] hearing the feet of doom that would pursue him to the end" (Tolkien C., 2007, p. 254). Mablung's words confirm Brandir's recitation of what Glaurung said to Niniel, and the full horror of what has happened drives Túrin to madness and suicide. This turn of Consolation is the dyscatastrophe. It may not fit smoothly, but the other options do not seem to involve Túrin. A better turn might be the reveal of Glaurung to Niniel of her name and lineage. She was in enchantment, unaware of the horror of knowing, until Glaurung lifted his spell. Further, if we are to see a turn in the entire *Narn*, it would be the capture of Húrin and curse of Morgoth because when that happens, the story foreshadows ruin, although it is not the sudden end. Some license must be taken depending on if we are looking at the whole tale or just those events as outlined here with the protagonist Túrin.

Conclusion

When looking at "Of Túrin Turambar," little good can truly be hoped for, and this started at the very beginning of the story. The family is beset with tragedy. The death of laughter and joy as Túrin's first sister Urwen, called Lalaith, "which is Laughter" (Tolkien C., 1977, p. 235) was killed by a pestilence "borne on an evil wind out of Angband" (Tolkien C., 1977, p. 235) sets the tone of loss, which is exacerbated by his father, Húrin, not returning from the Nirnaeth Arnoediad. If looking symbolically, the wind is an initial cursing of Túrin's family, since Angband was Morgoth's lair. Lalaith was replaced when Túrin's second sister was born. Her name was Niënor, "which is Mourning" (Tolkien C., 1977, p. 236). Túrin had no time with her as he was sent away to Thingol before she was born. Still, going from laughter to mourning cannot be lost in interpretation. Túrin continues to suffer with the loss of his best friend Beleg, made all the worse because it was by his Túrin's own hand. This is how the story goes. Further, the Narn î Hin Húrin is called by the elves, "The Tale of Grief, for it is sorrowful, and in it are revealed most evil works of Morgoth Bauglir" (Tolkien C., 1977, p. 236). Morgoth's curse was "doom of woe and a death of sorrow" (Tolkien C., 1984, p. 72). In the Introduction to *The Children of Húrin*, Christopher Tolkien gives his father's words on it as, "So ended the tale of Túrin the hapless; the worst of the works of Morgoth among Men in the ancient world" (Tolkien C., 2007, p. 18).

Tolkien leads us into the depths of despair throughout the story with the choices given to Túrin. Yet Túrin is not a bad person. This makes it all the more tragic. He suffers the loss of two sisters, father, mother, best friend, and wife. Not only that, he loses his primary family, his foster family, and ultimately his own family, as his sister/ wife was pregnant. The story is clearly a dyscatastrophe. To struggle and lose everything of worth and that you love or care for is the worst ending possible.

In this reworking of the story of 'Kullervo the Hapless' from the Kalevala, we see the inner consistency of a well-crafted fairy-story. As Shippey points out, "all four versions [of the tale of Turin[4]] differ from each other, but the outline remains surprisingly stable" (Shippey, 2000, p. 249). We also see how the spirit of Tolkien's theory of the four elements: Fantasy, Recovery, Escape, and Consolation are woven together into a poignant dyscatastrophe that does achieve in the reader "that particular emotion [...] quite unlike any other sensation" (Carpenter and Tolkien C., 1981, Letter 89, p. 100).

The one lingering question that needs further study is agency, as in free will. How much agency did Túrin have in light of what was thrown at him by Morgoth? Shippey has some theories proposed in *The Road to Middle-earth* (2003), but this topic merits further study throughout the Legendarium. Finally, is the tale of Túrin a fairy-story? Tolkien might say no because it is not given a happy ending or eucatastrophe of Consolation that is the specialty of fairy-story. He might ponder that is it more like a Drama due to the tragic end or dyscatastrophe, although not one to act out, one to recite. In *The Lays of Beleriand: The History of Middle-earth* part of the 'Lay of The Children of Húrin' can be found in alliterative verse (Tolkien C., 1985, pp. 5-56), which means Tolkien's thoughts appear to have been headed that way. While Tolkien says that fairy-stories are good at eucatastophe, he makes room for them to also have dyscatastrophe, as both terms fall under the blanket of Consolation, which is the final element of fairy-story. The tale of Túrin Turambar fits the perimeters of a fairy-story where each of the four elements: Fantasy, Recovery, Escape, and Consolation as defined by Tolkien can be found.

---

4. Listed by Shippey as 'Turambar and the Foalókë,' 'The Lay of the Children of Húrin,' 'Of Túrin Turambar,' and 'Narn î Hin Húrin'.

References

Carpenter, H. and Tolkien, C. eds., 1981. *The Letters of J. R. R. Tolkien*. Boston: Houghton Mifflin.

Fimi, D., 2010. *Tolkien, Race and Culture History: From Fairies to Hobbits*. London: Palgrave McMillan.

Flieger, V., 2003. *Splintered Light: Logos and Language in Tolkien's World*. Revised ed. Kent: Kent State Press.
—, 2005. *Interruped Music: The Making of Tolkien's Mythology*. Kent: Kent State University Press.
—, 2012. *Green Suns and Faerie: Essays on J. R. R. Tolkien*. Kent: Kent State University Press.

Harper, D., 2021. *Online Etymology Dictionary*. [Online] Available at: <https://www.etymonline.com/word/catastrophe> [Accessed 8 March 2021].

Shippey, T., 2000. *J.R.R. Tolkien: Author of the Century*. Boston: Houghton Mifflin.
—, 2003. *The Road to Middle-earth: How J.R.R.Tolkien Created a New Mythology*. Boston: Houghton Mifflin.

Tolkien, C., ed., 1977. *The Silmarillion*. London: Harper Collins Publishers.
—, 1984. *The Book of Lost Tales 2 – The History of Middle-earth Vol II*. New York: Ballantine Books.
—, 1985. *The Lays of Beleriand – The History of Middle-earth Vol III*. New York: Ballantine Books.
—, 2007. *The Children of Húrin*. Boston: Houghton Mifflin.

Tolkien, J.R.R., 1966. *The Tolkien Reader*. New York: Ballantine Books.
—, 1977. *Return of the King*. London: Allen and Unwin.

Vink, R., 2019. *(Un)happily Ever After: The Many Woes of Tolkien's Lovers*. s.l.:Lembas Extra.

Wood, R., 2011. J.R.R. Tolkien: His Sorrowful Vision of Joy. In: D. Hein and E. Henderson, eds., *C. S. Lewis and His Friends*. London: Society for Promoting Christian Knowledge. pp. 11-34.

"Master of Fate, yet by fate mastered" – Tolkien's Túrin Turambar and *Kalevala*'s Kullervo

Jyrki Korpua

> Wonder and little bewilderment were at any rate my experience when I first came upon the *Kalevala* – crossed, that is, the gulf between the Indo-European-speaking peoples of Europe into the smaller realm of those who still cling in queer corners to half-forgotten tongues and memories of an elder day. (Flieger, 2015, pp. 102-103).

As seen from the quote, *Kalevala*[1], at first, was something wild and different for J. R. R. Tolkien. From that wonder and bewilderment *Kalevala* build up to be an important starting point for Tolkien's fantasy fiction, his Legendarium as whole. From the mythical stories of *Kalevala*, the most important for Tolkien was the story of Kullervo, which Tolkien saw as a starting point of his own fiction (Carpenter and Tolkien C., 1981, Letter 75, p. 87). Tolkien's son Christopher Tolkien commented that the character of Túrin "was of deep significance to my father, and in dialogue of directness and immediacy he achieved a poignant portrait of his boyhood, essential to the whole: his severity and lack of gaiety, his sense of justice and his compassion" (Tolkien C., 2007, p. 13).

The importance and effect of *Kalevala* on Tolkien's creative work has been known for years. For larger audiences this has been shown ever since Humphrey Carpenter's authorised biography of Tolkien, published in 1977, addressing *Kalevala*'s influence on many occasions (e.g., Carpenter 1977, pp. 21, 49, 59, 73). Tolkien himself discusses *Kalevala* in his letters, of which a central part

---

1. *Kalevala*, here, refers to Elias Lönnrot's so-called "Standard Kalevala", which was published in 1848. The original publication process of *Kalevala* was slow: Elias Lönnrot published four *Kantele* notebooks, the so-called "Proto Kalevala" in 1833. Later in the same year Lönnrot compiled *Collected Songs about Väinämöinen*, known later as "the Pre-Kalevala". The first edition titled *Kalevala*, known later as *Old Kalevala*, came out in 1835 under the Finnish title *Kalewala taikka Wanhoja Karjalan Runoja Suomen Kansan muinosista ajoista*, containing 32 poems and 12078 verses. The version of *Kalevala* (1848 version) we nowadays refer to, the "Standard Kalevala", or "Kalevala Proper", contains 50 poems and 22795 verses (Korpua, 2016).

was published in 1981, edited by Carpenter with the assistance of Christopher Tolkien (see Carpenter and Tolkien C., 1981, Letters 1, 75, 163 & 257, pp. 7, 87, 214, 345). Those letters show interestingly, for example, that as early as 1914 Tolkien's then fiancé, and later wife Edith Bratt (later Edith Tolkien), was even then familiar with Tolkien's affection for the *Kalevala* (Carpenter and Tolkien C., 1981, Letter 1, p. 7).

Kalevala's influences on Tolkien's Legendarium have been studied before, but rarely by Finnish scholars. Interesting previous studies include, Tom Shippey's "Tolkien and the Appeal of the Pagan: Edda and *Kalevala*" (2007), Tom DuBois' & Scott Mellor's "The Nordic Roots of Tolkien's Middle Earth" (2002). In addition, linguistic similarities between *Kalevala* and Tolkien's Legendarium have been discussed by Luigi de Anna, among others, in his article "The Magic of Word: J. R. R. Tolkien and Finland" (1993). Tolkien's aesthetic similarities with Lönnrot's work, have also been studied by scholars such as Anne C. Petty, in her article "Identifying England's Lönnrot" (2004). I have also discussed Tolkien's intertextual references to *Kalevala* on some occasions (Korpua, 2015, pp. 162-169; Korpua, 2016; Korpua, 2018, pp. 175-178; Korpua, 2021, pp. 142-148).

Kalevala (1835/1849) is hailed as Finland's national epic, although the epic nature of *Kalevala* is something that can be debated. Tolkien himself wrote on the subject, discussing how one repeatedly hears *Kalevala* described as the Finnish National Epic. Tolkien does not see *Kalevala* as Finland's national epic, as he does not see it as an "Epic" at all (Korpua, 2018). Instead, Tolkien (Flieger, 2015, p. 103) describes *Kalevala* as "a mass of conceivably epic material [which] would lose all that is its greatest delight, if ever it were on unhappy day to be epically handled. The mere stories, bare events, alone could remain; all that undergrowth, that rich profusion and luxuriance, which clothe them would have to be stripped away."

Kalevala is the most known Finnish work of literature, translated to more than 60 languages, originally affecting greatly the beginning of Finnish national literature. Later, it has also inspired many Anglo-American fantasy writers such as Tolkien, Eileen Kernaghen, M. E. A. McNeil, Emil Petaja, Michael Scott Rohan, L. Sprague de Camp, Joan D. Vinge, and Ian Watson. For the fantasy writers and readers, *Kalevala* is one of the major works of literature to reactivate old

Nordic pagan myths for contemporary audiences. Finnish physicist and folklorist Elias Lönnrot (1802–1884) compiled, edited, and remodelled *Kalevala* from folk poetry that he had collected during his fieldtrips among poetry singers. Although *Kalevala* has its background and roots in oral poetry, Lönnrot is considered the single author of *Kalevala* (Korpua, 2016). But *Kalevala* is not just mimicking folk poetry and it is not a work of "forgery" (Korpua, 2021, p. 16). It is at the same time a work of national romantic biased editing of folk sources, and a showcase of highly skilful artistic invention by Lönnrot.

In *Kalevala*, Kullervo, Kalervo's Son, is an anti-hero with enormous physical strength and supernatural abilities, who grows up under inhuman circumstances as a slave in the aftermath of the bloody massacre of his entire tribe at the hands of Kullervo's uncle's Untamo's tribe. In *Kalevala*, Kullervo is at first a magical infant, capable, despite his age, of resisting attempts to kill him. He grows up to be a reckless child, who is sold into slavery to blacksmith god Ilmarinen; there, Kullervo is once again mocked and tormented, especially by the Wife of Ilmarinen, whom Kullervo later brutally kills with an evil spell. After the murder, he frees himself from his owners and becomes an aggressive revenant who is almost indifferent to its own environment.

Kullervo is a typical anti-hero: vigilant, aggressive, and abusive, but also superior to his own surroundings, as typical mythical heroes usually are (Frye, 1967, p. 33). Perhaps because of his neglecting character, Kullervo seduces a girl with money and sweet talks, in a scene which nowadays would read as forced sex and rape. Later, after the incident, an unknown girl turns out to be Kullervo's long lost sister, whom he had presumed dead. When the sister realises the incest, she commits suicide. With that, the fate of Kullervo is sealed. He revenges his family by killing Untamo's tribe, responsible for the death of own family members. But after that, perhaps because of the emptiness of his existence he, like his sister, takes his own life.

As I stated earlier, Tolkien acknowledged Lönnrot's *Kalevala* as a preliminary influence for his fiction. That is especially the case for the Kullervo cycle, which Tolkien describes as the actual "germ of my attempt to write legends of my own" (Carpenter and Tolkien C., 1981, Letter 257, p. 345). Tolkien had first read *Kalevala* in the 1907 English translation of W. F. Kirby, while he was a student at

Birmingham (Flieger, 2015, p. xi), Slightly contradictory to this, Tolkien's biographer Humphrey Carpenter writes that "as early as in the year 1911, before he was in his twenties, Tolkien discovered *Kalevala*, and he was thrilled about it". (Korpua, 2018, p. 178). Yet, no matter when Tolkien found *Kalevala*, he liked what he saw. As Tom Shippey puts it, *Kalevala* had a quality Tolkien admired (Shippey, 2007, p. 24). Also, from Oronzo Cilli's *Tolkien's Library. An Annotated Checklist* (2019, pp. 143, 170), we know that Tolkien owned a copy of both an English translation by Kirby, and an original Finnish version edited by Robert Wilhelm Ekman and Kai Linnilä.

At first, Tolkien's passion for *Kalevala*'s text was philological. He saw Lönnrot's literary creation as sort of mythology that he thought his home country England lacked (Carpenter, 1977, p. 59). It was because of *Kalevala* that Tolkien first tried writing a legend in verse and prose, when in 1914 he wrote his own version of "The Story of Kullervo" (Carpenter, 1977, p. 73), which then became the foundation of Túrin' story (Korpua, 2015, p. 162). Later, this story also became posthumously published as a *Kalevala*-inspired book fragment, *The Story of Kullervo* (2015), edited by Verlyn Flieger.

As a character, Kullervo was a central character in its own storyline of *Kalevala*. In the older Finnish folk tales, Kullervo was a tragic wizard or a powerful magician, a vengeful man, who is in some sources mentioned as one of the giants, "a Son of Kaleva". Then again, it should also be added that Kullervo was not important in Finnish pre-*Kalevala* folklore as such, since Kullervo is not mentioned on a list of "Kalewan Pojat" ("Sons of Kaleva") in Christfrid Ganander's classical *Mythologia Fennica* (1789), nor does his name appear in the book in any form. That is mainly because most of the poems connected with the Kullervo cycle were collected from further afield, from the area of Inkeri, by D. E. D. Europaeus, and re-used by Lönnrot in 1848's version of *Kalevala*. In 1848 *Kalevala*, Lönnrot also combined other separate Finnish and Karelian mythic stories of incest, vengeance, and family feuds, that originally did not include Kullervo as a character, into one complete story that makes up the Cycle of Kullervo as we nowadays know it. (Korpua, 2018, pp. 175-180) There, Lönnrot used cautionary tales, such as stories of siblings' incestuous relationships, and stories of vendettas, family feuds and *fratricides* (*frater cidum*), which means stories where brothers kill their siblings. In *The Story of Kullervo*, Tolkien's own version of Kullervo's story, he follows closely *Kalevala*'s *runos* (poems) 31 to 36 (Korpua, 2018, p. 180-182). From that, Tolkien built the base for the character of Túrin, Son of Húrin.

In Tolkien's Legendarium, the character of Túrin is one of the most important heroes of the First Age and Elder Days as a whole, since Túrin's story appears in Tolkien's *The Silmarillion*, in *Unfinished Tales of Númenor and Middle-earth*, and most importantly in *The Children of Húrin*, which contains the complete storyline of the character. Although these stories of Túrin were only published after Tolkien's death, which occurred in 1973, Tolkien still refers to Túrin in his most famous work, *The Lord of the Rings*, originally published in 1954-55. There, in the first part, *The Fellowship of the Ring*, Elrond, a leader of the Elves of Rivendell, says to Frodo, the main character of the book, that "though all the mighty elf-friends of old, Hador, and Húrin, and Túrin, and Beren himself were assembled together, your seat should be among them" (Tolkien, 1995, p. 264). That shows that Túrin is a central human character in the Legendarium.

For the readers, the first published version of Túrin's story called "Of Túrin Turambar", in *The Silmarillion* in 1977, or the longer later published version *The Children of Húrin*, are tragedies, following the model and tones of *Kalevala*'s Kullervo cycle. The story's central character Túrin wants to be a hero, wants to make something of himself and reclaim his family's higher position among Men; on the contrary though, his whole life is tragic from start to finish. Túrin's tale manifests the *Kalevala*'s story of Kullervo on many levels. Both the story of Kullervo from *Kalevala* and Túrin story in Tolkien's Legendarium are myths of slave-princes and stories of incest. They are Oedipalian cautionary tales, telling us – the readers – the terrible outcomes of even an unaware case of incest. Incest has of course been a popular mythological theme since the beginning of literature and human culture, a warning, as a myth of moral tuition (Korpua, 2018, pp. 178-182).

Narratologically, there are of course also significant differences in Túrin's tale and *Kalevala*'s Kullervo cycle. Tolkien's Túrin's tale also deals with the myths of heroic dragon slayers, deriving mostly from Scandinavian and Germanic myths, not connected at all with Kullervo's story.

Beside his heroic acts, still, Tolkien's tale of Túrin is dark, gloomy, and joyless. In a predestined story, after Túrin's mother has sent his young son away from his home, over the high mountains, Tolkien writes that "thus was the fate of Túrin woven" (Tolkien C., 1999, p. 236). Túrin is cursed and doomed from the beginning by an evil fate, constructed by the Dark Lord Morgoth, the evil god-like force in Tolkien's Legendarium. Túrin's life story, therefore, is predestined to fulfil his tragic fate. (Korpua, 2018, pp. 180-181).

Tolkien's stories concentrating on Túrin Turambar are usually called "The Children of Húrin", since they tell the story of human hero Húrin's two children, not just Túrin, but also of his sister Nienor, also known as Níniel. Túrin's fight with the great dragon inevitably suggests comparison with Germanic and English sources, such as myths of Sigurd or the heroic poem of Beowulf, while Túrin's unknowing incest with his sister and his suicide derive from *Kalevala*. Tolkien himself admits this in 1951, in his letter to publisher Milton Waldman, writing that "the tragic tale of Túrin Turambar and his sister Niniel of which Túrin is the hero: a figure that might be said (by people who like that sort of thing, though it is not very useful) to be derived from elements in Sigurd the Volsung, Oedipus, and the Finnish Kullervo" (Carpenter and Tolkien C., 1981, Letter 131, p. 150).

In Tolkien's story, just like in *Kalevala*'s Kullervo cycle, Túrin loses his family and is tormented by his oppressors, who have killed his people and taken over his father's lands. Like *Kalevala*'s Kullervo, Túrin seeks revenge, and finds it. He manages to kill the dragon Glaurung in a great heroic deed. But before that, in the middle of his journey, Túrin weds a woman, who is – unknowingly to both – his sister. In *Kalevala*, Kullervo only sleeps once with his sister in quite a brutal scene. He forces the girl into his sledge and then persuades her with the lure of money, and in an aggressive way, to have sex with him. In Túrin story the incestuous relationship is of a long-term nature, since the sister and brother fall in love and get married. Of course, also in Tolkien's story, they are both oblivious to the fact that they are siblings. When the truth is revealed, Nienor kills herself. Afterwards, when realising his doings and his dark fate, Túrin also commits suicide, fulfilling his tragic destiny. Despite calling himself "The Master of Fate" (*Turambar*), he is mastered by the Evil Lord Morgoth's dark fate, a curse that Morgoth had cast on all of Húrin's family.

Túrin's suicide depictions in Tolkien's Legendarium and
Kullervo's suicide in *Kalevala* are similar in style. Kullervo and
Túrin commit suicide because of their act of incest, and because
their sisters have also killed themselves. Túrin moreover, commits
further acts of evil. He kills – although accidently – the Elf-lord
Beleg. Later, in an act of brutality, unjustly kills Brandir, a leader of
Men who was at odds with him. Both heroes' sisters commit suicide
by drowning themselves. Túrin and Kullervo, finally, kill themselves
with their swords, by first asking the sword to take their lives.

Túrin's sword Gurthang is an interesting magical weapon in
Tolkien's Legendarium. Originally called Anglachel, it is a black
sword with edges of pale fire, worn by the malicious Dark Elf Eöl.
Eöl forged two swords, Anglachel and Anguirel, from meteorite,
"iron that fell from heaven as a blazing star" (Tolkien C., 1999, p.
239). Of these, he keeps Anguirel to himself, but he gives Anglachel
to the Elf-King Thingol (Elwë) as fee, because Thingol allows Eöl
to live in the forest of Nan Elmoth, part of Thingol's Kingdom of
Doriath in the First Age of Middle-earth. A powerful Maia-spirit,
Melian, King Thingol's wife and Queen of Doriath, comments that
"There is malice in this sword. The dark heart of the smith [Eöl]
still dwell in it" (Tolkien C., 1999, p. 240). Later, the sword is
given by Thingol to Beleg. When Túrin fights some orcs who attack
him, he mistakenly kills Beleg with his own sword. After Beleg's
unfortunate death, the sword is given to Túrin by the Elf-prince
Gwindor and renamed Gurthang, "Iron of Death". When wielding
the sword, Túrin is known to his friends and foes as Mormegil,
"The Black Sword". It is his signature weapon, yet it is a sword of
evil fate.

When Túrin commits suicide, he asks Gurthang, whether it will
kill him. For the first and last time in Tolkien's Legendarium, the
sword speaks and answers:

'Hail Gurthang! No lord or loyalty dost thou know, save the hand that
wieldeth thee. From no blood wilt thou shrink. Wilt thou therefore take
Túrin Turambar, wilt thou slay me switfly?' And from the blade rang a cold
voice in answer: 'Yea, I will drink thy blood gladly, that so I may forget the
blood of Beleg my master, and the blood of Brandir slain unjustly. I will
slay thee swiftly.' Then Túrin Turambar set the hilts upon the ground, and
cast himself upon the point of Gurthang, and the black blade took his life.
(Tolkien C., 1999, p. 270).

In *Kalevala*, in a similar way, Kullervo talks to his sword and the sword answers:

Kullervo Kalervon poika, tempasi terävän miekan;
katselevi, kääntelevi, kyselevi, tietelevi.
Kysyi mieltä miekaltansa,
tokko tuon tekisi mieli
syöä syyllistä lihoa,
viallista verta juoa. (*Kalevala*, 1992, p. 321)

In perhaps the best English translation, by Franchis Beabody Macoun Jr., the scene is as follows: "Kullervo, son of Kalervo, drew his sharp sword; he looks at it, turns it over, questions it, inquires of it. He asked the sword its wish, whether it wanted to eat guilty flesh, drink sinful blood" (Lönnrot, 1975, p. 255).

In Tolkien's fantasy world's grand narrative, Tolkien planned an important role for Túrin also after his death, in the "after life", as that earlier line from *The Lord of the Rings* in Elrond's words suggests. In the posthumous collection *The History of Middle-earth*, Tolkien writes that in the End of the World, in the so-called Last Battle, Túrin will be the avenger of all Men, and by that their greatest hero:

Then shall the last battle be gathered on the fields of Valinor. In that day Tulkas shall strive with Melko [Morgoth], and on his right shall stand Fionwë and on his left Túrin Turambar, son of Húrin, Conqueror of Fate, coming from the halls of Mandos; and it shall be the black of sword of Túrin that deals unto Melko [Morgoth] his death and final end; and so shall the children of Húrin and all Men be avenged. (Tolkien C., 2002, p. 76).

Even after his many anti-heroic acts and his tragic death by his own hands, Túrin's reputation inside the fictive world of Middle-earth is not just "anti-heroic". He is one of the great human warriors, "a mighty Elf-friend of Old", as Elrond in *The Lord of the Rings* calls him. Intertextually, that is, inside the story world, Túrin is a "hero", despite his many villainous acts. This has perhaps something to do with Tolkien's own sympathies for the misunderstood and mistreated tragic characters such as *Kalevala*'s Kullervo. For his humane flaws, he is the most interesting human and hero of the First Age.

References

de Anna, L., 1993. The Magic of Word: J. R. R. Tolkien and Finland. In: K.J. Battarbee, ed. *Scholarship & Fantasy. Proceedings of The Tolkien Phenomenon May 1992, Turku, Finland*. Turku: University of Turku. pp.7-20.

Carpenter, H., 1977: *J.R.R. Tolkien. A Biography*. Boston: Houghton Mifflin Company.

Carpenter, H. and Tolkien, C. eds., 1981. *The Letters of J. R. R. Tolkien*. London: George Allen & Unwin.

Cilli, O., 2019. *Tolkien's Library: An Annotated Checklist*. Edinburgh: Luna Press Publishing.

DuBois, T. and Mellor, S. 2002. The Nordic Roots of Tolkien's Middle Earth. *Scandinavian Review* 90(1), pp.35–40.

Flieger, V. ed., 2015. *The Story of Kullervo*. London: HarperCollins.

Frye, N., 1967. *Anatomy of Criticism: Four Essays by Northrop Frye*. New York: Atheneum.

Kalevala, 1992. Juva: WSOY.

Lönnrot, E., 1975. *Kalevala: Or Poems of the Kalevala District*. Translated by F. Beabody Macoun, Jr. Cambridge: Harvard University Press.

Korpua, J., 2015. *Constructive Mythopoetics of J.R.R. Tolkien's Legendarium*. Oulu: University of Oulu.
—, 2016. Elias Lönnrot: Kalevala. *Literary Encyclopedia*, volume 1.3.3: Finnish and Sami Writing and Culture. Available at: <https://www.litencyc.com/php/sworks.php?rec=true&UID=23237> [Accessed 27 August 2021].
—, 2018. The Germ of J.R.R. Tolkien's Fantasy. Elements of Kalevala in Tolkien's Fiction. In K. Alenius, et al, eds. *Transcultural Encounters* 2. Rovaniemi: Pohjois-Suomen historiallinen yhdistys, pp.175-186.
—, 2021. *The Mythopoeic Code of Tolkien. A Christian Platonic Reading of the Legendarium*. Jefferson: McFarland & Co.

Petty, A.C., 2004. Identifying England's Lönnrot. *Tolkien Studies: An Annual Scholarly Review,* 1(1), pp.69–84.

Shippey, T., 2007. Tolkien and the Appeal of the Pagan: Edda and Kalevala. In: T. Shippey. *Roots and Branches. Selected Papers on Tolkien by Tom Shippey*. Zollikofen: Walking Tree Publishers, pp.19-38.

Tolkien, C. ed., 1999: *The Silmarillion*. London: HarperCollins.
—, 2002. *The Lost Road and Other Writings – The History of Middle-earth Vol. V.*

London: HarperCollins Publishers.
—, 2007. *The Children of Húrin*. London: HarperCollins, pp.13-27.

Tolkien, J.R.R., 1995. *The Lord of the Rings*. London: HarperCollins.

Tal-Elmar: Tolkien's Unrepresented Natives

Renée Vink

The brief, abandoned tale of Tal-Elmar is the final text in *The Peoples of Middle-earth*, from *The History of Middle-earth* (Tolkien C., 1996, pp. 422-438). This does not mean it was Tolkien's last contribution to his Legendarium. The "Akallabêth" (the tale of the Fall of Númenor in *The Silmarillion*, Tolkien C., 1977) and "Aldarion and Erendis" (in *Unfinished Tales*, Tolkien C., 1980) were written later; they date from about 1958 (Tolkien C., 1996, p. 141f), and before 1965 respectively (Tolkien C., 1980, p. 7f). The first version of "Tal-Elmar", however, already existed before January 1955, when Tolkien embarked upon a continuation that soon loses itself in almost unintelligible, experimental passages (Tolkien C., 1996, p. 422). No *terminus post quem* is given, but the story may have begun after the completion of the Appendices to *The Lord of the Rings* (Tolkien, 1969). On a piece of paper dated 1968, Tolkien added a description, of which the first sentence is: "Beginning of a tale that sees the Númenóreans from the point of view of the Wild Men". (Tolkien C., 1996, p. 422). Which raises the question why he felt the need to write such a tale in the first place, a question I hope to address in the course of this paper.

The story is set in the Second Age, at a time when the Númenóreans used to visit the shores of Middle-earth. Most of its characters live in a town in the "green Hills of Agar" (Tolkien C., 1996, p. 423), located somewhere in the region of Langstrand, not far from the mouths of the Anduin (Tolkien C., 1996, p. 422), until Tolkien suggested it was somewhere near the estuary of the Isen, or alternatively, the Morthond (Tolkien C., 1996, p. 436). These people are represented by Buldar, his son, Hazad, Hazad's son, Tal-Elmar, and the town-master of Agar, Mogru. The story is told by an omniscient narrator, with frequent glimpses into a character's mind, predominantly Tal-Elmar's. Towards the end of the fragment, the Númenóreans make an appearance. As it turns out, the folk of Agar[1]

---

1. An interesting name: in the Bible, Hagarenes or Agarenes (from Greek *Agarenoi*) were the descendants of Hagar, the Ismaelites. They are often mentioned together

are a people in decline because of "ill weathers and pests" (Tolkien C., 1996, p. 426), something that may resonate rather ominously with the public of today. However, this does not have any consequences for the story fragment as we have it.

Hazad and Tal-Elmar have an interesting family history. Fighting in the army of his king[2], Hazad's father Buldar was wounded but survived to take a woman home from the defeated party, the "Fell Folk of the East". Her name was Elmar, and she was beautiful. "Having looked on her, Buldar desired no woman of his own folk" (Tolkien C., 1996, p. 424). He made her his slave and took her to wife, something she resented vocally, as she was already married and mother to a child. When Buldar refused to let her go, she took vengeance by foretelling that while she was alive, the "lot of all this folk shall worsen", and that after her death "in thy kin one shall arise who is mine alone. And with his arising shall come the end of thy people and the downfall of your king" (Tolkien C., 1996, p. 425).

The children she bore to Buldar all looked like him, even the youngest, Hazad, with whom she was closer than with any of the others. She died when Hazar was a child, but he never forgot her, and considering the women of his own people ugly compared to her, he married late. The narrator describes the folk of Agar as "broad, swarthy, short, tough, harsh-tongued, heavy-handed, and quick to violence" (Tolkien C., 1996, p. 423), with "thick legs and wide shoulders". In short, "base and unlovely" (Tolkien C., 1996, p. 425), to quote Elmar's judgement of them.

Hazad's youngest and dearest son, born when he is already getting on in age, was Tal-Elmar, named after his grandmother; in the fragment he is eighteen years old. In him, Elmar's prophecy comes true: being "fair of voice", "slender-built", "tall, and white-skinned", with fiery grey eyes that earn him the name of "Flint-eyes", he resembles her and has nothing in common with Buldar, Hazad, and the other the people of Agar. He is not talkative, and his face shows "the pride of one of alien race whom fate has cast away among ignoble people" (Tolkien C., 1996, p. 423). Unlike the folk of Agar, he believes the elderly should be treated kindly. From the get-go, he stands out as a good character.

---

with Saracens and Arabs, in other words, "infidel" Muslims <https://en.wikipedia.org/wiki/Hagarenes>; <https://en.wikipedia.org/wiki/Hagrite>. Tolkien's use of this name is in all probability no coincidence.

2. Assuming the unnamed "North King" who musters the army in which Buldar fights (424), is his own king.

Tolkien's genetics seem a bit off here. If a couple as unlike as Elmar and Buldar have children, it is possible that only one of them looks like Elmar. But if a Buldar-like son then takes a native woman of Agar for a wife, it is uncommon that one of their sons looks 100% like Elmar and not at all like Buldar, unless intermarriage with Elmar's people has taken place in the past or a mutation happens. Tolkien must have thought the same at some point, as he made a note that Buldar should be cut and Hazad should be the one to take Elmar for a wife (Tolkien C., 1996, p. 437, n. 5). As he made this note at the point where Hazad is said to have married late because Agarite women could not hold a candle to his mother, the reduplication of the beauty motif may have struck him as needless. However, eliminating the intermediate generation would have undermined the impact of the prophecy and demanded some drastic rewriting, like turning a sympathetic character Tal-Elmar was attached to into his mother's captor. Taking this into account would make analysing the tale even trickier than it is now. For that reason, I shall ignore the note in the rest of this paper

As for Elmar, when she and Buldar have an altercation about her capture and forced marriage, she tells him bluntly she dislikes his appearance and that of his people (Tolkien C., 1996, p. 425). Buldar retorts that Elmar's people "are cruel, and lawless, and the friends of demons. Thieves are they. For our lands are ours from of old, which they would wrest from us with their bitter blades. White skins and bright eyes are no warrant for such deeds" (Tolkien C., 1996, p. 425). From a modern, primary world point of view, Buldar's position is anti-racist, anti-imperialist and, especially in view of the accusation of land-theft, anti-colonialist. We certainly get the viewpoint of an Agarite here, though the Fell Folk of the East are not identified as hailing from Númenor. Later, Hazad will count them among the enemies of Agar, commenting that "they would not honour the kinship, if they came here with their swords" (Tolkien C., 1996, p. 427).

In *The Lord of the Rings* the East is the direction of evil; Mordor lies in the East, and the Variags of Khand, allied with Sauron, come from that direction. Earlier in the Third Age the Wainriders, foes of Gondor, also arrived from the East, while *The Silmarillion* mentions Easterlings fighting both for and against Morgoth. However, none of these are described as white-skinned, which makes the Fell Folk a notable exception. Are we dealing with bad white people versus darker-skinned people ("swarthy"), perhaps people of colour?

It turns out to be not that simple: in reaction to Buldar's allegation of land theft, Elmar points out that Buldar's people do not have a clean record either: "[A]re there not, as I hear men say, wild folk in the caves of the mountains, who once roamed here free, ere ye swart folk came hither and hunted them like wolves?" (Tolkien C., 1996, p. 425) So, there is another group here, "wild folk" oppressed by the people of Agar. Are they dark[3] people, or at least people ruled by one of the "Dark Kings" mentioned at the beginning of the story (Tolkien C., 1996, p. 423)?

No answers at this stage. To complicate things further, in addition to the victimized wild folk, the evil Fell Folk and his own, also evil swart folk, Hazad introduces yet another group, the "High Men of the Sea" (Tolkien C., 1996, p. 427) to bring Tal-Elmar's knowledge of the wider world up to date. And they are the worst of all. As Hazad says:

> Death they worship and slay men cruelly in honour of the Dark. Out of the Sea they came, and if they ever had any land of their own, ere they came to the west-shores, we know not where it may be. Black tales come to us out of the coast-lands, north and south, where they have now long time established their dark fortresses and their tombs (Tolkien C., 1996, p. 427).

Feigning friendship and offering gifts, they spy out the lands, to return in greater numbers in ships with black sails, taking away "captives packed like beasts" (Tolkien C., 1996, p. 427). This is reminiscent of the way slavers transported enslaved people from Africa to plantations in the West Indies. The practice was denounced by the former slaver Thomas Clarkson, who spread a print of one of these ships, the "Brookes", in 1788 (SHEC, 2021), thereby contributing to the abolition of the slave trade in 1807. Maybe Tolkien came across this or similar pictures and/or accounts and remembered them when he wrote "Tal-Elmar".

A horrible fate awaits the poor souls taken by the High Men of the Sea: some say they are eaten, while others say they are killed on "the black stones in worship of the Dark" (Tolkien C., 1996, p. 427). Those familiar with the story of Númenor will recognise the King's Men, evil Númenóreans in the final stage of their moral and spiritual

---

3. Henceforth, the word "dark", capitalised or not, will only refer to moral and spiritual darkness, not to skin colour.

decay, engaging in human sacrifice in the cult of Melkor introduced to the island by Sauron after his capture by the King, Ar-Pharazôn. The cannibalism, though, was probably a fabrication of the terrified natives.

The reason why Hazad tells all this to Tal-Elmar, is that his son has just sighted four ships on the horizon – one of which has ill-boding black sails[4]. Having heard the horror-story, Tal-Elmar tells his father they need to warn the townsfolk of Agar. At his point he turns into a real character and becomes the focus of the story. So far, readers have been told about his background and appearance, how he bears himself, and how he treats the vulnerable in society, personified by the elderly. Now Tolkien turns from telling to showing – for a while. Ignoring his father's plea for caution, Tal-Elmar returns to Agar with Hazad and informs Mogru, the Master of the town, about the ships. Mogru reacts disdainfully, insulting Hazad and dismissing the news. Hazad is cowed, but Tal-Elmar angrily defends his father and manages to talk Mogru into following him to the coast, at the same time deflecting the Master's irritation from Hazad onto himself. When they reach the sea, the ships are nowhere to be seen, but Tal-Elmar overrides Mogru's smug conclusion that there is nothing wrong by pointing out the inlet where they may be hiding.

The Master feels cornered and takes it out on Tal-Elmar and Hazad by sending the former on two errands: first he must convene a Moot, then he must spy out the people on the ships, a dangerous task. Tal-Elmar owes the Master of Agar his obedience, so he must go, leaving his father to Mogru's wrath. For a moment, he considers killing Mogru, but Hazad persuades him otherwise. Before he goes, Tal-Elmar issues a dire warning: he will wring the Master's neck if he returns to find his father in trouble. Then, taking Mogru's masters' staff and making the man cower before him, he leaves to convene the Moot and then seek out the people on the ships – and possibly meet his death.

A remarkable achievement for an eighteen-year-old. We know now that Tal-Elmar is not to be trifled with, difficult to cow, and just lacks experience in handling devious masters. It is obvious he takes after his Fell Folk mother in spirit as well as in body – that he is hers

---

4. This is vaguely reminiscent of European tales about mistakenly hoisted black sails which are then taken for harbingers of bad news, with tragic consequences (Theseus, Tristan and Isolde). As they do not function in this way in "Tal-Elmar", the reference is more likely to pirates.

alone, in the terms of Elmar's prophecy. He is brave to the point of
hot-headedness, in a way resembling Túrin Turambar: but for his
father's intervention, he would have killed Mogru. Setting out on his
errand, he is aware that his spying could lead him into mortal peril.
Then the possibility occurs to him that "I, who am a stranger in my
own people should find [the men on the ships] more pleasing than
Mogru and all others like him" (Tolkien C., 1996, p. 433).

Once he reaches the inlet and, according to expectation, sees the
ships and their crew, it dawns on him he has no news to take back: he
cannot count well enough to establish how many strangers there are,
and he has no way to find out what they want. Sobered, he thinks of
his childhood stories about "the 'blades' of the Cruel Men" (Tolkien
C., 1996, p. 433), which seems at odds with earlier claims he had
not been taught "much lore" and that Hazad's account was new to
him (Tolkien C., 1996, p. 426). The reference to the Cruel Men is in
the story continuation of January 1955; maybe Tolkien did not recall
everything he had written previously when he continued the story
and did not check his text. But who are they? The Fell Folk? The
High Men of the Sea? Other enemies Hazad forgot to count?

Staring at the strangers, Tal Elmar

> had that strange feeling, coming from where he knew not to this young lad,
> born and bred in a decaying, half-savage people: the feeling that he was not
> going to meet aliens but kinsmen from afar and friends (Tolkien C., 1996,
> p. 434).

If what Tal-Elmar feels is true, it now becomes clear who Elmar's
"Fell Folk from the East" are: Númenóreans.

Drawn to the men in the ships, who are obviously also
Númenóreans, Tal-Elmar steps forward "as if led or driven" (Tolkien
C., 1996, p. 435). At first, they take him for an Elf, but when he
greets them in the "half-savage language of the Men of the Dark",
they capture him, "but not with harsh handling" (Tolkien C., 1996,
p. 435). They are not King's Men but belong to his opponents, the
Faithful, as they will be called later in the "Akallabeth" portion of
The Silmarillion (*passim*). From here on, the text becomes more
fragmentary, with pieces of storytelling and dialogue in between
fragments and notes. The Númenóreans manage to convey they have
come "to occupy this land, and (...) to drive out the Dark People and
make a settlement to threaten the King" in alliance with "the Cruels

of the North" (Tolkien C., 1996, p. 436), who could be the Elves of
Lindon as seen from the viewpoint of the Dark People, in which case
they are not identical with "the Cruel *Men*".

Somewhere around here, Tolkien suggests that Tal-Elmar speaks
the tongue of these Númenóreans, which he has dreamed about. He
has him ask if they would "lure him to the black-winged boats and
give [him] to the Dark" (Tolkien C., 1996, p. 436). Their reply is
that he or in any case his kin belong already to the Dark. They tell
him the black sail represents "the fair night before the coming of
the Enemy", and that it is dotted with the stars of Elbereth (Tolkien
C., 1996, p. 346f). Tal-Elmar replies that his kin "fear the Dark, but
we do not love it nor serve it. At least so do some of us. So does my
father. And him I love" (Tolkien C., 1996, p. 437). They reply that
his "time of dwelling in these hills is come to an end. Here the Men
of the West have resolved to make their homes, and the folk of the
dark must depart – or be slain" (Tolkien C., 1996, p. 437). Tal Elmar
then offers himself up as hostage, as if he is not already their captive,
and the story breaks off.

To sensitive modern ears, the announcements of the Númenóreans
sound like blatant colonialism. Though an exploitation motive
is absent, it is obvious these men have come as conquerors and
occupiers, and the locals are no more than Dark People, so they will
have to go. Combined with Elmar's earlier accusation that the people
of Agar drove the previous occupants away (a colonialist trope
used by both Boers and English in South-Africa – SAHO, 2019)
this seems a rather flimsy excuse for conquest, and a rather boorish
way to announce it. Could it be Tolkien is engaging in anti-colonial
criticism here? If these men are indeed Faithful, this seems unlikely.
The subsequently written "Akallabeth" confirms that the Faithful
created a settlement in Middle-earth, Pelargir, although the author,
Elendil, declares that they "had little part" in the more exploitative
colonial endeavours of the other Númenóreans, the King's Men
(Tolkien C., 1977, p. 269). But being driven away and in the worst
case being slain is hardly better than being exploited, to put it mildly.
And these Númenóreans want more than just a foothold: this will
be a wholesale replacement of the current occupants of the area.
What is going on in this fragment that, as Tolkien wrote, "sees the
Númenóreans from the point of view of the 'Wild Men' of Middle-
earth"? (Tolkien C., 1996, p. 422)

The first thing that needs to be sorted out, is who the "Wild Men" are. Are they the people of Agar, who are exclusively described as "swarthy" or "swart" folk, or are they the "wild folk in the caves of the mountains" (Tolkien C., 1996, p. 425), as Elmar calls them, the natives driven away by the folk of Agar, and according to Hazad, their enemies? As these "wild folk" do not appear in the story fragment and therefore do not have a viewpoint, Tolkien's "Wild Men" can only be the swarthy folk – or his description would not apply to the available text.

In that case the next question is: why does Tolkien call the people of Agar "wild"? They do not live in temporary encampments, like hunter-gatherers or cattle-herding nomads, but in a town with a Master, like the people of Laketown in *The Hobbit* (Tolkien, 1975, pp. 189-93) They live in houses (Tolkien C., 1996, p. 428), and have a currency based economy that involves buying things (Tolkien C., 1996, p. 427). This is not a primitive society, though Tolkien seems to attempt to make the reader believe so by giving Tal-Elmar only a loin-cloth and a little cloak of fur to wear (Tolkien C., 1996, p. 431) and claiming he has never seen a bow and arrows (Tolkien C., 1996, p. 435)[5]. This implies the rest of the people of Agar do not know about them either – which is extremely strange, as they have been in contact with and done battle against people who do (the Fell Folk, for instance).

In short, even if they are still in an early stage of urbanisation, the people of Agar do not come across as "Wild Men". Did the elderly Tolkien – he was 75 when he commented on his story – fall back on the adventure books of his youth – Kipling and Rider Haggard come to mind – that tended to depict non-Western peoples, except a few East-Asian societies, as uncivilised, primitive and "savage" (the Latin-based term meaning "wild")? It seems best to ignore the designation "Wild Men" in the 1968 comment.

Another question is who can be thought to represent this people. Mogru is an Agarite, but his viewpoint is practically useless: he simply dismisses the "Go-hilleg", as he and Hazad call the Númenóreans, as a "crone-tale" (Tolkien C., 1996, p. 428). Elmar is obviously not from Agar, though she was probably born in Middle-earth. The Tolkien Gateway (2019)[6] suggests her people could be the colonial settlers of Pelargir, which does indeed lie East of the

5. Which is really peculiar, as only Australian Aboriginals did not use them.
6. See under "Mysteries of the Story".

locations proposed for Agar, and according to the "Akallabêth", those settlers were Faithful (Tolkien C., 1977, p. 269). In that case it is odd she does not object against Buldar's allegation that her people are "friends of demons" (Tolkien C., 1996, p. 425). This allegation is probably based on Sauron's alternative truth, that Melkor is good and the Valar are evil (Tolkien C., 1977, p. 271f). Elmar has a chance to enlighten her husband – and she does not use it!

Buldar, who considers her more beautiful than the Agarite women, has internalised her negative aesthetic judgement of his people as a whole: when she calls them "base and unlovely", he concedes she could be right (Tolkien C., 1996, p. 425). The narrator appears to suggest there is a universal standard of beauty to which Númenóreans conform, whereas the swarthy folk do not – except Tal-Elmar. This is especially clear in the following passage, from the part of the story where he approaches the men in the ships:

> Could he have seen himself he would have been struck with wonder no less than those who saw him now from the shore. His naked skin – for he wore only a loin-cloth, and little cloak of ... fur cast back and caught by a thong to his shoulder – glowed golden in the (...) light (Tolkien C., 1996, p. 435).

This is the omniscient narrator manifesting himself with a vengeance, showing a keen interest in a near-naked, fair youth, to the point where the author's personal esthetical preferences clearly shine through. This is rather problematic in a story purporting to show the viewpoint of the indigenous, swarthy people. Moreover, as the Númenóreans are white, this esthetical judgement also lends itself to suspicions of racism, to put it mildly.

Hazad's opinion of the Númenóreans is worse than Buldar's. Everything he tells Tal-Elmar is hearsay, but it is horrible, and it scares him deeply. Having described their practices of coming as friends first, then spying out the land, and later returning to take captives for the purpose of being sacrificed, he complains: "[I]s not our life hard enough without the vision of a black wing[7] upon the shining sea?" (Tolkien C., 1996, p. 427) Obviously, he has not connected his mother's folk with the abhorred Go-hilleg, or he might have been aghast to learn he is related to them. So, though he is only half indigenous, Hazad can be said to represent the viewpoint of the folk of Agar. In itself, his account is a telescoped,

---

7. The word the people of Agar use for "sail".

incorrect retelling of history: according to Appendix A(i) (Tolkien, 1969, p. 1073) and the "Akallabêth" (Tolkien C., 1977, pp. 263, 274), the earlier, benevolent visitors of Middle-earth were not the later, evil ones in disguise. Not that this makes it less credible as a native viewpoint.

But Hazad is not the main character. Tal-Elmar is, and he is *different*. Whether he is half or three quarters indigenous, as the fulfilment of a prophecy by a Númenórean woman, he is a Númenórean inside and out. His beloved father Hazad has just painted a pitch-black picture of the High Men of the Sea, but even before he has met any of them, Tal-Elmar ponders the possibility they will prove more sympathetic than the folk he has lived among for his entire life, but among whom he feels a stranger (Tolkien C., 1996, p. 433). Are the readers being manipulated?

That may be the case. The description of Tal-Elmar essentially eliminates anything native about him. He may be born 75% Agarite, but he has little or nothing in common with this people. Instead, he feels kinship with, and friendship for, the Númenóreans (Tolkien C., 1996, p. 434) even after Hazad has told him terrible things about them. He senses he knows their language (Tolkien C., 1996, p. 435), and later Tolkien suggest he speaks it: it is "the language of my long dreams", which returned to him when he heard it being used (Tolkien C., 1996, p. 436). This is reminiscent of the passage in "The Notion Club Papers", in which the Oxford scholars Lowdham and Jeremy suddenly speak a strange language which turns out to be Númenórean (Tolkien C., 1992, pp. 46-251) in an instance of inherited/genetic memories. There, it is peculiar enough, but in "Tal-Elmar" it comes right out of the blue, even given the fact that this part of the story is a somewhat fragmented draft.

Combined with two other elements in the story: 1) the armed hostilities between the people of Agar and the Faithful Númenórean settlers (the Fell Folk) that led to the capture of Elmar and 2) the framing of the Swarthy Folk as interlopers who chased their predecessors up the mountains, the "whitewashing" of Tal-Elmar turns the idea that the tale is written from the viewpoint of Middle-earth natives on its head. Even Tal-Elmar's defence of "his people", well-intentioned and courageous, is qualified. Some of them, including his father, do not love the dark, he says (Tolkien C., 1996, p. 437), implying that plenty of (depersonalised) others do.

In the end, against their expectations, readers are left with a predominantly negative view of the people of Agar. In the words of Dirk Wiemann: "The narrative (...) opens as a story of moral and ethical transvaluation but moves towards a reconfirmation of the dominant moral code of Tolkien's universe." The dark picture of the Númenóreans painted initially is a "bait" to be switched for a confirmation of the "polarizing worldview" that characterises Tolkien's whole Legendarium (Wiemann, 2014, pp. 693-4).[8] Wiemann's article identifies a tendency to bait and switch on Tolkien's part discussed extensively by Verlyn Flieger (2021), and the polarizing view is certainly present.

However, it is not merely a matter of dark folk of Middle-earth versus enlightened Númenóreans. Appendix A(i) of *The Lord of the Rings* describes two groups of Númenóreans representing opposite moral codes; the later "Akallabêth" does so more extensively. There, the followers of Sauron are as evil as Hazad's account claims, while the Númenóreans Tal-Elmar meets on the shore are their opponents (Tolkien C., 1996, p. 436) and can be identified as Faithful, who are good people. Meanwhile, the intention of the "good" Númenóreans to colonize the land of Agar, and their announcement that they will kill those who refuse to leave peacefully, seems morally debatable. Their excuse that the people of Agar are Dark people and "our Enemies" (Tolkien C., 1996, p. 436) does not play out in the fragment as published. They are not aligned with the King's Men: they are their victims, and it feels quite unfair they are relegated to the dark side of Tolkien's world.

However, it may have been Tolkien's intention to make the people of Agar allies of Sauron: the announcement by the Númenóreans that they intend to make a settlement "to threaten the King" is followed by: ("Or is this while Sauron is absent in Númenor?") (Tolkien C., 1996, p. 436). In the last note to the text, Christopher concludes that "the King is Sauron" (Tolkien C., 1996, p. 438, n. 14). But in the absence of textual evidence that the folk of Agar are all as morally depraved as Orcs, instead of being caught between Sauron, the Anvil (as an evil King[9] in Middle-earth) and Sauron, the Hammer (as the High Priest of Melkor in Númenor), these Númenóreans come across as very heavy-handed. From a sceptical

---

8. Which Wiemann simplifies further by calling it Manichean (p. 694), which is debatable. But that debate falls outside the scope of this paper.
9. He could be the "North" King in whose army Buldar fights.

point of view, they sound less reasonable than the Conquistadors presenting their conquest of Mexico as a just war, having a right to punish the Aztecs for "not keeping the law of nature or being idol worshippers" (Restall, 2017, p. 81). Their announcement that they wanted to "make a settlement to threaten the King" sounds like the fledgeling Dutch Republic justifying its ruthless colonial endeavours as a necessary move against their enemies, including the King of Spain (Van der Heijden, 2020).

Why would Tolkien embark on such a tale in the first place? My suggested answer involves the (pseudo)historical account of the final years of the Second Age as published in Appendix A(i) of *The Lord of the Rings*. There, Elendil and his sons are declared to have "established (...) the Númenórean realms in exile, Arnor and Gondor" (Tolkien, 1969 p. 1074) after the Downfall of Númenor. Previously, Elrond already made a statement to this effect at the Rivendell Council (Tolkien, 1969, p. 260). Who lived in these realms, apart from the small group of Faithful who reached Middle-earth? Reading between the lines of *The Lord of the Rings* suggests that people were living there, but we are not invited to give it a great deal of thought. After all, the people escaping from Númenor needed a place to settle, while Aragorn was descended from a line of Kings, not refugees.

But what if Tolkien started giving it some thought? Around the independence of India and Pakistan from the British Empire in 1947 and into the 1950s, when more former colonies became independent, debates about colonialisation and colonialism undoubtedly became a recurrent item in British news. This cannot have escaped Tolkien, who was subscribed to three newspapers, read the news every day and took "a strong interest in what was going on" (Ordway, 2021, p. 17f). At some point, he may have realised that the colonisation debate had implications for the establishment of what now looked to be colonial realms in Middle-earth by his Faithful, and that there had to be a reason why Númenóreans were lording it over the original inhabitants of these lands. Middle-earth, however sparsely populated, was no *terra nullius* when the survivors of the Downfall set foot there. The *terra nullius* doctrine was used by modern colonising nations to lay claim to areas whose inhabitants did not live in states acknowledged by European powers; prime examples of it are Australia (AHO, 2021) and South-Africa[10].

10. See footnote 2.

Tolkien may have wondered if he had not written himself into a corner, and felt the need to extricate himself. In which case "Tal-Elmar" could be an attempt to deal with the matter in story form, as was his habit. As the first part of the text dates from before January 1955, writing began about a year before 20 October 1955, when *The Return of the King* was published[11], including the Appendices. Set in a populated region that would become part of Gondor, the story may be intended to answer the question of what people lived in Middle-earth during the late Second Age, and give them an identity and a bit of history. At the same time, it had to explain why they ended up as subjects of realms, established by people who were not of Middle-earth and had not been so for thousands of years.

If this was what Tolkien tried to do, the attempt was unsuccessful.[12] Thirteen years later he remembered it as a story seen from the viewpoint of the "Wild Men". But though this may have been his intention, it is not what it is – if only because the narrative viewpoint is not "third person limited native": there are too many intrusions by an omniscient narrator. It is prejudiced: as the Númenóreans who established realms in Middle-earth were good, the natives of Middle-earth had to be bad. It is confusing, with a King who is secretly Sauron, and a maze of peoples that seems intended to prepare the readers for shocking and revelatory twists and turns: Swart(hy) Folk, Fell Folk of the East, Wild Folk, Go-hilleg[13], Men from the Sea, Cruel Men, Cruels of the North, Dark People, a pureblood crossbreed – and in the end a Bewildered Public, sniffing at the many red herrings Tolkien the Trickster has scattered about.

Readers are confronted with a group of aggressive sounding Númenóreans who seem poster-boys for colonial arrogance, invaders who displace and kill native peoples by framing them as bad and

---

11. This may look like wild speculation, but what if he though his story could function as an addition to Appendix A (i) and this was the reason he began writing it?

12. As someone put it less diplomatically: "Tolkien's familiar cartoon mythology about Evil Men who are apt to Sauron's rule has run smack into Tolkien's own desire to sympathetically imagine the actual lives of such men." (TORN, 2011)

13. The only indigenous term (the meaning is not given) for any people in "Tal-Elmar", though the others must also have had names in the language of Agar. It raises the question who wrote the story (down). Were the people of Agar literate? That *Go-hilleg* is the only indigenous word for any of the peoples referred to, suggests the narrator was not one of them. So, even the use of this term undermines the idea the events are seen from a Middle-earth viewpoint.

morally inferior. To Tal-Elmar, they may explain their black sail as a symbol of beauty and purity (Tolkien C., 1996, p. 437), but for the people of Agar they are as threatening as pirates. The character readers are invited to identify with feels drawn to these men for reasons that appear to be fated, genetical, and esthetical – but hardly realistic. Tal-Elmar starts out showing some potential but ends up as a puppet manipulated by an author whose moral and spiritual agenda overrules his narrative instincts. Far from representing any Wild Men, he is "mine alone", as Elmar predicted, and he even seems poised to become a weapon *against* the Wild Men. With his contrived identity, he is a symbol for an equally contrived story exposition that soon turns into an idiosyncratic echo chamber. One can only hope Tolkien realised this would not work and discarded "Tal-Elmar" for that reason.

However, the reason could also be that Tolkien gave up soon after he wondered if Sauron was already in Númenor – as he had to be, or Hazad's tale about human sacrifices would make no sense. In that case, the newcomers lost their pretext of having to make a "settlement against the King" (Tolkien C., 1996, p. 437) and were reduced to mere colonial bullies. That it was the evil Ar Pharazôn who had rid Middle-earth of Sauron, complicated matters to the point where the story became an impossible mess.

A few years later (~1958) Tolkien wrote the "Akallabêth". He abandoned the novelistic approach and opted for a more straightforward piece of legend without explicitly dominating white Western aesthetics, peculiar genetics, obfuscating designations, and an unconvincing attempt to depict a "primitive" society. Admittedly, the natives are still a little dark, and the Faithful are still colonizers in all but name, but it remains low key and understated, in a way that helps to take the edge of Tolkien's polarising worldview if one does not look too closely. And it works better in the mythological/legendary sphere with its air of inevitability and necessity, than in a novelistic story like "Tal-Elmar".

With thanks to Pamina Fernandez Camacho for some useful comments and suggestions.

References

AHO (Aboriginal Heritage Office), 2021. *A Brief Aboriginal History* [online]. Available at <https://www.aboriginalheritage.org/history/history/> [Accessed 27 August 2021].

Flieger, V., 2021. *Annual Guest of Honour Talk of the Tolkien Society* [online]. Available at <https://www.facebook.com/watch/live/?v=266992551776700&ref= watch_permalink> [Accessed 28 August 2021].

Ordway, H., 2021. *Tolkien's Modern Reading: Middle-earth Beyond the Middle Ages*. Park Ridge: World on Fire Academic.

Restall, M., 2018. *When Montezuma met Cortés: The True Story of the Meeting that Changed History*. London: HarperCollins.

Thomas, C., 2021. *Stowage of the British slave ship Brookes under the Regulated Slave Trade Act of 1788*. SHEC: Resources for Teachers. [online] Available at <https://shec.ashp.cuny.edu/items/show/1226> [Accessed 29 August 2021].

SAHO (South-African History Online), 2019. *The Empty Land Myth* [online]. Available at <https://www.sahistory.org.za/article/empty-land-myth> [Accessed 25 August 2021].

TORN (The One Ring.Net), 2011. *Middle-earth under the Shadow: the abandoned Tal-Elmar story* [online]. Available at <http://newboards. theonering.net/forum/gforum/perl/gforum.cgi?do=post_view_ printable;post=356064;guest=155467592> [Accessed 24 September 2021].

Tolkien, C. ed., 1977. *The Silmarillion*. London: George Allen & Unwin.
—, 1992. *Sauron Defeated – The History of Middle-earth Vol. IX*. London: HarperCollins. The Notion Club Papers, pp.145-327.
—, 1996. *The Peoples of Middle-earth – The History of Middle-earth Vol. XII*. London: HarperCollins. Tal Elmar, pp.422-438.
—, 1980. In: C. Tolkien, ed. *Unfinished Tales*. London: George Allen and Unwin. Aldarion and Erendis, pp.173-217.

Tolkien, J.R.R., 1969. *The Lord of the Rings*, Deluxe Edition. London: George Allen & Unwin.
—, 1975. *The Hobbit*. London: George Allen & Unwin.

Tolkien Gateway, 2019. *Tal Elmar (chapter)* [online]. Available at <http:// tolkiengateway.net/wiki/Tal-Elmar_(chapter)> [accessed 24 August 2021].

van der Heijden, C., 2020. Het verhaal van de anderen. *De Groene Amsterdammer*, Dossier: Ons koloniaal verleden [online]. Available at <https:// www.groene.nl/artikel/het-verhaal-van-de-anderen> [Accessed 1 September 2021].

Wiemann, D., 2014. Tolkien's Baits: Agonism, Essentialism and the Visible in The Lord of the Rings. In: G. Sedlmayer and N. Waller, eds. *Politics in Fantasy Media. Essays on Ideology and Gender in Fiction, Film, Television and Games*. [e-book] Jefferson (NC): McFarland. pp.685-749.

Wikipedia, 2021. *Hagarenes; Hagrite* [online]. Available at <https://en.wikipedia. org/wiki/Hagarenes; https://en.wikipedia.org/wiki/Hagarenes> [Accessed 3 September 2021].

Éowyn as Light Bearer

Catherine A. Coundjeris

J.R.R. Tolkien describes Éowyn in terms of light and beauty:

> "Grave and thoughtful was her glance, as she looked on the king with cool pity in her eyes. Very fair was her face, and her long hair was like a river of gold. Slender and tall she was in her white robe girt with silver; but strong she seemed and stern as steel, a daughter of kings." (Tolkien, 1965b, p. 152).

Éowyn and her brother Éomer have lost their parents and are living in the court of King Théoden who, under the debilitating influence of Wormtongue, spy to Saruman, exists only as a corrupted shell of his former self.

Tolkien himself lost both his parents as a young boy. He knew the throes of grief first-hand. His father's loss was sudden—a bad case of rheumatic fever back in Bloemfontein, South Africa. Mabel had returned to England with her two young sons, visiting her family. Left with few resources after her husband's death she was rejected by her family due to her ardent Catholic faith. Despite that, Mabel was able to give her sons eight memorable years filled with precious moments spent in the beauty of the English countryside, but she eventually developed diabetes and died soon after. She was able to entrust her sons into the guardianship of a Catholic priest, Father Francis Morgan to ensure they would grow up in the Catholic faith. His mother's devotion to her faith and her sons had a great impact on Tolkien:

> "My own dear mother was a martyr indeed, and it is not to everybody that God grants so easy a way to his great gifts as he did to Hilary and myself, giving us a mother who killed herself with labour and trouble to ensure us keeping the faith." (Carpenter, 1977, p. 39).

His great devotion to his mother influenced his view of womankind and the female power to abide through great sorrow in honour and nobility, which can be seen in the development of Éowyn's character who is also besieged by overwhelming tragedy.

The death of Théoden's son Théodred threw the king and his family into a deeper sorrow than the loss of Éowyn's parents. Indeed, Éowyn is in a great depression and suffering from an aching sense of loss and grief. Grief over the diminishment of her family, grief over the aging deterioration of Théoden, and grief over the loss of the grandeur that was Rohan. She served as a caregiver to Théoden, her king and uncle and kept the home fires burning through her protective nature. "Behind his chair stood a woman clad in white." (Tolkien, 1965b, p. 148). Ever at his side to protect him from the deceitful Wormtongue whom we know as wicked by how he refers to the Lady Galadriel of Lothlórien. "Then it is true, as Eomer has reported, that you are in league with the Sorceress of the Golden Wood?" said Wormtongue. "It is not to be wondered at: webs of deceit were ever woven in Dwimordene." (Tolkien, 1965b, page 150) Throughout the ages, men like Wormtongue have diminished good women by wicked names, in this case intimating that Galadriel is only a sorceress and in league with Gandalf for nefarious purposes. In this atmosphere, Éowyn watches over her uncle with solicitous care, "The woman hastened to the king's side, taking his arm," (Tolkien, 1965b, p. 152). Despite her homey talents she is not by nature domestic and her heart bridles under the weight of such caregiving necessities. Her worst fear is, "A cage. To stay behind bars, until use and old age accept them, and all chance of doing great deeds is gone beyond recall or desire." (Tolkien, 1965c, p. 68).

Inevitably, she falls in love with Aragorn who cannot return her love since he is betrothed to another. Éowyn's love is real and honest and is only reasonable for one so noble to love nobility in others.

"As she stood before Aragorn she paused suddenly and looked upon him, and her eyes were shining. And he looked down upon her fair face and smiled; but as he took the cup, his hand met hers, and he knew that she trembled at the touch. 'Hail Aragorn son of Arathorn!' she said. 'Hail Lady of Rohan!' he answered, but his face now was troubled and he did not smile" (Tolkien, 1965b, p. 162).

The readers wonder at this, for Arwen is kept quietly in the background and Éowyn is so lovely and real and present. Indeed, Éowyn seems to be a perfect match for Aragorn and this reader was disappointed when her love for him is not returned in kind.

It is interesting to note that there were several drafts of the Éowyn story. According to scholar Morgan N. Fontenot (2019), Tolkien actually wrote in another character, Théoden's daughter Idis, then removed her upon several rewrites. He also had Éowyn die in the first versions and Aragorn never married, but pining after Éowyn his whole life. However, this did not suit Tolkien's vision of Middle-earth. A powerful presence in this work of Tolkien's is his desire to write a mythology for England. Family lineage is very important in Tolkien's contemporary world as it is in the world of Middle-earth. He wanted to show the grace and majesty of the line of the Dúnedain through Aragorn's link with the elvish line. Therefore, he rewrote his initial drafts to reveal this through Aragorn's betrothal to Arwen daughter of Elrond.

Yet the obstacle is the same, and this new love cannot come to fruition, for not only is he not free to pursue such a course of action, but there is no time for a gentle parting. Thus, in the face of imminent war, Éowyn endures another loss. She suffers through the passing of a new love into the shadow of death when Aragorn chooses to depart from the Rohirrim to journey from Dunharrow to the Paths of the Dead at the crucial moment of the mustering of Rohan. Just like many others in her life, "[Aragorn] has passed into the shadows from which none have returned. I could not dissuade him. He is gone." (Tolkien, 1965c, p. 82).

Nonetheless, Éowyn is a much beloved Lady of Rohan, and King Théoden and his people trust her with their lives. When the King rides into battle, he turns to this pillar of womanly virtues and gives her the duty to rule in his place. He was uncertain of who to choose, but Háma a warrior of Rohan suggests, "There is Éowyn, daughter of Éomund, his sister. She is fearless, and high-hearted. All love her. Let her be as lord to the Éorlingas, while we are gone." (Tolkien, 1965b, p. 163). Even then the lords knew that Éowyn was full of courage and goodness and more than capable of leading the people of Rohan. Their love for her is like a bright flame. Her joy at Théoden's recovery through Gandalf's ministrations is short-lived. Her response is to accept, but she voices her sentiments plaintively, "A year shall I endure for every day that passes until your return.' But as she spoke her eyes went to Aragorn who stood nearby." (Tolkien, 1965b, p. 163) She has fallen for this Ranger from the North and longs for better days.

Now Éowyn's role changes again and she must act as Steward in the King's absence and take over the rule of her people. Théoden would not have chosen her for this role if he did not think her worthy and capable. The people love her and she loves her people. Then why in the end would she abandon her post and go to war? The answer is very complicated, but can be found in the history of those times that Tolkien alludes to in his lore coloured by his own experience:

> "Beyond the trenches no-man's land was littered with bloated and decaying bodies. All around was desolation. Grass and corn had vanished into a sea of mud. Trees, stripped of leaf and branch, stood as mere mutilated and blackened trunks." (Carpenter, 1977, p. 91).

Wars in this primitive time were brutal especially to the women who were left behind. This war with the East is considered hopeless and Éowyn herself is without hope for a good conclusion, as already all her private hopes have been shattered. Aragorn leaving is the last straw. She reasons rightly that the end of the women and the old and the children would be death by burning, torture, and other atrocities:

> "you are a woman, and your part is in the house, but when the men have died in battle, and in honour, you have to be burned in the house, for the men will need it no more. But I am of the House of Eorl and not a serving-woman. I can ride and wield blade, and I do not fear either pain or death." (Tolkien, 1965c, p. 68).

She would rather die as a shieldmaiden than as a queen who could be carried off or worse. Instead, since she cannot dissuade him, she requests to join Aragorn on his journey onto the Paths of the Dead, "Lord, if you must go, then let me ride in your following. For I am weary of skulking in the hills, and wish to face peril and battle.'" (Tolkien, 1965c, p. 67). His response is to remind her of her duty to the King and her people. She bristles at this and declares that she is not a dry nurse, but in the end, she does stay in her role until Théoden arrives at Dunharrow:

> Her explicitly-stated charge is fulfilled, and the reader does not find out if she is given another. When Théoden left Edoras for Helm's Deep, his farewell to and appointment of Éowyn as his deputy was public, but he conducts his farewell to Éowyn at Dunharrow in private–it is a scene that neither the reader nor those within the story witness.
>
> It may be objected that even if Éowyn was not specifically commanded to serve as ruler after Théoden's departure for war in Gondor, she did her people a disservice by leaving them leaderless. Yet, this speculation is not

based on solid evidence from the text. Simply because Tolkien writes no scene in which Éowyn hands her authority to someone else does not mean that she leaves without making arrangements." (Catanach, 2005).

This interpretation is quite spot on as oath breaking is considered anathema in this mythology, and her commitment to her people could be seen as a type of oath. She gave her word to protect them, reminiscent of the oath made long ago between Eorl of Rohan and Cirion the Steward of Gondor to ride to his aid in time of war. This oath was so solemn that it made the land it was invoked on hallowed ground because they called upon the names of the Valar making the spot Háligfirgen, meaning Holy Mountain (Hostetter, 2021, p. 392). Thus the Rohirrim and Éowyn in kind hold sacred their word.

Her decision to ride to war is not suicidal. She has a pure heart and one that sees clearly: "I would not see a thing that is high and excellent cast away needlessly" (Tolkien, 1965c, p. 68). This she says to Aragorn, but she must also see it true of herself as well. She is honest and comes close to declaring her love for Aragorn. In a last effort to change his mind she states, "They go only because they would not be parted from thee—because they love thee" (Tolkien, 1965c, p. 68). A clear and bold declaration of her love reveals her open nature.

She is a generous hearted person and when she sees that Merry will be denied his place with the Rohirrim she comes to his aid while disguised as Dernhelm. She allows Merry to ride with her into battle. First, in her rightful position as Lady of Rohan she arms him for battle: "here is also a stout jerkin of leather, a belt and a knife" (Tolkien, 1965c, p. 90). She also gives him a shield with a white horse and a helmet, wishing him good fortune. He begs Théoden to allow him to go to war at his side, but the king refused saying that Merry's little pony could not keep up with the war horses. Merry begs saying, "And as all my friends have gone to battle, I should be ashamed to stay behind" (Tolkien, 1965c, p. 90). This sentiment could very well belong to Éowyn, echoing the young men of Tolkien's time who signed up for the war effort during the Great War. In fact, it was considered a great dishonour to shirk one's duty, which is illustrated by all Tolkien's schoolboy chums going to war.

Furthermore, one could argue that Éowyn is fated to join the battle and her greater purpose lies in following her heart. She is meant by some unseen hand to go to war. For in the darkest hour when the Lord of the Nazgûl rises up as "a great black shape against the fires" (Tolkien, 1965c, p. 125) the Lady of Rohan rides into the storm not as a warrior, but as a guardian spirit, remaining close to the King. In his hour of need, when the Nazgûl steed, perching on the body of Snowmane and digging its claws into the steed of Théoden would devour the King, Éowyn springs forth. Steadfast Dernhelm alone standing against the enemy she calls out, "Begone, foul dwimmerlaik, lord of carrion! Leave the dead in peace!" (Tolkien, 1965c, p. 141). She stands there with all her womanly virtues intact, defending family and home and country. Even in a moment of pure adrenalin rush the womanhood of Éowyn calls for peace. A peace she is willing to die for.

Her love for her King as father gives her courage to withstand the darkness. When told that "no living man may hinder me" (Tolkien, 1965c, p. 141) Éowyn does not quail, but draws her sword to defend the body of her father king identifying herself as a woman and daughter:

> "But no living man am I! You look upon a woman. Éowyn I am, Éomund's daughter. You stand between me and my lord and kin. Begone, if you be not deathless! For living or dark undead, I will smite you, if you touch him." (Tolkien, 1965c, p. 141).

One cannot help but enjoy Tolkien's play with words. As he was a philologist, he wrote a riddle to describe the terror of the Nazgûl Lord. He was so awful that no man could defeat him. One might assume that no one could defeat him, but one would be wrong. Women are overlooked in Tolkien's time as they often were in days of old. It is powerful that Tolkien argues Éowyn can defeat the Nazgûl because she is a woman not a man. In Tolkien's world, a woman is tied with the bounty of nature. "This love for the memory of the countryside of his youth was later to become a central part of his writing, and it was intimately bound up with his love for the memory of his mother" (Carpenter, 1977, p. 40). Éowyn represents the goodness of the natural order where kin defends kin and the Nazgûl Lord is an aberration, a thing that lives that should have died. It is an immortality that goes against the laws of nature. Éowyn is changed in an instant and becomes not just herself but a fulcrum for the feminine power. Kin is fostered at home and hearth where a woman rules. The Nazgûl is the antithesis of this long ago rent from his natural origins. Thus, only a woman could defeat him with the natural light of home.

Merry her compatriot witnesses the transformation and notes the light that Éowyn bears into battle:

> "her bright hair, released from its bond, gleamed with pale gold upon her shoulders. Her grey eyes as the sea were hard and fell, and yet tears were upon her cheek. A sword was in her hand, and she raised her shield against the horror of her enemy's eyes." (Tolkien, 1965c, p. 142).

In her hour of greatest need she is not alone, for accompanying her is the one whom she had aided who now will give her aid. She who is "fair yet terrible" (Tolkien, 1965c, p. 142) slays the steed of the Nazgûl. Then Merry deals the Lord of the Nazgûl a blow to his knee and Éowyn finishes him off. Together maiden and hobbit did what no man could do. Éowyn's light gives courage to the hobbit and the hobbit helps her to defeat the enemy. Women often work together with others to assure domestic tranquillity.

Alas, Théoden is not rescued in time and he perishes upon the field of battle. Tolkien is no stranger to loss on a battlefield. His young friends from the T.C.B.S. club from King Edward's prep school and Oxford did not survive the war and many in Tolkien's battalion were killed. "Tolkien never forgot what he called the 'animal horror' of trench warfare" (Carpenter, 1977, p. 91). Tolkien himself was struck down with pyrexia of unknown origin, which the soldier's called *trench fever* and could very well be the genesis of the "dark breath" which struck down Éowyn, Merry and Faramir.

Éowyn is victorious over the Nazgûl; however, it is not without a great cost to her health, for she is wounded terribly. Faramir son of Denethor has also been paralysed by a similar malady. Both lie in the House of Healing victims of the dark breath that only athelas and the healer-king can remedy. There are more similarities between them. Both are orphans, Faramir has lost his mother and now his father, and both have served as Stewards of a great kingdom. Even still both have witnessed loved ones diminish through sorrow and madness, one because of the evil of Saruman and the other through a plantír connection to Sauron. In the end of all that is known to them, both are prisoners of the healers and have Aragorn to thank for their recovery. Faramir sees her beauty and bravery and she is drawn to his prowess, a natural impulse, for two such individuals would seek each other to find comfort in a war-torn world: "She did not answer, but as he looked at her it seemed to him that something in her softened, as though a bitter frost were yielding at the first faint presage of Spring." (Tolkien, 1965c, p. 296). Gradually they walk together and wonder at the darkness in the East while the light grows between them. Days pass until news of the victory comes to them just as Faramir declares his allegiance to Éowyn White Lady of Rohan.

One might call Éowyn fickle for choosing another so soon after falling in love with Aragorn. Courtly love, or the idea of a soul mate, was unheard of during these times. According to Tolkien, they lived in times of great stress; yet with the threat of death hanging over their heads they chose life. A path he himself endured when he married Edith Bratt. Tolkien came to realise that "'the real soul-mate' is the one you are actually married to" (Carpenter and Tolkien C., 1981, Letter 43, p. 51).

Tolkien himself tackles criticism about the love affair between Éowyn and Faramir:

> "It is possible to love more than one person...at the same time, but in a different mode of intensity. I do not think that Éowyn's feelings for Aragorn really changed much; and when he was revealed as so lofty a figure, in descent and office, she was able to go on loving and admiring him. He was old, and that is not only a physical quality: when not accompanied by any physical decay age can be alarming or awe-inspiring. Also, she was not herself ambitious in the true political sense. Though not a 'dry nurse' in temper, she was also not really a soldier or 'amazon', but like many brave women was capable of great military gallantry at a crisis." (Carpenter and Tolkien C., 1981, Letter 244, p. 323).

Even though Éowyn loves Aragorn, her love for him matures into more of a spiritual devotion to a king than the love of an equal. Faramir is her equal. Together the Steward of Gondor and the Lady of Rohan make the best choices as rulers of Ithilien. This appointment is no small consolation prize. In fact, Tolkien again clears the air about it:

> "Also, to be a Prince of Ithilien [and princess] the greatest noble after Dol Amroth in the revived Númenórean state of Gondor, soon to be of imperial power and prestige, was not a 'market-garden job' as you term it. Until much had been done by the restored King the P. of Ithilien would be the resident march-warden of Gondor, in its main eastward outpost - and also would have many duties in rehabilitating the lost territory, and clearing it of

outlaws and orc-remnants, not to speak of the dreadful vale of Minas Ithil (Morgul)." (Carpenter and Tolkien C., 1981, Letter 244, p. 323)

On the other hand, Faramir

"read the hearts of men as shrewdly as his father, but what he read moved him sooner to pity than to scorn. He was gentle in bearing, and a lover of lore and of music, and therefore by many in those days his courage was judged less than his brother's. But it was not so, except that he did not seek glory in danger without purpose." (Tolkien, 1965c, p. 419).

He would make a wise ruler and Éowyn an excellent queen for she too was moved to pity and love for others as was seen in her treatment of an aging king and her solicitous care for Merry as they marched to war. Her people would not have loved her so if she were lacking in the social graces of kindness and compassion. The nuances of her character are formidable and lift this fantasy into the realm of mythic lore and fine literature, entering a place where the spiritual becomes real flesh and blood.

Éowyn is a light bearer in the world of Middle-earth, but she is not the only one. It is interesting to note that women are not represented in the Fellowship, but are relegated to the "minor" character roles. Yet each woman who is part of Middle-earth has a connection to the world of light and goodness despite their flaws. That is because women are creators and bring life into the world whether through birth or through sacrifice or through wielding a sword to defend family and kin. When Frodo was in Shelob's Lair, the Light of Eärendil's Star given to him by the Lady Galadriel saved his life and gave him hope. "May it be a light to you in dark places, when all other lights go out" (Tolkien, 1965a, p. 488). Galadriel, Lady of Light and of the Galadhrim, gave to each member of the Fellowship a gift. She freely gave them the light of her friendship. Éowyn gifting Merry with his sword and his armour is an echo of this earlier gift giving. Such hospitality is a warm and human manifestation, bringing the ethereal elven realm into sharper focus, and also alluding to the light of Tolkien's faith,

"The woman is another fallen human-being with a soul in peril. But combined and harmonized with religion (as long ago it was, producing much of that beautiful devotion to Our Lady that has been God's way of refining so much our gross manly natures and emotions..." (Carpenter and Tolkien C., 1981, Letter 43, p. 49).

Tolkien's Catholic faith informs upon his creation and he portrays women in a way reminiscent of the role of the Virgin Mary: bearing the light of home and hearth and family into the fray of everyday life.

> Tolkien cast his mythology in this form because he wanted it to be remote and strange, and yet at the same time not to be a lie. He wanted the mythological and legendary stories to express his own moral view of the universe; and as a Christian he would not place this view in a cosmos without the God that he worshipped…So while God is present in Tolkien's universe, He remains unseen. (Carpenter, 1977, p.99).

Truly, the women in *The Lord of the Rings* take on a level of divinity for members of the Fellowship, and the others who struggle against the Eye of Sauron. Although Tolkien warns his son Michael against the vagaries of courtly love that "tends to make the lady a kind of guiding star or divinity," (Carpenter and Tolkien C., 1981, Letter 43, p. 49) he portrays the women in *The Lord of the Rings* with an important role as light bearers. Perhaps this emerges from his desire for his mother who died so young or his long wait for his wife's hand and then his endurance through war to live in matrimony with her. Nevertheless, the women do shine with a guiding light in this story. The supporting role of women in *The Lord of the Rings* shows that as fellow "companions in shipwreck" (Carpenter and Tolkien C., 1981, Letter 43, p. 49) they can lead the men in their lives towards their goal through their handiwork and off-stage support. Remember, Galadriel supplies her guests with special gifts, not least is the waybread that is indeed a form of Communion which sustains body and soul in the darkest hour:

> "Out of the darkness of my life, so much frustrated, I put before you the one great thing to love on earth: the Blessed Sacrament…. There you will find romance, glory, honour, fidelity, and the true way of all your loves upon earth…" (Carpenter and Tolkien C., 1981, Letter 43, p. 53).

In addition,

> "Arwen fought for her people by inspiring Aragorn to aid in leading the Fellowship and remaining strong in the fight for his crown, to pursue goodness, truth, and beauty despite a world darkened by evil. Arwen is the delicate balance to the roughness of men, a soothing reminder of hope and love" (Vincent, 2019).

In the movies she is more present; however, in Tolkien's text she does make the banner that Aragorn displays in battle, showing her unfailing and quiet support. The reader finds out more about her in the Appendix, discovering Arwen's long wait for Aragorn to come into his own as King. Despite this conventional role of women, Éowyn breaks the mould and joins the fray. Her calling is different and her role is in effect foretold. Her greatest weakness, a fear of being caged, is transformed into an opportunity for fate to play a role in those dire times. No man can defeat Sauron's henchman, only a woman and her companion hobbit. Éowyn was meant to face the Nazgûl Lord in battle.

Moreover, this absence of women in the Fellowship mirrors Tolkien's childhood growing up in the care of a parish priest. He speaks of his mother in warm terms to his son Michael,

"Your grandmother, to whom you owe so much—for she was a gifted lady of great beauty and wit, greatly stricken by God with grief and suffering, who died in youth (at 34) of a disease hastened by persecution of her faith—died in the postman's cottage at Rednal, and buried at Bromsgrove" (Carpenter and Tolkien C., 1981, Letter 44, p. 54).

He lived through the darkness of disease and persecution and war. Meeting Edith Bratt when he was 16 years old and forbidden by his guardian to pursue his love until he was 21 at which point, he promptly contacted Edith and confessed his love and proposed marriage on January 8, 1913. War broke out the following year and Tolkien still had a year to go of college. Finally in July of 1915 he was 'bolted' into the army. He married on March 22, 1916.

"May found me crossing the Channel (I still have the verse I wrote on the occasion!) for the carnage of Somme. Think of your mother! Yet I do not now for a moment feel that she was doing more than she should have been asked to do" (Carpenter and Tolkien C., 1981, Letter 43, p. 54).

Tolkien and his wife were made of stern stuff, too, as were Éowyn and Faramir.

It is interesting to note that a man accustomed to the rowdy company of men, revered and understood some important aspects of women. He had a daughter, Pricilla, and one would think that she too wanted to have a stake in the stories that she listened to as a child at her father's knee. One can only guess at this, but she lets

her fondness for her father's work show in her position as Honorary
Vice President of the Tolkien Society since 1986. This quote from
Gandalf is very telling to Tolkien's own position as a father:

> My friend, you had horses, and deed of arms, and the free fields; but she,
> being born in the body of a maid, had a spirit and courage at least the match
> of yours. Yet she was doomed to wait upon an old man, whom she loved as
> a father, and watch him falling into a mean dishonoured dotage; and her part
> seemed to her more ignoble than that of the staff he leaned on. (Tolkien,
> 1965c, p.174).

By all accounts Tolkien was a devoted father and began *The
Hobbit* (1937) as a story to entertain his children. Thus, a character
like Éowyn who has appealed to many young women may indeed
have appealed to Tolkien's daughter. Her creation emerging from
Tolkien's real experience with hearth and home.

On a final note, we should see how Éowyn's love for Aragorn
is transformed into an allegiance to her king. She asks for his
blessing, "Wish me joy, my liege-lord and healer!" And he answers,
"I have wished thee joy ever since first I saw thee. It heals my heart
to see you now in bliss!" (Tolkien, 1965c, p. 316). According to
Paul H. Kocher, "Never has Tolkien looked into the human heart
to better purpose than in this inset tale of Éowyn and Aragorn"
(Kocher, 1972, p. 147). In truth, Tolkien examines the nature of
good and evil within his epic story and with the character of Éowyn,
revealing how the weakness of a character can be their source of
greatest strength. Éowyn's despair and grief led to her moment of
glory against the Nazgûl Lord. All of Tolkien's experiences and
background came to bear in his characterisation of Éowyn. Even
his nature as a consummate writer unearths the Éowyn we know
and love. Tolkien's various drafts of this substory reveal his respect
for Éowyn as a character. "Clearly, Tolkien first envisioned Éowyn
as a powerful, wise, respected woman who easily took up the
leadership of her people and rode openly into battle as one of the
army's more valiant warriors" (Fontenot, 2019). His later drafts
are more subtle, showing the complicated circumstances of women
throughout history; hence, he creates a woman who must ride to
war in disguise, standing against the custom of her time. However,
Tolkien reveals his ultimate respect and sense that women are called
to illuminate the world in which they live through remaining true
to their inner nature. A nature that is attuned with the greater nature

of the universe and the only true power which can disrupt the plans of evil. Tolkien's mythology about Éowyn is more an illustration of this truth than a fabrication.

> You call a star a star, and say it is just a ball of matter moving on a mathematical course. But that is merely how you see it. By so naming things and describing them you are only inventing your own terms about them. And just as speech is invention about objects and ideas, so myth is invention about truth. (Carpenter, 1977, p.151).

Éowyn's story feels true down to its roots and thus she rides into legend. Ultimately, Éowyn's tale comes full circle and she emerges out of the darkness a light bearer to her family, friends and to Faramir who sees within her a grace and honesty that he can admire and embrace, betrothing himself to her and crowning her his queen.

References

Carpenter, H., 1977. *The Biography of Tolkien*. Houghton Mifflin Company: Boston.

Carpenter, H. and Tolkien, C. eds., 1981. *The Letters of J.R.R. Tolkien*. Boston: Houghton Mifflin Harcourt.

Catanach, D., 2005. *The Problem of Éowyn: A Look at Ethics and Values in Middle-earth*. [online] Available at: <scholar.google.com> [Accessed on July 7, 2021].

Fontenot, M.N., 2019. *Exploring the People of Middle Earth: Éowyn Shieldmaiden of Rohan*. [online] Available at <https://www.tor.com/2019/04/04/exploring-the-peoples-of-middle-earth-eowyn-shieldmaiden-of-rohan/> [Accessed on September 11, 2021].

Foster, R., 1971. *Tolkien's World from A to Z The Complete Guide to Middle-earth*. Ballantine Books: New York.

Hostetter, C.F. ed., 2021. *The Nature of Middle-earth*. C.F. Hostetter ed. Houghton Mifflin Company: Boston.

Kocher, P.H., 1972. *Master of Middle-earth*. Ballantine Books: New York.

Koloski, P., 2020. *Tolkien Was Trying to be A Good Dad When He Created Middle-earth*. [online] Available at: <https://voyagecomics.com/2020/06/08/tolkien-was-trying-to-be-a-good-dad-when-he-created-middle-earth/> [Accessed September 14, 2021].

Tolkien, J.R.R., 1937. *The Hobbit*. London: Allen & Unwin.
—, 1965a. *The Fellowship of the Ring*. Ballantine Books: New York.
—, 1965b. *The Two Towers*. Ballantine Books: New York.
—, 1965c. *The Return of the King*. Ballantine Books: New York.

Vincent, H., 2019. *Two Sides of Womanly Beauty: Character Studies of Éowyn and Arwen*. [online] Available at <https://fellowshipandfairydust.com/2019/06/05/two-sides-of-womanly-beauty/> [Accessed July 7, 2021].

The Last Prince of Cardolan: Memory and mediation in the mortuary archaeology of Middle-earth

Scott Chaussée

The geographic and historical context of the Barrow-downs in Middle-earth

The Barrow-downs is the western terminal sub-region of the much more extensive South Downs, a hilly upland region in central Eriador, north-western Middle-earth (Figure 1). The Old Forest borders the Barrow-downs to the west; the Great Road and Bree-land to the north; the stretch of the north-south Greenway road, called 'Andrath' and the rest of the South Downs to the east; a meander of the River Baranduin (Brandywine) to the south-west. The barrow-downs are open to the plains of Minhiriath to the south, between the Baranduin and the Greenway.

The Barrow-downs were used for burial since the First Age, before the Edain traversed the Blue Mountains and entered Beleriand. After the cataclysm that ended the Second Age (SA 3319), the Númenóreans which were not destroyed established two kingdoms (so-called 'Realms in Exile') in the west of Middle-earth (Tolkien C., 1997, p. 191): Arnor was ruled by Elendil from Annuminas in the north-west, and Gondor was ruled by his sons from Osgiliath in the south. Appendix A states: 'Those hills were therefore revered by the Dúnedain after their return; and there many of their lords and kings were buried', indicating that they held the barrows in reverence for their antiquity, which may have survived in actual or invented lore about the place (Tolkien, 2007, p. 1362). The interaction of landscape and memory created a sense of political or dynastic legitimacy for the fledgling kingdoms after the ruin of Númenór. It reinforced territorial claims to the region despite millennia of absence.

The northern royal line persisted unbroken until the end of the reign of Eärendur (TA 640-861) (Tolkien C., 1997, p. 193). Eärendur's sons established smaller independent kingdoms within Arnor: Arthedain in the north-west, ruled from Fornost; Cardolan between the River Baranduin in the west and the Rivers Gwathló (Greyflood) and Mitheithel (Hoarwell) in the south and east; Rhudaur north of the Great Road between the Weather Hills and the River Bruinen (Loudwater). The claim by the royal line of Arthedain of supremacy over Cardolan and Rhudaur was disputed by the two other kingdoms, and all three realms struggled for mastery of the palantír kept at Amon Sûl. The Witch-king used that disunity to establish the realm of Angmar during the reign of Malvegil of Arthedain, who ruled between TA 1272-1349. Malvegil's successor, Argeleb I, was slain in battle against a combined force of Rhudaur and Angmar in TA 1356 (Tolkien C., 1997).

The Tale of Years entry for TA 1409 states: 'The Witch-king of Angmar invades Arnor. King Arveleg I slain. Fornost and Tyrn Gorthad (the Barrow-downs) are defended. The Tower of Amon Sûl destroyed' (Tolkien, 2007, p. 1425; Tolkien and Tolkien, 2009, p. 194). In Appendix A, the episode is less brief:

> 'A great host came out of Angmar in 1409…The Tower of Amon Sul was burned and razed;… Cardolan was ravaged. Araphor son of Arveleg was not yet full-grown, but he was valiant, and with aid from Círdan he repelled the enemy from Fornost and the North Downs. A remnant of the faithful among the Dúnedain of Cardolan also held out in Tyrn Gorthad (the Barrow-downs), or took refuge in the Forest behind.' (Tolkien, 2007, p. 1362).

It may have been at the time of their refuge that some of their number met Tom Bombadil (discussed in more detail below). The Cardolanians appear to have held out for over 200 years, until the Dark Plague of TA 1636-1637, during which 'most of the people of Cardolan perished, especially in Minhiriath… It was at this time that an end came of the Dúnedain of Cardolan, and evil spirits out of Angmar and Rhudaur entered into the deserted mounds and dwelt there' (Tolkien, 2007, p. 1362). The haunted downs were abandoned until TA 1851 when Argaleb II won a victory over Angmar. Though the king sought to reoccupy Cardolan, 'the evil wights terrify all who seek to dwell near' (Tolkien C., 1997, p. 195). The northern kingdoms of Arnor ended in TA 1974 when the Witch-king of Angmar overran Arthedain and took Fornost. Arvedui (surnamed Last-king) attempted to save the *palantíri* of Amon Sûl and Fornost, but he drowned in the Ice-bay of Forochel in TA 1975. From then on, the line of Arnor was carried by a Chieftain of the Dúnedain rather

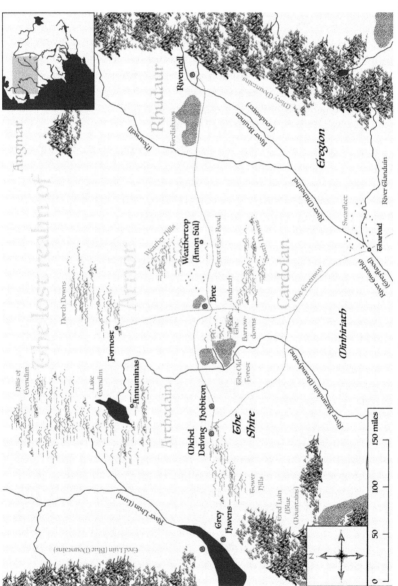

Figure 1: Map showing the location of the Barrow-downs and other locations mentioned in the text. ©Scott Chaussee 2022.

than a king; a line which culminated in the personage of Aragorn II Elessar, who was crowned High King of Gondor and Arnor after the War of the Ring (TA 3019) (Tolkien C., 2009, pp. 195-196, 202).

Identification of the barrow-wight as the Last Prince of Cardolan

The actual encounter with the barrow-wight is remarkably brief, and there is no immediate identification of it as a Cardolanian prince. The figure is only described from the perspective of Frodo:

> 'Trembling, he looked up, in time to see a tall dark figure like a shadow against the stars. It leaned over him. He thought there were two eyes, very cold though lit with a pale light that seemed to come from some remote distance' (Tolkien, 2007, p. 182).

It was not until Tom Bombadil rescues them that the reader is given a clue to the identity of the wight. When the other hobbits under the spell came to, Merry exclaimed, 'of course, I remember!... the men of Carn Dum came on us at night, and we were worsted. Ah! The spear in my heart!' (Tolkien, 2007, p. 187). After he saved the hobbits, Tom Bombadil chose a knife 'forged many long years ago by Men of Westernesse' for each of them. Tom then lamented that 'few now remember them... yet still some go wandering, sons of forgotten kings' (Tolkien, 2007, p. 190). The wandering sons of forgotten kings are clearly the rangers, the remnants of the Dúnedain of the north scattered after the death of Arvedui, discussed above (Tolkien, 2007, pp. 1352-1395).

There is no direct identification of the Great Barrow or the barrow-wight in the narrative, but the entry in the Tales of Years explicitly stated that 'some say that the mound in which the Ring-bearer was imprisoned had been the grave of the last prince of Cardolan, who fell in the war of 1409' (Tolkien, 2007, pp. 1362-1363). Indeed, the identification of the occupant of the Great Barrow is not that much of a mystery. More enigmatic is the quite recollection that came to Tom when he came across a brooch from the spoils of the barrow, which he later gave to Goldberry (Tolkien, 2007, p.190), which suggested he knew of the remnant of Cardolanians which constructed the barrow in the first place. It was perhaps a woman, the owner of the brooch, which led the band after the death of the last prince.

This paper accepts the identity of the barrow-wight as the last prince of Cardolan; Rather than focus on proving the identity, this paper will introduce the cultural influences that Tolkien drew from to construct the narrative surrounding the Barrow-downs and the wights. This discussion reinforces the suggestion that the barrow-wight was indeed the last prince of Cardolan, and this association influenced the later events of the War of the Ring.

Burials mounds elsewhere in Middle-earth

Eriador is not the sole region of Middle-earth where burial mounds were found. It has been remarked above that the earliest barrows in Minhiriath dated to the First Age. After the conclusion of the War of the Last Alliance (SA 3441), Isildur laid the remains of Elendil within a burial mound at the treeless summit of an isolated mountain – formerly called Eilenaer, afterwards Amon Anwar ('the hill of awe') (Tolkien C., 2009).

Amon Anwar laid at the centre of a formerly enlarged Kingdom of Gondor. The strength of Gondor waned through the Third Age, and so Amon Anwar was no longer the centre of the South Kingdom but amid a de-populated region, Calenardhon. In TA 2510, after the victory at the Field of Celebrant, Eorl the Young swore an oath to the steward Cirion at the tomb of Elendil and the land, which afterward was called Rohan, was granted to his people the Éothéod. Cirion subsequently removed Elendil's remains to the Hallows of Minas Tirith. Still, both peoples revered Amon Anwar which became known as Halifirien ('Holy Mountain') to the Rohirrim (Tolkien C., 2009). The concept of reverence for a particularly high-status individual is interwoven into early medieval communities' pre-Christian and conversion-period ideologies of the mortuary landscape, discussed in the next section below.

Apart from the Great Barrow, the other apparent mortuary architecture is that of the Barrow-fields of Rohan. Burial mounds are indelibly linked to the identity of the kings of Rohan, perhaps by association with the tomb of Elendil and the oath of Eorl the Young on Amon Anwar. Territorial legitimacy of the Riddermark itself is derived from an oath at the burial mound of Elendil, and his grave provided a model of mortuary architecture within which all subsequent Kings of Rohan utilised. As they approached the gates of Edoras, Gandalf pointed out the royal barrows to Aragorn, Gimli, and

Legolas, who observed the carpet of white flowers – Simbelmynë, or 'Evermind' (Tolkien, 2007, p. 662). Again, the importance of remembrance for the dead is central here – in this case, the very name of the flower which covers the mounds of past kings.

The Rohirrim are most clearly drawn from Tolkien's knowledge of early medieval society and Old English literary culture. It was early medieval communities in Britain between the fifth and eighth centuries that utilised prehistoric burial mounds as a fitting locale to build their burial mounds and accessing an extant mortuary landscape already filled with meaning (Williams, 1997; Semple, 1998; Williams, 1999; Semple, 2008; Williamson, 2008; Williams and Sayer, 2009; Semple, 2013). The following two sections will introduce the textual and archaeological contexts which arguably influenced Tolkien's ideas of the power of the special dead over communities of the living.

The powerful dead in the early medieval mind: textual references

As a professor of the Old English language, Tolkien would have been acutely aware of the manifold mentions of mortuary architecture in the Old English sources that he studied and taught. *The Lord of the Rings* is full of allusions to the corpus of Old English poetry and prose; not least of these is his partially reworked insertion of a fragment of the elegiac poem 'The Wanderer' as Aragorn, Legolas, and Gimli approach Edoras (Tolkien, 2007, p. 662). More implicitly, Tolkien intertwined ideologies of remembrance of the powerful dead and the danger of forgetting. Perhaps through his Catholicism, he would have been particularly attuned to the perceived power of the corporeal relics of saints and the sites associated with them, as well as the fear of unhallowed places. Early medieval and contemporary attitudes towards the powerful dead influenced the invention of the barrow-wights and how individuals and communities engaged with the dead throughout the story.

The Ecclesiastical History of the English People was written by a monk named Bede in the second quarter of the eighth century and is a cornerstone text for understanding the development of the Christian church in Britain and cultural attitudes to, and the spiritual power of, the special dead. As a churchman himself, Bede sought to amplify the miracles relayed to him regarding specific spiritually powerful individuals which, in turn, buoyed the still tenuous relationship between Christianity and the non-elite secular community.

The material power of the special dead is observed throughout the text. Still, it is particularly salient in the stories about King Oswald of Northumbria (ca 605-641/642), in which some parallels can be drawn with the prince of Cardolan and other aspects of the mortuary archaeology of Middle-earth. Oswald was a Christian king but was killed in battle against a pagan, King Penda of Mercia. The place where he died became notable for its potent curative ability, healing a horse and, later, the paralysis of a nearby innkeeper's daughter. Another man noticed the ground was greener and more beautiful than the rest of the field and conjectured that a holier man than the rest of the army must have died there (Bede, 2008, 125, *HE III*.10). The soil of the place brought away from the site was still potent and capable of exorcising demons (Bede, 2008, 127-128, *HE III*.11). Although Elendil died in battle at Dagorlad, the hallowed nature of a place where Oswald was killed bears a resemblance to the summit of Amon Anwar. Elendil's tomb was established on this hill before it became Halifirien and a site of reverence for both the Rohirrim and Gondorians (Tolkien C., 2009).

Oswald's bodily remains were also capable of miracles through active manipulation of the bones themselves and their proximity. Oswald's bones were discovered and taken to a church in the kingdom of Mercia, which was often at war with Northumbria. Through a miracle, the brethren accepted the sanctity of Saint Oswald, washed the bones, and placed them in a shrine; the water which washed the bones had the power of exorcising demonically possessed individuals. Later, at the same monastery, a little boy suffered from recurrent fevers and was told to sit at the tomb of Oswald, and when he did, 'the disease did not venture to attack him; indeed, it fled away in such terror that it did not dare to touch him… at any time afterwards' (Bede, 2008, 129, *HE III*.12). The dedication to the recovery, anointing, and preserving the remains of a saint suggests that if left unhallowed, lacking reference, they could have become a vector for a malign

The power of publicly memorialised and consecrated burials was firmly linked with the ideology of early medieval Christianity. Graves and barrows of unknown individuals, by the same token, had the potential for detrimental effects. The latter part of the *Beowulf* poem features two barrows that bookend the section. It opens with the description of a thief who entered 'the steep vaults of a stone-roofed barrow' and disturbed a dragon; the thief escaped with a gem-studded cup, and the dragon became enraged (Heaney, 2002, p. 56). While Bilbo's encounter with Smaug in *The Hobbit* echoes this episode (Tolkien, 2011, pp. 204-213), the other circumstances bear a more remarkable resemblance to the barrow-wight encounter.

The *Beowulf* poet conjectured an identity for the individual interred in the barrow, which later became the home of the dragon. The passage was a clear model for the destruction of Cardolan and the barrow of the Last Prince. The past was even envisioned by the poet, who described the newly constructed barrow and an unnamed individual who despondently filled it with treasure. The poet imagined the person said:

> 'My own people / have been ruined in war; one by one / they went down to death... / ... I am left with nobody / to bear a sword... /... the companies have departed. ... / the coat of mail that came through all fights, /. Through shield-collapse and cut of sword, / decays with the warrior. .../ ... Pillage and slaughter have emptied the earth of entire peoples.'/ and so he mourned as he moved about the world, / deserted and alone, lamenting his unhappiness, day and night, until death's flood/ brimmed up in his heart. (Heaney, 2002, pp. 57-58).

The memory, or an insufficient capacity to reproduce it, is the context for why the barrow or the goods within are dangerous. A few lines later in *Beowulf*, it is stated '... there were many other/ heirlooms heaped inside the earth-house,/ because long ago, some forgotten person had deposited the whole/ rich inheritance of a highborne race/ in this ancient cache' (Heaney, 2002, p. 57). This mournful illustration parallels the Great Barrow and the lost community of Cardolan. Much like the remnant of the Cardolanian refugees, the community that built the barrow in *Beowulf* was decimated by war. Because there was no longer a living community to mediate the memory of the dead, a dragon could infest the barrow in *Beowulf*; in *The Lord of the Rings*, the spirits from Angmar were able to infest the downs and become the barrow-wights because the living community which buried the Prince of Cardolan died off.

Although the spirits were able to occupy the barrows and the remains of the individuals therein, the mounds themselves were not evil places. Pope Gregory, who sent Christian missionaries to Britain in AD 597, wrote that the pagan temples were not to be destroyed, only the idols in them (McClure and Collins, 2008, p. 57). The priests were to take 'holy water and sprinkle it in these shrines, build altars and place relics in them. For if the shrines are well built, it is essential that they should be changed from the worship of devils...' (*ibid*). The washing of St Oswald's bones and the conversion of pagan sanctuaries to the provision of Christian practice is similar to the purification of the Great Barrow and its relics by Tom Bombadil. By converting places and objects worthy of reverence to a perceived greater purpose, the hobbits and the mission of the West vis-à-vis that purification process.

One of the more unequivocal stories from Old English sources of this exorcism and conversion process, is that of Guthlac of Crowland (AD 674-714). The hagiography of Guthlac embodies the interface between secular and divine and the role of burial mounds in mediating struggles for social power. Guthlac spent his young adulthood as the leader of a warband. Guthlac, his hagiographer wrote, 'thought about the valiant deeds of the heroes of old and of the great men of the world', leading his troop to plunder and destruction of his enemies (Swanton, 1979, p. 42). After 9 years of war-making, Guthlac awoke one morning with a thought of 'the ancient kings of old, who forsook this world with a wretched death and with a miserable departure left this wicked life'; at 24 years old, he forsook his noble heritage and his material goods and joined the monastery at Repton (modern Derbyshire, England) (Swanton, 1979, pp. 42-43).

After two years as a monk at the monastery in Repton, Guthlac resolved to become a hermit in the wilderness of the fens of eastern England. On an island in the fens, 'a great burial-mound built over the earth, which men of old had dug into and broken up looking for treasure' (Swanton, 1979, p. 44). It was there that Guthlac built himself a house. Once he occupied the burial mound, the hagiographer uses the language of spiritual warfare in describing Guthlac's conduct which suggests the wilderness generally, and the mound, in particular, was a contested place:

> So that he might shield himself against the darts of the wicked spirits with spiritual arms, he took the shield of faith...dressed himself in the mail of heavenly hope; and he put on his head the helmet of pure thoughts; and he continually shot and fought against the accursed spirits with the arrows of holy psalms. (Swanton, 1979, p. 45).

Guthlac was almost immediately set upon by demons ('the ancient foe of mankind') and struck by a phantom weapon, wounding him with despair; on another day, two devils tempted him with false teachings; finally, on another night, Guthlac was accosted by 'great multitudes of accursed spirits' that spoke in Celtic [Brythonic, or Old Welsh] – Guthlac understood their speech for having been exiled among Brythonic-speaking peoples – but it was the fact that Guthlac 'fought and contended with the accursed spirits so frequently, they realised that their power and activity was vanquished' (Swanton, 1979, pp. 45-50).

Guthlac's experiences at the burial mound demonstrate the centrality of active agency in mediating spiritual power at these contested places and gaining territorial legitimacy, even in a small way. The barrow wights bear a striking resemblance to Guthlac's 'Celtic' demons. The demons against whom Guthlac strove were perhaps ghosts of the earlier populations settled in Britain and buried their dead in mounds, but they were forgotten. Guthlac's mound was in a fen, unsuited for agriculture, but the spirits therein had to be contended with and defeated for the legitimacy of Guthlac to be demonstrated. Once Crowland Abbey was founded at the mound site, it housed a cartulary; that is, the monks recorded transactions of land within the territory of the secular kings; through Guthlac's hagiography, his dominance of the spirits at the barrow is remembered (Sawyer, 1998). Through its later Christian appropriation – first, through the spiritual contest of Guthlac and second, the establishment of the abbey – the burial mound became a tool of social power that the kings of Mercia utilised to negotiate territorial legitimacy.

Where burial mounds were not or could not be consecrated through the actions of holy individuals, they remained a threat to physical and spiritual security. Indeed, by the ninth and tenth centuries AD, burial mounds became a source of social power in a different way (Semple, 1998). Rather than a delicate matter of shifting pagan practice endorsed by Pope Gregory centuries earlier, the attempt by the Christian sources to portray the barrow as a dangerous place, but not one that was out of the hands of the Christian church to conquer, or the secular elite to use as a tool of fear and punishment.

Archaeological influences on the imagery of the Great Barrow and the Barrow-downs

The previous section has demonstrated that the links between mortuary architecture, memory, and legitimacy are crucial to understanding early medieval communities, as well as the attitudes of later communities to evident but enigmatic archaeological remains (Williams, 2005; 2007; Reynolds, 2018), and it is posited that these themes are fundamental to critical interactions in the mythos of Middle-earth. The influences from Old English textual sources on the mortuary behaviour of the societies of Middle-earth were also demonstrated. This section will explore the influences of the physical landscape and the materiality of the Great Barrow episode, drawn from Tolkien's postulated interactions with archaeologists and early medieval material culture while at Oxford in the 1930s.

The Great Barrow episode recounted above indicates the topographic situation, orientation, and morphology of at least some of the mounds (Tolkien, 2007, pp. 178-179). In the geography of Middle-earth, Tolkien has stated that Rivendell should be viewed as on the same latitude as Oxford. In a 1937 letter to Stanley Unwin postulating a sequel to *The Hobbit*, Tolkien questioned whether Tom Bombadil, 'the spirit of the (vanishing) Oxford and Berkshire countryside, could be made into the hero of the story' (Carpenter and Tolkien C., 1981, Letter 19, p. 32). So, while burial mounds exist all over Britain, the inspiration for the Barrow-downs should be sought in areas south of England, particularly the counties of Berkshire, Oxfordshire, Hampshire, Surrey, and Sussex.

Burial mounds occur in diverse shapes and sizes. While the chalk downland of the English south downs provides the topographic context for the Barrow-downs, the description of the Great Barrow appears to reference an extant monument known as 'Waylands Smithy', 30 miles south-west of Oxford (Figure 0.1). Wayland's Smithy belongs to a class of burial monuments termed 'long barrows' and dates to the Neolithic period (ca 4,000-2,500 BC). Fourteen people (11 men, two women, and a child) were discovered when archaeologically examined in 1962-1963 (Whittle, 1991). Interestingly, radiocarbon dating placed the burials within the span of a single generation, perhaps as short a period as 15 years. Multi-generational mixed burials are features of long barrows and chambered tombs (such as a similar but earlier site at West Kennet, Wiltshire (Thomas &Whittle, 1986), but the short and intensive construction and inhumation suggest some type of catastrophe. Three or more people potentially suffered lethal arrowhead strikes, and the remains of two individuals were subject to animal scavenging before final burial (Whittle, 1991).

Although there are many chambered tombs in the chalk downland of southern England, the proximity of Wayland's Smithy to Oxford makes it the most likely candidate as forming a component of the visual influence, though the interior bears more resemblance to a chambered tomb similar to West Kennet, but several orders of magnitude larger than any surviving monument in England. In size, the Great Barrow is more likely akin to the massive mortuary structures of Ireland, such as at Newgrange, which is 86 m in diameter and 13 m tall (Eogan and Doyle, 2010). Despite its internal differences, Wayland's Smithy is set within a landscape rich in archaeology such as the hill-fort and chalk figure at Uffington, as well as the prehistoric routeway and political boundary between rival early medieval kingdoms, known as the Ridgeway (Pollard and Reynolds, 2002). Wayland's Smithy is so named due to associations with a supernatural smith in Anglo-Saxon legends, Wayland (Grinsell, 1976).

The association of Wayland's Smithy with the production of metalwork items with supernatural power dovetails finely with the relics taken away by the hobbits to the end of their respective journeys. The daggers taken by the hobbits from the tomb were described as 'long, leaf-shaped, and keen, of marvellous workmanship, damasked with serpent-forms in red and gold' (Tolkien, 2007, p. 190). Intertwined beasts and serpent forms are common features of high-status early medieval metalwork, predominantly ascribed to related decorative styles known as Sahlin's Style I and II (Hoilund Nielsen, 1999). One of the most celebrated assemblages of Sahlins-style metalwork ever discovered until the Staffordshire Hoard (in 2009) came from the early seventh-century ship Burial at Sutton Hoo, Suffolk, which was excavated between 1938-1939 (Bruce-Mitford, 1978; Carver, 1998). In particular, the grandest examples of metalwork from these hoards were decorated with garnet-inlaid cloisonné, forming rich imagery of serpent-like creatures in red and gold.

In a later draft letter to Peter Hastings dated 1954, Tolkien further clarified the nature of Tom Bombadil as 'an exemplar, a particular embodying of pure (real) natural science: the spirit that desires knowledge of other things, their history and nature, because they are 'other' and wholly independent of the enquiring mind' (Carpenter and Tolkien C., 1981, Letter 153, pp. 207-208). One can presume that the materiality of the Anglo-Saxon period would have interested Tolkien, and he would have followed the news of the excavations at Sutton Hoo keenly. The Ashmolean Museum in Oxford is only a few hundred metres from the Eagle and Child pub, which hosted meetings of the Inklings literary club. Deep time, and how later communities reckoned with the extant remains of past societies is a constant through-line in the narrative of *The Lord of the Rings* and is central to modern academic studies of archaeology.

Tolkien was describing the modern principles of archaeology when Tom Bombadil, the embodiment of the enquiring mind and natural science, recovered artefacts from the great barrow. Perhaps he was channelling an Oxford contemporary, J.N.L. Myres, an early and still-influential scholar of the archaeology of early medieval England. In addition to the textual material which influenced Tolkien's construction of the episode at the Great Barrow, awareness of the rapidly expanding and increasingly scientific discipline of archaeology gave him a rich assemblage of artefacts that he may have used to develop his vocabulary. In his masterful way, he synthesised landscapes, sites, and individual objects to create an evocative setting that became integral to the success of the other hobbits through the recovery of the ancient knives from the barrow.

Discussion: the importance of active remembrance for the living and the dead

The episode of the Great Barrow from *The Lord of the Rings* fits into millennia-old traditions of mythmaking which surround mortuary architecture and fits the fictional societies of Middle-earth into wider contexts regarding perceptions of funerary behaviour and burial sites in contemporary Earth. The active reproduction of memory by living communities was central to protecting the powerful dead and living communities from them. The evil spirits could only enter the Barrow-downs after it was de-populated. The power of the active role of individuals in preserving the memory of the buried. The purification of the site and the mediation of its contents through the actions of the hobbits in the rest of the story is central to the narrative theme of the power of memory and active agency.

Artefacts, recovered through the means of genuinely enquiring minds, and curated with sympathy to the memory of the original owners is a central tenet of modern archaeology and speaks to the desire of Tolkien to produce a unifying narrative across deep time. The warning of the episode in the barrow is against the dangers of forgetting, and the power of active agents in the reproduction of memory. Current archaeological theory considers burial mounds to be focal points for the mediation of territory. Tom Bombadil represents the landscape, and the barrows of the Cardolanians represent the legitimate claim to territory. Without the active engagement of people and their agency in the reproduction of the memory of those claims, the territory becomes lost; a liminal place that can then become infested with supernatural monstrosities, just as the fenland barrow where the Anglo-Saxon saint Guthlac made his hermitage.

When the Gondorians at the end of the Second Age removed Elendil's remains from Amon Anwar at the end of the Second Age, they placed them in sepulchral isolation within the Houses of the Dead, in the highest level of Minas Tirith. This created insularity in the reproduction of their memory. The territorial integrity of Gondor, perhaps as a consequence of this insularity, began to weaken. A parallel might be drawn between the final years of Númenor before the advent of the worship of Sauron, when the Númenoreans converted their active memorialisation of their dead to an envy of the Eldar and an obsession with immortality. Though the Númenoreans filled their land with tombs, the remains were preserved uncorrupted, in mockery of death and not ever submitting to it (Tolkien C. 2009, pp. 274-275).

At the end of the Third Age, the divergent nature of the mortuary behaviour exhibited by the rulers of Rohan and Gondor mirrored the relative successes of their ruling classes. The Rohirrim actively *remembered* their kings, through the presence of the burial mounds at the foot of, but not within, the walls of Edoras. Rather than an outward-looking, public memorial originally conceived by Isildur, the memory of the kings and later stewards of Gondor became an insular practice, removed from frequent acts of public memorialisation which marked the remembrance of the kings of Rohan. The final mockery occurred during the period of Denethor's madness when he tried to burn a still-living Faramir in the Houses of the Dead, an act of, perhaps sacrilegious, sacrifice which ultimately caused the death of Denethor and the end of the Stewards of Gondor.

In archaeology and history, burial mounds have proven themselves as potent symbols for claims to legitimacy in the landscape and the mediation among living communities and between the living and dead. The hobbits were active agents in the mediation of the last prince's memory. This mediation was crucial in mending the world broken by Sauron. Tolkien's narrative is too considered to allow for coincidence; therefore, it is significant that Pippin used the knife from the Great Barrow to swear service to Denethor, the steward of Gondor. Also, it was the knife that Merry recovered from the Great Barrow which injured the Witch-king at the Battle of the Pelannor Fields. As a descendent people of a northern folk, it may also be significant that Eowyn landed the killing blow, in recognition of the grief of the woman who led the Cardolanian band after the death of the prince. But, just as the Anglo-Saxon King Oswald's corporeal remains united formerly opposed kingdoms through the perceived virtue of their blessedness, the memory of the Last Prince, through the active agency of the hobbits and the purification of relics from the Great Barrow, finally prevailed against the ancient enemy of Cardolan. By activating the memory of Cardolan, the hobbits connected past and present, bridged the rift between the realms of Arnor, and ultimately forged the reunification of the Northern and Southern kingdoms.

References

Alexander, M., 1972. *The earliest English poems*. London: Penguin Books.

Bede, 2008. *Historia Ecclesiastica*, trans. Colgrave, B. In: McClure, J. and Collins, R., trans. and eds., *The Ecclesiastical history of the English people, the greater chronicle, Bede's letter to Egbert*. Oxford: Oxford University Press.

Bruce-Mitford, R., 1978. *The Sutton Hoo Ship Burial: Volume II, arms, armour, and regalia*. London: British Museum Press.

Carpenter, H. and Tolkien, C. eds., 1981. *The Letters of J. R. R. Tolkien*. London: George Allen & Unwin.

Carver, M., 1998. *Sutton Hoo: Burial ground of Kings?* Philadelphia, PA: University of Pennsylvania Press

Davidson, H., 1950. The hill of the dragon: Anglo-Saxon burial mounds in literature and archaeology. *Folklore* 61(4), pp.169-185.

Eogan, G. and Doyle, P., 2010. *Guide to the Passage Tombs at Brú na Bóinne*. Dublin: Wordwell.

Grinsell, L.V., 1976. *Folklore of Prehistoric Sites in Britain*, London: David & Charles.

Heaney, S. and Donaghue, D., trans. and ed., 2002. *Beowulf: A new verse translation*. New York: W.W. Norton & Company.

Høilund Nielsen, K., 1999. Style II and the Anglo-Saxon elite. *Anglo-Saxon Studies in Archaeology and History* 10, pp.185-202.

Pollard, J. and Reynolds, A., 2002. *Avebury: The biography of a landscape*. Stroud: Tempus.

Reynolds, A., 2018. Lineage, genealogy, and landscape: a high-resolution archaeological model for the emergence of supra-local society from early medieval England. *World Archaeology*, 50(1), pp.121-136.

Sawyer, P.H., 1998. *Anglo-Saxon Lincolnshire*, Lincoln: History of Lincolnshire Committee.

Semple, S., 1998. A fear of the past: The place of the prehistoric burial mound in the ideology of middle and later Anglo-Saxon England. *World Archaeology* 30(1), pp.109-126.
—, 2008. Polities and princes AD 400-800: New perspectives on the funerary landscape of the South Saxon kingdom. *Oxford Journal of Archaeology* 27(4), pp.407-429.

152   Scott Chaussée

—, 2013. *Perceptions of the prehistoric in Anglo-Saxon England: Religion, ritual, and rulership in the landscape*. Oxford: Oxford University Press.

Speake, G., 1980. *Anglo-Saxon Animal Art and its Germanic Background*. Oxford: Clarendon Press.

Swanton, trans., 1979. The life of St Guthlac. In: Swanton, ed. *Anglo-Saxon Prose*. London: J.M. Dent & Sons.

Thomas, J. and Whittle, A., 1986. Anatomy of a tomb: West Kennet revisited. *Oxford Journal of Archaeology* 5, pp.129-156.

Tolkien, C., ed., 1997. *The peoples of Middle-earth – The History of Middle-earth Vol. XII.* London: HarperCollins.
—, 1999. *The Silmarillion*, London: HarperCollins.
—, 2009. *The unfinished tales of Numenor and Middle-earth*. London: HarperCollins.

Tolkien, J.R.R., 2007. *The Lord of the Rings*. 50th Anniversary Edition. London: HarperCollins.
—, 2011. *The hobbit, or, there and back again*. 75th Anniversary Edition. London: HarperCollins.

Whittle, A., 1991. Wayland's Smithy, Oxfordshire: excavations at the Neolithic tomb in 1962-63 by RJC Atkinson and S Piggott. *Proceedings of the Prehistoric Society*, 57(2), pp.61-101.

Whittle, A., Bayliss, A. and Wysocki, M., 2007. Once in a lifetime: the date of the Wayland's Smithy long barrow. *Cambridge Archaeological Journal*, 17 Supplement S1, pp.103-121.

Williams, H., 1999. Identities and cemeteries in Roman and early medieval archaeology. In: Baker, P., Forcey, C., Jundi, S. and Witcher, R. eds. TRAC 98: *Proceedings of the Eighth Annual Theoretical Roman Archaeology Conference*, pp.96-108.
—, 2005. Keeping the dead at arm's length: Memory, weaponry, and early medieval mortuary technologies. *Journal of Social Archaeology* 5(2), pp.253-275.
—, 2007. Introduction: themes in the archaeology of early medieval death and burial. *Anglo-Saxon Studies in Archaeology and History*, 14, pp.1-11.

Williamson, T., 2008. *Sutton Hoo and its landscape: The context of monuments*. Oxford: Windgather Press.

What is so fabulous about Smaug?

A J Dalton

The fabulous beast that is the dragon is pretty much as old as writing itself, perhaps older if it represents an ancestral memory of the prehistoric giants who once ruled the Earth. As with such a memory, the literary motif or fable of the dragon endures up to the current day, in popular works such as George R.R. Martin's *A Game of Thrones* (1996), Paolini's *Eragon* (2002), and many more. We might ask how and why the dragon has endured, since finding answers to such questions will allow us to understand the 'nature' of the dragon, what value(s) it represents for us, what function it serves, and what truths, directly or indirectly, it reveals about us. This article will trace and consider the literary origins and tradition of the dragon, from the New Testament of the Bible, through the legend of St George, to the epic poem *Beowulf* and up to Tolkien's novel *The Hobbit* (1937), in order to answer the questions just immediately asked, then to conclude by identifying just what is so fabulous about Smaug.

The term 'dragon' derives from the Greek 'drakōn', with the original meaning 'serpent'. Similarly, the New Testament (NT) claims the serpent of the Old Testament's (OT) Garden of Eden to be one of Satan's avatars, and then describes him variously as 'an enormous red dragon with seven heads and ten horns and seven crowns', 'a dragon that can spew water like a river', 'the beast', a demon who can possess humans, one who can mark the heads and hands of his followers and 'a thorn in the flesh' (Biblica, 1978).

We might wonder why the NT chooses to demonise the serpent or snake so literally. The snake, of course, was synonymous with the Greco-Egyptian god Serapis, as a symbol of rulership and power, as well as the Greek god of healing and doctors, Asclepius (Dalton, 2020, p. 7). Therefore, in demonising the snake or dragon, personifying it as Satan, the Bible is effectively engaged in a certain propaganda against non-Christian faiths, particularly those which are described in the Book of Revelation as, due to the influence and leadership of Satan, responsible for the persecution of Christians.

> To the angel of the church in Pergamon write:
> These are the words of him who has the sharp, double-edged sword. I
> know where you live – where Satan has his throne. Yet you remain true
> to my name. You did not renounce your faith in me, not even in the days
> of Antipas, my faithful witness, who was put to death in your city – where
> Satan lives. (Biblica, Revelation 2: 12-13).

The Christian priest Antipas, whose name translates as 'against all', was horrifically tortured and executed in 92AD in the ancient Greek city of Pergamon (now in eastern Turkey) by pagan priests and the followers of Serapis for refusing, when tested, to declare the Roman emperor as lord and god above all (Renner, 2010). Consequently, we begin to understand Satan and his acts as both a metaphorical personification and actual description of the physical and political persecution that Christians were suffering during the extended period of the NT's writing. Just as the nature of that persecution of and the opposition to Christianity changes with time, so the qualities of Satan shift and expand so that all anti-Christian acts may be included. Ultimately, Satan must come to be the antagonist (the Dark Lord) set against everything that Christianity represents, and must perform the attempt to bring down heaven itself to replace God the King in some sort of military coup. Thus, the dramatic climax or the 'story' of the war in heaven at the end of the Bible (Revelation), when Satan attempts a coup, is logically inevitable.

> Then war broke out in heaven, Michael and his angels fought against the
> dragon, and the dragon and his angels fought back. But he was not strong
> enough, and they lost their place in heaven. The great dragon was hurled
> down – that ancient serpent called the devil, or Satan, who leads the whole
> world astray. He was hurled to the earth and his angels with him. (Biblica,
> Revelation 12).

As above, having been hurled down to the earth, Satan made his home in the city of Pergamon, turning that city into the place of 'dark' torture and moral ruination that Satan sought to visit upon heaven's shining 'city' (Matthew 5). Yet, Pergamon was more than just a city: it was a centre for the pre-Christian Roman Empire, and it worshipped the Roman Emperor in a number of temples. The pre-Christian Roman emperors, therefore, particularly those who persecuted Christians (and saw to Jesus being sent to his death), are effectively agents of Satan, or Satan himself, presiding over a dark and evil empire. The ambition of such agents and agency is/was to extinguish Christianity throughout the world of Man, and to rule the human earth entirely.

Naturally enough, the Bible cannot allow or afford to have the Satanic dragon and its influence continuing to thrive in Pergamon and, thereby, throughout the wider Roman Empire. The will of God has to be seen as ultimately prevailing. As the NT was completed in c.120AD, approximately two hundred years *before* the Roman Empire converted to Christianity, the writers and compilers of the Bible were faced with a particular 'creative' difficulty since, at that time, Pergamon was still ruled by its (Satanic) Roman emperor. The only way out of that difficulty, of course, was for there to be a vision (or prophecy) of the future in the book of Revelation, a vision in which we see Satan defeated once more, this time once and for all. There has to be a final, climactic, all-consuming battle, with the complete annihilation of the enemy, thus eliminating any possible threat thereafter. In short, there must be an end of days and an end to all possibility of human sin. Inevitably, the earth as it currently is must end, with the Kingdom of Heaven triumphing over all.

> I saw heaven standing open and there before me was a white horse, whose rider is called Faithful and True. With justice he judges and wages war. […] The armies of heaven were following him, riding on white horses and dressed in fine linen, white and clean. […] Then I saw the beast and the kings of the earth and their armies gathered together to wage war against the rider on the horse and his army. But the beast was captured, and with it the false prophet who had performed the signs on its behalf. With these signs he had deluded those who had received the mark of the beast and worshiped its image. The two of them were thrown alive into the fiery lake of burning sulfur. […] And I saw an angel coming down out of heaven, having the key to the Abyss and holding in his hand a great chain. He seized the dragon, that ancient serpent, who is the devil, or Satan, and bound him for a thousand years. He threw him into the Abyss, and locked and sealed it over him, to keep him from deceiving the nations anymore until the thousand years were ended. After that, he must be set free for a short time. (Biblica, Revelation 19-21).

It is from the Bible, then, that we not only get the character of Satan as the dragon and Dark Lord, but also the character of the heavenly warrior as a virtuous knight upon a white horse (the 'white knight' or 'Chosen One'). And this knight fights the dragon and defeats it. Surely, we are put in mind of the later character of St George, who similarly defeats the 'dragon of the abyss', a dragon who (according to the seventh century hagiography of St George (Société des Bollandistes, 1895)) is a monarch that persecuted the saint for his Christianity. Historically, St George (c.256-303AD) was a Roman officer-soldier of Greek origin called Georgius. He was a Christian and was martyred (on 23 April) in eastern Asia Minor by Emperor Diocletian, for not recanting his faith.

There are strong echoes of the persecution of Antipas in Pergamon in the life story of St George. However, where the bloody and sacrificial death of Antipas served to personify, celebrate and witness that Dark Lord who is Satan, the stoic death of Georgius served to inspire witnesses to convert to Christianity, to see him beatified and to see the dragon ultimately defeated. Less than a decade after Georgius's martyrdom, in 313AD Emperor Constantine issued the Edict of Milan, and Christianity quickly became the official religion of the Roman Empire. It is at this point that Satan's dark empire is overthrown, the holy Roman Empire begins, and Rome becomes the 'holy city' (Revelation 21) at the centre of God's new kingdom on earth.

It is for the above reasons that St George became a patron saint in England, Georgia (the country named after him, where the first medieval account of St George fighting a physical, rather than metaphorical, dragon was written), and 22 other countries. It is why he is venerated in Anglicanism, Eastern Orthodoxy, Lutheranism, Oriental Orthodoxy, Roman Catholicism and Umbanda. It is why there are chapels and places of worship dedicated to him around the world. And it is why this soldier-saint became the symbolic figurehead of the Christian crusades, Rome's attempt to claim Jerusalem for Christianity. For Christian soldiers, bravery, suffering and sacrifice would see Christianity defeat the dragon and save the kingdom from its fire and torment forever. Success in Jerusalem would see the entire known world brought within Christianity, and Satan's own ministry and kingdom put to an end. The earth as it was would be ended and Jerusalem would be the 'new Jerusalem' of Revelation 21, when the earth would be a heaven and all those who had given their lives would live in the eternal city and kingdom.

For the writers, editors and compilers of the Christian Bible, the white knight who defeats the Satanic dragon or Dark Lord in a climactic battle, thereby seeing the kingdom of earth saved and made a paradise (the Kingdom of Heaven), was dramatically satisfying, powerful political propaganda, a persuasive mix of historical fact and prophetic fiction, and ideologically coherent, compelling and complete. It was a masterpiece in thematic, creative and even literary terms.

For the newly-Christianised Rome, its subsequent popes and soldiery, the Bible was an inspiring historical narrative, a political manifesto, a mission statement, a visionary guide for self-improving day-to-day conduct, legal and moral justification for the Christianising of Rome, legitimacy for all Church-sanctioned actions, and a contract with a priceless reward-upon-completion. As a result, Pope Urban II understood the Bible's description of Satan being chained in the abyss for a thousand years (Revelation 20) as literal. He understood the warning '[Satan] could not fool the nations anymore until 1000 years were completed' and 'After this he must be free a while' as an all-too-real clear-and-present-danger, and as a literal instruction to act without delay once the thousand years were up. Therefore, precisely a thousand years after the writing of the Book of Revelation, Pope Urban II launched the first crusade to 'free' Jerusalem, in 1095 A.D. His soldiers had St George (upon 'a white horse') as their figurehead and rallying cry, they wore the 'fine linen, white and clean' and the red cross of 'a robe dipped in blood' (as described in Revelation 19-21), and they were considered the actual holy army of the Bible's white knight 'called Faithful and True'. This was no metaphor. Fantasy and reality, history and the future, the physical and the spiritual, mortal life and eternity were all one and the same. Thus, at the time of the crusade, Satan, the dragon and his numerous demonic agents were considered real and loose in the world.

Naturally, it was around the time of the first crusade that the legend of St George and the Dragon became most popular and current. Icons and images started to proliferate as a vivid and visual retelling of the Bible narrative that would reach the illiterate and those who had no direct access to the text of the Bible. The legend served as dehumanising propaganda concerning the alien, bestial, dark-skinned and lowly enemy (we may be put in mind of the goblins in Tolkien's *The Hobbit*), and it readily lent itself to shifts in symbology so that it could be tailored or personalised to the soldiery and customs of the different nations of Christendom. By way of example, there are two obvious shifts in the telling or depiction of the legend. First, the dragon is sometimes instead portrayed as a giant snake, better understood by those of a Greco-Roman culture and tradition, as per the cruel pagan gods of Pergamon previously mentioned, as per the original Greek meaning of 'dragon', and as per the Garden of Eden narrative. Second, the green-hilled kingdom that is being saved is sometimes instead portrayed as a princess-bride suffering the lascivious and rapine attentions of a sexualised dragon (complete with penetrative barbed tail, overbright eye and extended forked tongue).

Tellingly, the figure of the princess-bride does not exist in the original Georgian text or visual depictions of the legend (10th-11th cent.), but she is quickly introduced to the Latin versions that circulated in France and England during the 12th and 13th centuries (Jacobus de Voragine's *The Golden Legend*, c.1260, and Vincent de Beauvais's *Speculum Historiale*, at about the same time, just two of many examples). The figure of the princess-bride of course performs a range of symbolic and propagandist functions: she humanises the quest to free Jerusalem, just as the dragon dehumanises the enemy; she represents a more personal promise of reward and motivation for the crusaders than the simple claiming of foreign hills. With St George defending her honour (as per the medieval traditions of 'courtly love'), she enables the representation of a moral and superior set of behaviours that justify and legitimate the destruction of the enemy, while romanticising, spiritualising and validating the male struggle and sacrifice the crusaders must endure in order to see her protected and enshrined in a blessed future. These functions are entirely understood in Jacobus de Voragine's *The Golden Legend*, for the confrontation is replete with both religious and psycho-sexual imagery. At first, the princess-bride tries to send St George away, so that he might be spared and to show she is not one to 'court' others for selfish gain, to show that she is an 'honest' woman. Then the venom-spewing dragon emerges from the nearby pool, intent on having the princess-bride, St George makes the sign of the cross and charges on horseback, wounding the dragon with his 'lance'. He calls for the princess-bride to throw him her 'girdle' and he loops it around the dragon's neck, so that it will follow her as a 'meek beast' upon a leash. They lead the dragon to the city and St George offers to kill the dragon upon condition the terrified King and people convert to Christianity, which they duly do. Upon the spot where St George slays the dragon, the King then builds a church to the Virgin Mary, and a spring flows from its altar with water that cures all the disease originally caused by the dragon's venom.

It is from this version of the St George legend, which can be interpreted as another version of the Book of Revelation chapters 19-21, that the character of Satan is first furnished with the particularly venal and carnal ambitions with which modern audiences are familiar, those Satanic desires that inevitably tempt and corrupt humankind. In the Book of Revelation, 'the Whore' of Babylon is largely synonymous with Satan, but she does not possess the sexually proactive and predatory qualities that are exhibited by the dragon in *The Golden Legend*. It is the latter narrative, then, that represents the full sexualisation of Satan, the moment when audiences begin to think of hell as potentially being full of all sorts of sexual degradation, decadence and perversion. This characterisation adds to the image of Satan as some sort of Great Seducer testing and tempting us towards our own doom (which might also represent an echo and evolution of the Old Testament function of the adversarial 'satan', a nameless member of God's holy court who acts as a testing Divine Prosecutor). At the same time, this construction of Satan invests him with a greater physicality than previously, making him even more real, and making immediate one of the ways in which he seeks to possess us and make his desires our own desires. More than that, we come to understand even better how he also has shape-changing abilities, for is he not able to adopt any form or gender with which to seduce us most? He could be anyone around us, which is a terrifying thought, one that can only inspire greater faith.

All the seductions and temptations offered by Satan in both the Bible and the St George are also represented in the epic poem *Beowulf* (700-1000CE), the true date of which is disputed, with the debate seeing the poem as either contemporaneous with the (earliest) Georgian hagiography of St George or with the first crusade. However, the poem ascribes sexual temptation and corruption to Grendell's mother (the implied seducer and mistress of the adulterous King of Denmark, Hrothgar, their corrupting sexual act seeing the monstrous Grendell born, and horrific murder and punishment consequently visited upon the wider community/body politic) and a selfish or avaricious desire for gold, personal wealth and power to the dragon (the sort of corruption described during Jesus's 'cleansing of the Temple', when he throws out the merchants and money-lenders, described in each of the Synoptic Gospels). The hero Beowulf defeats Grendell and then, prepared to sacrifice himself if necessary, descends into the lake of the vengeful 'hell-dam' mother (Heaney, 1999, l.1292) when none else will. Beowulf's sword fails him during the (implied) psycho-sexual combat, but he ultimately triumphs. Hrothgar rewards Beowulf, warning him 'not [to] give way to pride' (1.1760) and always to reward his thanes unselfishly, after which Beowulf returns home and becomes king of his own people. Yet Beowulf proves to be a less generous king than Hrothgar ever was, proud of the treasure that he sees as mainly having been won by himself, meaning that the upshot (or offspring born) of his final encounter with Grendell's mother is a dragon hoarding the wealth of his kingdom. A desperate 'slave fleeing the hand the heavy hand of some [ungenerous] master' (1.2224) is forced to hide in the dragon's burrow and steals a 'gold-plated cup' (1.2282) and, against the natural order of gift-giving within society, gives the cup to his master, in order to be better accepted and treated. Discovering the theft, the dragon, in righteous vengeance, sets to harrowing the kingdom, and Beowulf proudly insists on facing the dragon alone, spurning his thanes further still. Yet, as Grendell was of Hrothgar's own making, so too is the dragon of Beowulf's making. Thus, in destroying the dragon, Beowulf suffers a mortal wound and undoes himself also.

The biblical parallels and symbolism (concerning the corrupt and corrupting female, as well as the dragon) within *Beowulf* should be apparent from the above; the poem also makes regular, explicit references to Cain and Abel, Noah and the flood, the devil, hell and the Last Judgement, along with providing imprecations to God. At the same time, the narrative is set in a pre-Christian, sixth-century Scandinavia, and is written in the West Saxon dialect of Old English, rather than the more scholarly Latin of Christian monks or transcribers. Hence, we can understand why there was such debate concerning the historical (rather than literary) origin of the poem, and why the poem is described as a 'transitional' poem in terms of social and religious change within both the British Isles and western Europe. Significantly, it was Professor of Anglo-Saxon at the University of Oxford J.R.R. Tolkien, himself a devout

Roman Catholic, who in his 1936 lecture entitled 'Beowulf: The Monsters and the Critics' made the case for a literary (rather than historical) appreciation and consideration of the poem. The lecture is understood as a (trans)formative work in modern studies of the poem (Niles, 1998; Shippey, 1998; Lerer, 1998; Solopova, 2009).

> Beowulf's dragon, if one wishes really to criticize, is not to be blamed for being a dragon, but rather for not being dragon enough, plain pure fairy-story dragon. There are in the poem some vivid touches of the right kind— as *þa se wyrm onwoc, wroht wæs geniwad; stonc æfter stane*, 2285—in which this dragon is a real worm, with a bestial life and thought of his own, but the conception, none the less, approaches *draconitas* rather than *draco*: a personification of malice, greed, destruction (the evil side of heroic life), and of the undiscriminating cruelty of fortune that distinguishes not good or bad (the evil aspect of all life). But for Beowulf, the poem, that is as it should be. In this poem the balance is nice, but it is preserved. The large symbolism is near the surface, but it does not break through, nor become allegory. Something more significant than a standard hero, a man faced with a foe more evil than any human enemy of house or realm, is before us, and yet incarnate in time, walking in heroic history, and treading the named lands of the North. And this, we are told, is the radical defect of Beowulf, that its author, coming in a time rich in the legends of heroic men, has used them afresh in an original fashion, giving us not just one more, but something akin yet different: a measure and interpretation of them all. (Tolkien, 1936, p. 7).

A year after Tolkien gave his seminal lecture, *The Hobbit* was published, and we are presented with his terrifying vision of the fire-breathing, demonically malign, jealous, power-hungry, winged 'worm' Smaug. And Smaug is just as jealously treasure-hoarding – and vengeful when robbed – as the dragon found in *Beowulf*, a dragon which in turn draws upon the New Testament's narrative concerning Satan as the dragon (in addition, perhaps, to a Norse tradition, as noted in Tolkien's lecture). Where Bilbo Baggins (the Chosen One) is the smallest and weakest individual in Middle-earth, Smaug is the largest and most fearsome, and the greatest test (the Dark Lord of the New Testament, but also the adversarial 'satan' and testing Prosecutor of the Old Testament) Bilbo must face, a test that not even the selfishly treasure-hungry dwarves have the courage to face. Yet the 'contest' between Bilbo and Smaug is a battle of wits, riddles (Tolkien, 1937, p. 234) and moral courage, rather than a physical match:

'It was at this point that Bilbo stopped. Going on from there was the bravest
thing he ever did. The tremendous things that happened afterwards were as
nothing compared to it. He fought the real battle in the tunnel alone, before
he ever saw the vast danger that lay in wait' (Tolkien, 1937, pp. 225-26).

Fortunately, Bilbo has already overcome the character flaw of his
own self-interest, having learnt from the near-fatal sin or mistake
of trying to steal gold from the pockets of trolls, and later resisting
the temptation to murder Gollum beneath Mount Doom in order to
keep the ring he has found by mere good fortune, thereby becoming
capable and willing to self-sacrifice in a near Christ-like manner
(making him the Chosen One of 'The Hero's Journey' (Campbell,
1990). Thus, he is 'rewarded' with the initial success of stealing 'a
great two-handled cup', *precisely* like the slave in *Beowulf*, then to
return to the less brave dwarves. Later, when bandying words with
Smaug, and almost coming under the beast's insidious, undermining
'dragon-spell' (p. 235), Bilbo's selfless determination 'to remain
loyal to his friends' (p. 236) instead enables him to provoke Smaug
into boasting and unwittingly revealing the gap in his armour of
gemstones and scales.

What a shame that, unlike Bilbo, the hero Beowulf could not
remember to reward and be so loyal to his thanes, particularly as
Beowulf's personal failure and subsequent demise then sees his
kingdom less defended, his 'nation invaded [and] enemies on the
rampage' (l.3153-3152). For the demonic threat of selfishness does
not just threaten to undo individuals alone, but all of society, just
as Satan looks to replace God's kingdom on Earth with his own
dark empire. Discovering his treasure looted (by Bilbo *et al*), and
incorrectly thinking that the perpetrators are the human inhabitants of
Lake-town, Smaug descends to destroy the entire population. Even
during that terrible confrontation, we see the cowardly and treasure-
hungry Master of the town, the political leader, looking to escape with
his unwieldy and burdensome gold, rather than remaining to lead the
defence and provide some chance of saving the wider community.
Here, we see the potentially devastating consequences of self-
interest at political levels, as well as an individual nation's selfish
hunger for power, wealth and resources, for all humanity. But for the
selfless heroism of Bard of Lake-town, who has been informed of
Bilbo's selfless discovery concerning Smaug's weakness, all would
be lost to the ancient rage, fire and destruction of the Satanic dragon.

It would be the end of world, in a final hell-like conflagration, an end of days which would see the Satanic dragon triumph in its war against Heaven.

The vision described above is what the Satanic dragon threatens to bring about via his malign influence and unhesitating use of power for selfish gain, no matter the genocidal consequences. Nor are such a vision and description inappropriate, for Tolkien witnessed the world's First World War, a war in which he watched his boyhood friends massacred in Orvillers, France, and where he saw the great cities of European civilisation(s) brought to ruination by the weapons and technology of our own devising. As Tolkien himself stated, he began writing the language and mythology for his second-world fantasy in canteens, crowded wooden huts, 'by candle light in bell-tents, [and] even [...] down in dugouts under shell fire' (Carpenter and Tolkien C., 1981, Letter 66, p.90). Furthermore, with regard to *The Lord of the Rings* (1954-55), 'The Dead Marshes and the approaches to the Morannon owe something to Northern France after the Battle of the Somme' (Carpenter and Tolkien C., 1981, Letter 226, p.321).

Tolkien saw us lose our humanity and all human 'fellowship' during such times of war and geopolitical competition, when we forgot to guard against temptation, malign influence and *our own selves*. Even once Smaug is defeated by Bard, each of the races of Middle-earth then rushes to claim the dragon's treasure for their own selves, and the Battle of the Five Armies begins, a battle where there can be no true winners, and a battle during which many a hero is lost, including the leader of the dwarves, Thorin Oakenshield (who must sacrifice himself to redeem his former greed). Indeed, it is all but the Last Battle and Final Judgement visited upon them.

Smaug, then, can be read as a later manifestation of the Bible's Satanic dragon, yet he is also the allegorical embodiment of the destructive force, horror and damnation our own actions can bring about in the wider world. His territory is termed the Desolation, a barren wasteland where nothing grows, where God's creation is undone. The destruction he brings about via his agency and 'dark' agents, is genocidal and apocalyptic. Smaug can be seen as the entire world's War Machine, a science and technology which uses the same Latinate language as is used to describe his territory as the 'Desolation', and the same Latinate language as is used by the political and conniving Master (in an echo of Smaug's own insidious and manipulative 'dragon-spell' that conjures 'an unaccountable desire [to] seize' (p. 235) Bilbo). By contrast, the home of Bilbo Baggins (our Chosen One) is described via the Anglo-Saxon-based term 'The Shire', describing a place in harmony with nature (God's creation), a place where friends can sit (drinking tea, smoking a pipe and) speaking the emotional, Anglo-Saxon-based language of good 'fellowship'. And it is a home to which Bilbo gratefully returns.

> 'You are a very fine person, Mr. Baggins, and I am very fond of you; but you are only quite a little fellow in a wide world after all!'
> 'Thank goodness!' said Bilbo laughing, and handed him the tobacco-jar. (Tolkien, 1937, p. 315).

Having been informed by all of the above, the question of just what is so *fabulous* about Smaug may now be more concisely answered. Smaug is a Satanic dragon and intelligence that is far more ancient than humanity can ever entirely know. At the same time, he is a part of a clear duality, in terms of good and evil, the Chosen One and the Dark Lord, and, importantly, separate from humanity (as an enemy) while also potentially being a part of us (as a leader). Even when he is not physically or locally present, his jealous influence continues to work widely upon human society, to tantalise, tempt, sway and seduce us with his blandishment, threats, false promises and lies, all to bring such conflict (war) that will guarantee humanity's damnation or self-destruction. Indeed, one of the roots of the word 'fabulous' is 'fabula', which has various etymological meanings, including 'story' and 'lie'. Tolkien implicitly understands and expresses such when considering those (like 'Gandalf the White') who oppose the likes of Smaug and Sauron:

> Why they should take such a form is bound up with the 'mythology' of the 'angelic' Powers of the world of this fable. At this point in the fabulous history the purpose was precisely to limit and hinder their exhibition of 'power' on the physical plane, and so that they should do what they were primarily sent for: train, advise, instruct, arouse the hearts and minds of those threatened by Sauron to a resistance with their own strengths; and not just to do the job for them. (Carpenter and Tolkien C., 1981, Letter 156, p.216).

The Satanic dragon Smaug, then, is a story as old as time, and also the means by which humanity can or will be deceived and destroyed.

He also represents the duality of a raging, venal, irrational 'beast' and an intelligence that tests (and can easily surpass) humanity's own. The latter represents the mesmerising, seductive and awe-inspiring set of meanings associated with 'fabulous'. Smaug is indeed 'a fabulous beast' in all the meanings of the words.

Do you mourn for Smaug's passing? Do not. Remember, his influence or temptation continues to work even when he is not physically or locally present. Even though the Satanic dragon in the Bible was 'thrown alive into the fiery lake of burning sulfur' following the war in heaven, and Smaug is similarly lost to the fiery lake around Lake-town, the Book of Revelation promises it will only be for a thousand years. Then the beast will rise from the pit once more, and humanity will again know strife, war and the prospect of a fiery apocalypse. Smaug is there waiting in our future!

References and Bibliography

Beauvais, V., 2018. *Speculum Historiale*. [online] Available at: <http://www. vincentiusbelvacensis.eu> [Accessed: 14 March 2018].

Biblica, 1978. *Holy Bible: New International Version*. London: Hodder & Stoughton.

Campbell, J. 1990. *The Hero's Journey*. London:

Carpenter, H. and Tolkien, C. eds., 1981. *The Letters of J. R. R. Tolkien*. London: George Allen & Unwin.

Dalton, A. J., 2020. *The Satanic in Science Fiction and Fantasy*. Edinburgh: Luna Press Publishing.

Heaney, S., 1996. *Beowulf: A New Verse Translation*. London: W. W. Norton & Company.

Martin, G., 1996. *A Game of Thrones*. New York: Bantam Spectra.

Lerer, S., 1998. *Beowulf* and Contemporary Critical Theory. In: R. Bjork and J. Niles, eds. *A Beowulf Handbook*. Lincoln (NE): University of Nebraska Press. p.5.

Niles, J.D., 1998. *Beowulf*, Truth, and Meaning. In R. Bjork and J. Niles, eds. *A Beowulf Handbook*. Lincoln, Nebraska: University of Nebraska Press. pp.328-30.

Paolonini, C., 2002. *Eragon*. East Bridgewater (MA): Paolini LLC.

Renner, R., 2010. *A Light in Darkness* Vol.1. Tulsa, Oklahoma: Harrison House Publishers.

Société des Bollandistes, 1895. *Bibliotheca Hagiographica Graeca*. Bruxelles: Apud editories.

Shippey, T., 1998. Structure and Unity. In R. Bjork, R and J. Niles, eds. *A Beowulf Handbook*. Lincoln, Nebraska: University of Nebraska Press, p.163.

Solopova, E., 2009. *Languages, Myths and History: An Introduction to the Linguistic and Literary Background of J. R. R. Tolkien's Fiction*. New York: North Landing Books.

Tolkien, J.R.R., 1936. *Beowulf: The Monsters and the Critics* [pdf] Available at: < https://jenniferjsnow.files.wordpress.com/2011/01/11790039-jrr-tolkien-beowulf-the-monsters-and-the-critics.pdf> [Accessed 13 June 2021]
—, 1937. *The Hobbit*. London: Allen & Unwin.
—, 1954-55. *The Lord of the Rings*. London: Allen & Unwin.

Voragine, J., 2003. *The Golden Legend*. London: Aeterna Press.

Contributors

Amie Angèle Brochu has over 15 years of direct social and residential care experience working with vulnerable populations in mental health, education and the non-profit sector. Her educational background in social work, women's and gender studies and psychology nurtures her research interests in critical theory, reflexivity, and social justice. Amie is currently a sessional lecturer with the School of Social Work at Dalhousie University in Atlantic Canada.

From a young age, stories of wizardry and magic have captivated her. Even as she completed a master's degree in social work, Amie skilfully wove fantasy narratives into her research project. She is currently undertaking a PhD at Middlesex University London, UK exploring the progressive potential of fantasy literature in fostering a trans-liminal space contributing to individual, collective and social transformation. When Amie is not researching, writing or teaching she enjoys beachcombing, live theatre, and exploring historical medieval sites. You can usually find her writing in her favourite Muskoka chair with a glass of Korean Boba milk tea.

Scott Chaussée is an archaeologist who specialises in understanding communities and the power of the landscape in shaping people's beliefs and actions. He completed his PhD in Landscape Archaeology at University College London and is active in teaching, research, and professional practice. His research particularly explores how early medieval communities situated themselves within the landscape and utilised the relict landscape in constructing their social and territorial identities. He teaches archaeology courses in the lifelong learning department at Aberystwyth University in Wales, hoping to inspire the next generation of archaeologist researchers.

When not writing his own dark fantasy and horror fiction, Scott most likely is re-reading *The Lord of the Rings*, as he has done annually for the last 20 years. Middle-earth is another home for him, and the richness of Tolkien's world, with its linguistic, mythological, material and landscape influences has been a source of wonder and inspiration. The detail of its construction is so clear and consistent that it allows for an archaeological interpretation of its material culture, as one could with any past society.

Scott is originally from Lawrence, Kansas in the USA but has lived in the United Kingdom for the last 11 years. He lives with his beautiful wife, Anna, in the leafy city of Winchester in the heart of southern England.

Catherine A. Coundjeris holds an M.F.A. in Creative Writing from Emerson College and a Masters in Children's Literature from Simmons College. A former elementary school teacher, Catherine has also taught writing at Emerson College and ESL writing at Urban College in Boston. Her poetry is published in literary magazines, including *The Dawntreader*, *Visions with Voices*, *Nine Cloud Journal*, *Academy of the Heart and Mind*, *Bombfire*, *Paper Dragons*, *Kaleidoscope*, *North* *of Oxford, Shift, Halcyon Days, Blue Moon, Jalmurra, Calla Press, Stick Figure, Last Leaves, Open Door Magazine, Bewildering Stories, Raven Review* and *Loud Coffee Press.* She also has stories published in *Proem* and *Quail Bell.* She is very passionate about adult literacy.

A J Dalton (the 'A' is for Adam) is a prize-winning author of science fiction and fantasy. He has published twelve books to date, including *The Book of Orm, The Book of Angels, The Book of Dragons* and *The Book of Witches* with Kristell Ink, the *Empire of the Saviours* trilogy with Gollancz, *I am a Small God* with Admanga Publishing, and *The Satanic in Science Fiction and Fantasy* with Luna Press Publishing. His website is www.ajdalton.eu, where there is much to entertain fans of SFF.

Brendan Dyer writes Speculative Fiction and currently teaches writing at Western Connecticut State University, where he earned his MFA in Creative and Professional Writing. His poetry and short fiction appear in *SERIAL Magazine, The Black and White Journal, Havik,* and *The Esthetic Apostle.*

PhD, Docent (Associate professor) **Jyrki Korpua** is a reseacher of literature and cultural studies at the University of Oulu. He has edited many special issues of journals and published articles on literature, video games, graphic novels, and film studies. He is the author of non-fiction books "The Bible and Literature" (2016, in Finnish, published by Avain), "Kalevala and Literature" (2017, in Finnish, Avain), and *The Mythopoeic Code of Tolkien: A Christian Platonic Reading of the Legendarium* (2021, McFarland). He is one of the editors with Saija Isomaa & Jouni Teittinen of the antology *New Perspectives to Dystopian Fiction* (2020, Cambridge Scholars Publishers).

For Luna Press, Korpua wrote an article on the female roles in Peter Jackson's Tolkien adaptation for *Gender Identity and Sexuality Current Fantasy and Science Fiction* in 2017, on representation of evil in television series Babylon 5 and Mass Effect game series for *A Shadow Within: Evil in Fantasy and Science Fiction* in 2019, and on Nordic Countries in worldbuilding of Frozen and Frozen II movies for *Worlds Apart: Worldbuilding in Fantasy and Science Fiction* in 2021, all edited by Francesca T. Barbini.

Elise Caemasache McKenna is a Course Director in the Creative Writing Department at Full Sail University. She earned her Master's at University of Central Florida and is pursuing a PhD in Tolkien studies. She has been studying Tolkien for over thirty years and has presented and guest lectured on the Professor and his Legendarium, Harry Potter, and H. P. Lovecraft at conferences all over the United States, England, Australia, and New Zealand. Her articles appear in *How We Became Middle Earth, Loremasters and Libraries in Fantasy and Science Fiction, Lembas Extra, Mythlore,* and Conference Proceedings for the Tolkien Society. She has been a recipient of local awards & grants to continue her research. She teaches fantasy, science fiction, horror fiction, story development, and creating new worlds.

She is currently writing articles on Tolkien and Romanticism and presenting at various conferences. She is working on a collaborative fantasy novel set in late 1800s Australia. Her publications on H.P. Lovecraft in Florida, Tolkien and gaming, and horror in Tolkien's works are scheduled for 2022. Aside from sharing Tolkien's love of trees, she enjoys making small furry animals from wool roving, living with small furry animals, and rescuing small furry animals. Her favorite book is *The Silmarillion*, but she allows ghost stories of M. R. James, Cynthia Asquith, and Neil Gaiman to creep in occasionally. She loves traveling and plans to live in New Zealand when she grows up.

Angela P. Nicholas graduated in Latin at London University (Royal Holloway College) in 1971 and subsequently gained post-graduate qualifications in Librarianship and Information Technology. She is now retired after a career first in higher education as a librarian, and then in local government as an IT specialist.

In 1973 a friend persuaded her to read *The Hobbit* and *The Lord of the Rings* thereby triggering a lasting interest in J. R. R. Tolkien's Middle-earth writing. She is the author of *Aragorn: J.R.R. Tolkien's Undervalued Hero* (2nd edition, Luna Press, 2017), a work which arose from her dissatisfaction with the portrayal of Aragorn in Peter Jackson's *Lord of the Rings* films. She also contributed a chapter to *Music in Tolkien's Work and Beyond* (edited by Julian Eilmann and Friedhelm Schneidewind, Walking Tree Publishers, 2019).

Angela has lived in Portsmouth (UK) for many years with husband, Chris MacArthur, and various feline companions. As well as a shared enthusiasm for Tolkien and cats she and Chris enjoy the countryside and do regular local walks, as well as going on walking holidays further afield.

They are also members of the 1745 Association, a historical society whose aims are to study the Jacobite Movement and preserve the memories of those involved in it.

Enrico Spadaro is an Italian young researcher with a passion for J.R.R. Tolkien. Born in Catania (Italy) in 1991. When he watched Peter Jackson's adaption of *The Fellowship of the Rings* he fell in love with Tolkien. Thus, he started studying foreign languages and literatures at university. In 2014 he obtained a master in Literary Translation at the University of Pisa, in Tuscany. In his final dissertation, Tolkien's tale *The Lost Road* was translated into Italian. He continued his research on Tolkien in France at Aix-Marseille Université and he defended his PhD thesis in November 2018: the title of the thesis is *La Littérature-Monde de J.R.R. Tolkien: pertinence, discours et modernité d'une oeuvre originale*, under the supervision of Pr. Joanny Moulin. The thesis has been published in March 2021 by the French publisher L'Harmattan.

In summer 2019, he applied for the postdoc Teach@Tübingen fellowship at the University of Tübingen in Germany, which started in October 2020, with a duration of six months.

He took part in congresses about literature and fiction: in May 2017, he communicated at the meeting *Chemins de Traverse en fiction*, held in Paris at École Normale Supérieure. In August 2019, he attended Tolkien 2019 in Birmingham, where he presented a paper entitled "To the Origins of Fairy-tales".

He is currently a language teacher and member of the Italian group "Tolkieniani Italiani", that analyses and comments Tolkien's themes and works. A radio podcast "La Voce di Arda" is broadcast every Friday evening (https://www.spreaker.com/show/lo-show-di-radio-la-voce-di-arda) on such themes. The podcast was presented at the Association for Digital Humanities and Digital Culture (AIUCD) 10th annual conference in January 2021 and during the Prancing Pony Podcast Moot in May 2021.

Mauro Toninelli has been passionate of Tolkien since high school, back in the 1990s, when he first read The Lord of the Rings. Those days when he immersed himself in Middle-earth were the beginning of a passion that gradually turned into something greater.

Born in Brescia (Italy) in 1977, he graduated in modern literature after classical high school. He is a member of the Lombardy Order of Journalists and works at *La Voce del Popolo*, a diocesan weekly newspaper in Brescia, with which he still collaborates. He teaches Religion in Secondary Schools and holds a Master's degree in Religious Sciences. He is the author of *Perché ci vuole Cuore*, a reflection on school, of *Io, papà? 9 mesi coi baffi*, diary of the father between the serious and the facetious in a pregnancy, of *Siate fedeli alla terra!*, hints of anthropological reflection between Nietzsche and Hadjadj. His last work is *Colui che raccontò la Grazia. Una rilettura de Il Signore degli Anelli di J.R.R. Tolkien*, published by the Cittadella publishing house, in which he offers ideas concerning the Catholic themes in Tolkien's work. After the publication of this work, which had already been preceded by meetings on Tolkien in the Brescia area, he participated in several meetings about Tolkien and published articles on tolkienitalia.net.

He is a member of the Italian group "Tolkieniani Italiani" and occasionally participates as an expert guest in the radio broadcasts "La Voce di Arda" (https://www.spreaker.com/show/lo-show-di-radio-la-voce-di-arda).

In summer 2021 he was among the speakers at the international conference "The Tree of Tales" held at the Rimini Meeting in collaboration with University of St Andrews, University of Oxford, Associazione Newman e King Edward's School of Birmingham (Tolkien, The Tree of Tales Conference – The Tree of Tales).

Renée Vink lives in The Hague (Netherlands) and has been an avid Tolkien reader for five decades. In 1981 she co-founded the Dutch Tolkien Society Unquendor, and in 1985 its scholarly journal *Lembas Extra*, of which she is currently one of the editors (again). She has written numerous essays on J.R.R. Tolkien and Arda for *Tolkien Studies*, volumes of Walking Tree Publishers, TS conference proceedings, and other publications. In 2012 her monograph *Wagner and Tolkien: Mythmakers* was published, in 2020 *Gleanings from Tolkien's Garden*, a volume of selected essays (nominated for the Tolkien Society Best Book Award 2021).

Her profession in the primary world is translator, and from 2009 onwards she has been the official translator of works by Tolkien into Dutch, among them *The Legend of Sigurd and Gudrún, Tolkien's Beowulf, Beren and Lúthien* and *The Fall of Gondolin* – but regrettably not *The History of Middle-earth*, which was never published in Dutch. In between, she wrote a number of historical mysteries about medieval Dutch noblemen and Holy Roman emperors, featuring runaway beguines, troubadours, and Dante as sleuths.

Lightning Source UK Ltd.
Milton Keynes UK
UKHW021538140622
404414UK00009B/1664